CONTEMPORARY INDIA WITH CONTROVERSIAL NEIGHBOURS

CONTEMPORARY INDIA WITH CONTROVERSIAL NEIGHBOURS

Dr. Rajkumar Singh

GYAN

Contemporary India with Controversial Neighbours

Rs. 750

ISBN: 978-81-212-1129-1

Published in 2011 in India by
Gyan Publishing House
23, Main Ansari Road, Darya Ganj,
New Delhi-110002
Phones : 23282060, 23261060
Fax : 011-23285914
E-mail: books@gyanbooks.com
Website: www.gyanbooks.com

Laser Type Setting by : Square Vision, New Delhi

Printed at : Chawla Offset Press, Delhi

Dedicated to

Smt. Lalmani Devi
Mother-in-law

CONTENTS

PART TWO
CONTROVERSIAL NEIGHBOURS

LIST OF ABBREVIATIONS

AD	–	Annie Domini
ADB	–	Asian Development Bank
AIORC	–	Association of Indian Ocean Rim Countries
AGP	–	Awareness Generation Programme
AoA	–	Agreement on Agriculture
AJK	–	Azad Jammu and Kashmir
APRC	–	All Party Representative Committee
ASEAN	–	Association of South East Asian Nations
BC	–	Before Christ
CAARD	–	Committee on Administrative Arrangements for Rural Development
CBM	–	Confidence Building Measures
CDP	–	Community Development Programme
CENTO	–	Central Treaty Organisation
CPNUML	–	Communist Party of Nepal United Marxist Leninist
CSWB	–	Central Social Welfare Board
CWC	–	Ceylon Workers Congress
D-CP	–	Dudley Senanayake – Chelvanayagam Pact
DDC	–	District Development Council
DMC	–	Disaster Management Committee
DPA	–	District Political Authority
EFTA	–	European Free Trade Area
ENLF	–	Eelam National Liberation Front
EPRLF	–	Eelam Peoples Revolutionary Liberation Front
EROS	–	Eelam Revolutionary Organisation of Students
ESCAP	–	Economic and Social Commission for Asia and Pacific

EU	–	European Union
FP	–	Federal Party
GDP	–	Gross Domestic Product
GATT	–	General Agreement on Tarrif and Trade
HM	–	Hizbul Mujahideen
ICRISAT	–	International Crops Research Institute for the Semi Arid Tropics
IMF	–	International Monetary Fund
IPKF	–	Indian Peace-keeping Force
IRBM	–	Intermediate Range Ballistic Missile
JKG	–	Jai Krishna Goit
JKLF	–	Jammu and Kashmir Liberation Front
JRC	–	Joint Rivers Commission
JTMM	–	Janatantrik Tarai Mukti Morcha
JVP	–	Janatha Vimukti Peramuna
JWG	–	Joint Working Group
LAC	–	Line of Actual Control
LoC	–	Line of Control
LTTE	–	Liberation Tigers of Tamil Eelam
MAD	–	Mutual Assured Disagreement
MCNS	–	Media Centre for National Security
MJF	–	Madhesi Janadhikar Forum
MoU	–	Memorandum of Understanding
MUF	–	Muslim United Front
NAFTA	–	North American Free Trade Area
NAM	–	Non Aligned Movement
NC	–	National Conference
NATO	–	North Atlantic Treaty Organisation
NMD	–	National Missile Defence
NORDA	–	Norwegian Development Agency
NSS	–	National Service Scheme
NWFP	–	North West Frontier Province
NYKS	–	Nehru Yuva Kendra Sanghathan

OAS	–	Organisation of American States
OAU	–	Organisation of African Unity
OPEC	–	Oil Producing European Countries
PA	–	Peoples Alliance
PLO	–	Palestinian Liberation Organisation.
PoK	–	Pak-occupied Kashmir
PLOTE	–	Peoples Liberation Organisation of Tamil Eelam
PRC	–	People's Republic of China
PRIs	–	Panchayati Raj Institutions
SAFTA	–	South Asian Free Trade Area
SAPTA	–	South Asia Preferential Trading Arrangement
SAARC	–	South Asian Association for Regional Cooperation
SARIE	–	South Asia Regional Initiative / Energy
SCOR	–	Security Council Official Record
SEATO	–	South East Asia Treaty Organisation
SFG	–	Strategic Foresight Group
SLFP	–	Sri Lankan Freedom Party
SPA	–	Seven Party Alliance
STEP	–	Support to Training and Employment
TELA	–	Tamil Eelam Liberation Army
TELO	–	Tamil Eelam Liberation Organisation
TMD	–	Threat Missile Defence
TMLP	–	Tarai Madhes Loktantrik Morcha
TNT	–	Tamil New Tigers
TUF	–	Tamil United Front
TULF	–	Tamil United Liberation Front
UN	–	United Nations
UNCIP	–	United Nations Commission for India and Pakistan
UNHRC	–	United Nations Human Rights Commission
UNP	–	United National Party
UPFN	–	United Peoples Front of Nepal
WTO	–	World Trade Organisation
USAID	–	United States Assistance for International Development

PREFACE

The book 'Contemporary India with Controversial Neighbours' properly takes into account the real position of India's political system adopted in 1947 with its effectiveness in the age of liberalisation and globalisation. With the change of society and the nature of Indian political system like other developing countries, India also faces the aspects of good governance and needed to take a number of remedial steps at its level. India, as a emerging strong nation along with its other strengths and potentialities take active part, from the start, in international affair and is effortful to make the world peaceful and prosperous. Its international stature also adds to its internal strength and the both united symbolised India as an ideal and responsible state of the world arena regionally and globally.

Independent India is heavily ladden with problems and some of them have taken decades in negotiations without any result at hand or in sight. Its problem of the State of Jammu and Kashmir with Pakistan is as old as independent India itself is and four Kashmir-centered declared wars have already been fought between India and Pakistan the latest one in 1999 at Kargil. Border dispute with the People's Republic of China began at the close of 1950s and after an India-China war in 1962 the thorny border problem is still continuing which has plagued New Delhi's relations with the Beijing despite understandings on several counts. Controversies with Sri Lanka, Nepal and Bangladesh are too hindering India's good relations with them in a globalised world which has opened a vast dimension of inter-state relations. Contemporary India is doing its level best to solve its problems with neighbours but strategic considerations - regional and global have marred the prospect of their resolution. We hope a good sense would prevail sooner or later and they would come to terms with India.

I wish to thank the institutions and individuals for their encouragement, cooperation and good wishes that I received and staff of the central libraries at New Delhi and other places where I got a lot of information and analytical / critical views of different subject experts. They all concerned deserve cordial thanks.

I am deeply grateful to several persons and colleagues. Among teachers Dr. D.N. Mallik, Dr. Kirtyanand Singh, Dr. R.N. Kumar and Dr. M.R. Kazami, retired Professors of the University Department of Political Science, BRA Bihar University, Muzaffarpur, have been constant source of guide and encouragement at every stage. Colleagues Dr. Dhirendra Narayan Singh, Department of Political Science MLT College, Saharsa, Dr. Chandra Prakash Singh Department of History, Dr. Kumar Jyotivardhan, Dr. Usha Singh Department of Hindi, West Campus P.G. Centre, Saharsa and departmental colleagues, Dr. Bijay Kumar Verma and Dr. Pawan Kumar are thankful for their cooperation and goodwishes. Eldest brother the late Suryanath Singh, elder brother Bhuvneshwar Prasad Singh, father-in-law Shri Ramanand Singh, retired Professor and Head, University Department of Physics, BRA Bihar University, Muzaffarpur, deserve deep sense of gratitude for their sincere goodwishes. The author is also grateful to colleagues and staff of the B.N. Mandal University, West Campus, P.G. Centre, Saharsa.

I would be failing in my duty if I do not record my honest goodwishes and gratitude to the family members including my wife Dr. Hemlata Singh, son Aditya Priyadarshi and Apurv Adarsh in the completion of the book.

However, for the facts, analysis, views and misjudgements contained in the book I alone am responsible.

02 June 2010 **Rajkumar Singh**

INTRODUCTION

India celebrated its Independence on 15th August 1947 when the British Imperial power voluntarily abdicated their rule in India unlike the Mughals who died of its own self-inflicted wounds. The new occasion represented for its people the start of an epoch that was imbued with a new vision of political stalwarts – Mahatma Gandhi and Jawaharlal Nehru. Their 'inclusive' vision had shaped country's political framework and was enshrined as the essence in the newly enacted constitution. Interestingly in the summer of 1947 Gandhi referred to himself as a Sindhi and a Punjabi, as a lover of all socialists and a father to young communists. He was a true symbol of multiple identities and strove strenuously to include all India in his family. It was Jawaharlal Nehru who, of those who followed or came after Gandhi, best upheld his inclusive patriotism. Like the Mahatma, in his person and in his faith he transcended the divisions of race and religion, caste and class, gender and geography. He was a Hindu who was befriended by Muslims, a Brahmin who did not observe the rules of caste, a north Indian who would not impose Hindi on the south, a man who could be trusted and respected by women. Above all, Nehru was of the view that an ideological dispute, or political disagreement apart, the power of a state was to be exercised in the public domain and all were to be anchored in the public interest. Nehru noted on August 15, 1947 : It must be clearly understood that the interests of our long suffering masses must come first and every entrenched interests that come in their way must yield to them.

Like the early 1950s today, after six decades of independence, the nation-state is honing and defining its place in the sun, formulating the internal dynamics of a new democratic idiom, and stumbling upon ways to graft an inclusive social order - a crying need of every developing state. The present crises in Indian democracy have prompted and propelled every one of the conscious citizens of this country to think of an alternative to remedy the situation. Politics and Administration are looked at by the people contemptuously and its deeper implications have affected the society as politics and society are not functioning in a vacuum and in isolation, but they are parts of the society. In the circumstances it is necessary to look at the crisis and understand what it is, how it is and why it is ? Democracy cannot survive and will not deliver the intended goods and services to the society when the society has intense social conflicts. However by the time India became independent the concept of democracy has moved on since the time when the right to vote was a restricted privilege, determined by wealth, education and gender. Today, theoretically every adult with a fixed address has the right to vote in a democracy.

With these perceptions and objectives in view the tasks of nation-building were taken up by the Indian people and their leaders with a certain elan and determination and with confidence in their capacity to succeed. The initial broad framework was based on social consensus that was to be built on the values of nationalism, secularism and democracy and the goals of rapid economic development and radical social changes. Political system, when understood as the state, is characterized by an ensemble of institutional patterns and political organisation. In general the state is distinguished from other organisations in society by its capacity to monopolise the legitimate use of violence within a given territory. In this context even the concept of governance has undergone a change. It now extends beyond the conventional law enforcing service; providing domain of the state to imply process of development, which is participatory and takes into consideration the interests of the stakeholder groups in society especially of the most excluded and disadvantaged sections. This is of great importance in the developing world where many governments appeared to have failed in performing their duties and major changes were considered necessary for arranging new patterns of interactions between government and citizens.

So under Indian polity, at first, the national state was made an instrument of development and social transformation. Indian unity, it was realised, had to be strengthened by recognising and accepting India's immense regional, linguistic, ethnic and religion's diversity. It was to be further developed by acknowledging and accommodating the Indian's multiple identities and by giving different parts of the country and various sections of the people an adequate space in the Indian union. In other words the founders of the Indian Republic had the courage to two major innovations of historical significance in nation building and social engineering : first, to build a democratic and civil libertarian society among an illiterate people and second, to undertake economic development within a democratic political structure.

From the beginning India viewed economic progress as an unalienable ingredient of the political development. Jawaharlal Nehru voiced in the Constituent Assembly the fundamental national proposition and argued, 'We have given the content of democracy in this resolution and not only the content of democracy but the content, if I may say so, of economic democracy. Well, I stand for Socialism. I hope India will stand for Socialism and that India will go towards the constitution of a Socialist state.' After six decades the same socialist theme was renewed in the form of a wake-up call given by President Pratibha Patil in her Republic Day-eve address in January 2008 in which she said that the disadvantaged 'too should find a place to enjoy the sunshine of the country's growth and development. She added further', our efforts and our commitment, while pursuing the goal of high growth rates, should be to ensure that all people of our country benefit from it. Our pledge will remain unfulfilled until, as Gandhi had said 'we have wiped every tear in every eye'.

In the situations, independent India had to begin its upward economic climb from an abysmally low level. The technological and productivity levels of Indian agriculture and industry were to be constantly and rapidly raised. As the Indian economy was an integral part of the world economy, it was to be based on self-reliance, free of subordination to the metropolitan interest or domination by foreign capital. To meet the challenge India, especially after 1955, set out to achieve an integrated national economy based on an indigenous industry, catering primarily to its domestic market. In line Nehru did organise basic institutions and instrumentalities such as the planning commission, public sector enterprises, strategic state-managed industries and river projects. The initial economic policies and their implementation with some success and failures worked for three five year plan periods, it however needed a radical shift in mid-sixties due to national and international constraints and was in the grip of massive crisis in many respects. The then situation changed India's image from a model developing country to a 'basket case'.

The period around the mid-sixties economic crisis apart also witnessed a shift in the social basis of Indian politics. There began a gradual power seepage from urban to rural and within rural from upper castes to OBCs. The year 1967 revealed something more basic – a combination of social conflict within the traditional caste hierarchy and widespread public discontent with the Congress itself. The new situation was warranted by social inequality, aloofness of Indian intelligentsia, internal tension, decline of morality and decency in public life. The political system adopted in free India is Parliamentary democracy which has seen several ups and downs in Indian context. In recent decades role of religion has increased in Indian politics compelling the social system for its reordering. By 1971 a clear shift in both the social basis of Indian politics and its party and governmental apparatus began to take place. It was the time when the people at large started receiving the economic and administrative performance of the Party in power in terms of how it affected their day-to-day life and related this to their own electoral decision making. The changed context saw the launching of a series of radical economic policies which were to have long-term effects on India's developmental efforts.

In early nineties (1991) the long-term constraints that were building up over a few decades and debilitating the Indian economy combined with certain more recent and immediate factors led to a massive fiscal and balance of payments crisis that climaxed later and in the meantime the minority congress government headed by P.V. Narasimha Rao took over power with Manmohan Singh as finance minister. The process of reforms in Indian economy started in 1991, involved, inter alia, an immediate fiscal correction; making the exchange rate more realistically linked to the market, the liberalisation of trade and industrial controls like freer access to imports; a considerable dismantling of the industrial licensing system; reform of the public sector including gradual privatisation etc. In short it was an attempt to free the economy from stifling internal controls as well as equip it to participate in the world wide globalisation process to its advantage. It led to the economic development based on micro-chip, bio-technology, information technology, new resources of energy and advanced managerial techniques. In the current phase, it is not proper to say that the earlier Nehruvian strategy was wrong. But, over time, certain negative features developed. That, and the response to the changed world conditions required a shift in strategy for the achievement of the same goal. The economic globalisation commenced since 1980s has resulted in unprecedented technological boost and faster flow of capital.

Globalisation, in broader term, is a complex social, economic, cultural, technological, and political process in which the mobility of capital, ideas, technology, organisations and people has acquired a growing global and transnational form.The process is multidimensional. Advances in new technology, cheaper and quicker transport, trade liberalisation, the increase in financial flows and the growth in the size and power of corporations are its distinctive features. The global economy stresses economic objectives of free trade, growth, employment and sustainable development. Liberals claim that globalisation promotes development, democracy, personal empowerment and global governance. Development is not only about growth of GNP per head, but also about the expansion of human freedom and dignity.

In this age of globalisation the process of politicisation and mobilisation has been intensified and the continuous ongoing process has sometimes taken the form of popular agitations posing a challenge for democratic values and governance have been difficult to reconcile in a country where socio-economic relativities can be altered only through political mobilisation. A polity devises through painful experiences and sometimes through joyful energy, an operative work culture commensurate with the state's objective interests and designed to deepen its legitimacy. The emergent political culture is a sum total of preferred habits, style, values, and predilections for dialogue, conversations, contestations through disputes, disagreements, and conflicts. The decline of political culture began to appear in the mid-1970s and continued unabated one after another which led a structural crisis, and the result was the 1991 makeover to a market economy.

The departure from the 'care for the public commandment to market magic' instigated fundamental changes in the polity's architecture: decline of a pan-Indian party, rise of the regional parties, the strong culture making way for a cooperative federalism, the resuscitation of constitutional institutions-Presidency, judiciary, media, election commission, etc. In the circumstances it became difficult to mobilise democracy's energy, emotions, ideas, imagination, and passions in pursuit of national goals. Now the governing classes owe it to themselves to attend the task of re-energising the political culture. The task is urgent because of the polity's grand paradox on the one hand, mass democratic movements have run out of steam and stamina, and on the other, those groups that believe in violence have placed themselves beyond the reach of the state in large parts of the country.

At present related to the whole issue is the concept of governance which is neither new nor static. Governance is the process of decision making and implementation of those decisions, governance focuses on the actors who make decisions and the structures that are involved in decision making. Governance clearly refers to political accountability, transparency in government procedures and openness in government transactions and rule of law. It is associated with effective, efficient and responsive administration in a democratic framework. Participation by civil society, together with information disclosure and transparency can help in monitoring policy decisions and implementing accountability of public authority resulting in good governance. Keeping these facts in active consideration the base of democratic set up in India has been broadened to fulfil the requirements of good governance. To make ours a truly just society we ally economic reforms to governance reforms through the panchayats and women empowerment so as to translate accelerated growth into 'inclusive' growth – the overarching objective of the Eleven Five Year Plan.

Taking experiences from its long history and recent past, at Independence Jawaharlal Nehru gave voice and shape to India's policy of non-alignment. It was India's aspiration for freedom and liberty that was responsible for the development of free India's new foreign policy. India, a new comer to the world scene, was confronted with not only the need to initiate relations with dozens of countries of which it had no recent direct knowledge but a global bipolarity in international politics or the rise of the United States and the Soviet Union as two Super Powers. India under Jawaharlal Nehru decided to keep away from Super Power squabbles and thus keep its foreign policy options open. In addition India went far beyond just neutrality or staying out of military blocs. Nehru rejected the charge of immoral neutrality hurled at India by John Foster Dulles and made it clear that Non-alignment meant having the freedom to decide each issue on its merit, to weigh what was right or wrong and then take a stand in favour of right. In larger perspective the policy of Non-alignment came to symbolised the struggle of India and other newly independent nations to retain and strengthen their independence from colonialism and imperialism. India being the first to become independent, rightly gave the lead to other ex-colonies in this respect.

At the start of the new epoch Nehru also visualised a resurgent Asia where India would play a central role. He confidently declared. 'India is going to be and bound to be a country that counts in world affairs, not I hope in a military sense, but in many other senses, which are more important and effective in the end.' This situation continued up to the early 1990s, i.e. the end of the cold war period. The late 1980s and the early 1990s, witnessed a radical change in the scenario of international politics. The disintegration of the Soviet Union left the United States as the only Super Power on the scene. However, the change of scenario in international arena makes no difference to the basic themes of the policy of Non-alignment. Its main thrust being the protection of India's autonomy in international relations and contributing to improvement of international system through befriending as many countries as possible in general and the super powers in particular. The real purpose of Non-alignment was to promote peace, disarmament and development. These issues are still relevant and the challenge is how to attain these goals today? India can meet this challenge by playing a role of bridge power. New Delhi must pursue a policy of multi-partnership with all major powers of the world.

Since Independence the contemporary India has achieved significantly through various forms of affirmative action and economic incentives. In the economic arena it is emerging as a major player in the global market and can now even afford to selectively abandon its proverbial beggings bowl. Its progress in the arena of military technology has been impressive as have been its achievements in the spheres of nuclear, missile, and space technology. But in spite of half a century of achievements in the political, economic, and military fields, one fact can not be ignored. The gulf between potential and performance is particularly unbridgeable and yawning in the arena of foreign policy and security. Neither the assertive Indira Doctrine nor the conciliatory Gujral Doctrine succeeded in instilling trust among its neighbours. Apprehensions over India's 'hegemonic' intentions continue to undermine its influence in the region. It has serious political disputes, differences, or disagreements with all its neighbours. India is saddled with two nuclear rivals with whom it has serious and seemingly irresolvable border disputes – Pakistan and China. They both have a shared interest in containing India. Problem of Indian origin settlers in Sri Lanka, emergence and spread of Maoism in Nepal and Bangladesh's unfriendly attitude on Farakka issue and other matters of national interest still continue to be a challenge/threat for the internal security of India. Efforts for resolving them are ongoing with all the controversial neighbours with no concrete results in sight.

With Pakistan the problem of the predominantly State of Jammu and Kashmir has been a bone of contention between India and Pakistan which caused four wars since the days of the partition of the subcontinent. It began because the State of Jammu and Kashmir remained undecided on the eve of India's independence whether to join with India or Pakistan. In a certain set of circumstances created by Pakistan, Raja Hari Singh, the king of the state, in October 1947, decided to join Indian union through the Instrument of Accession, which was signed by the Maharaja and accepted by the Defence Committee and the Governor-General of

India. Pakistan argues that the question of Jammu and Kashmir was a part of the general decolonisation and hence it was a question of right of self-determination of the people the State. India and Pakistan have been talking on the issue since then intermittently through mediation and direct talks as well but they have not been able to find an amicable solution as yet. Kashmir is more a consequence than a cause of ideological and power-centered conflict between the two countries. As Islamabad had rightly stated after Kargil War in 1999 that conflicts and tensions with India would remain even after the Kashmir issue is resolved. It showed that Kashmir is not the cause of the India-Pakistan conflict, rather the result of bitter India-Pakistan relations. The primary image of India in Pakistan is that of a hostile nation and the primary threat to Pakistan's security.

Notwithstanding considerable improvement in political ties, the lack of final settlement on the boundary dispute between the two neighbours – India and China makes it difficult to totally dispel the mutual suspicion that has characterised bilateral ties for long. New Delhi wants Beijing to speed up the process as the dispute is the final hurdle in boosting bilateral ties, while the Chinese are persisting with their claims over entire Arunachal Pradesh of India specifically Tawang, which are not acceptable to India. Following the 1962 border war, information about India in China became virtually non-existent. With no direct flights for over thirty years and an absence of any significant trade and investment, the average Chinese person knew more about the United States all the way across the Pacific Ocean than India, a close neighbour. Senior-level border negotiations had been going on since 1981 and despite 30 years of continuous border talks – the longest between any two states in modern history, India is the only country with which China has not settled its land frontiers or even fully defined a line of control.

After commencement of the Border negotiations in 1981 it received a breakthrough in 1988, 1993 and 2003. In 1988 Rajiv Gandhi, the then Prime Minister of India, went to China and during the visit the mechanism of talks was reclassified as joint Working Group (JWG), although there was nothing new or joint about it. More success professedly came India's way when Narasimha Rao signed an agreement with Beijing to maintain 'peace and tranquility along the Line of Actual Control (LAC), a line that the Chinese had refused to define. It was perhaps done to maintain military pressure on India and pin down large numbers of Indian troops along the Himalayas. Eight round of border talks had been held between 1981 and 1987 and an additional 14 Joint Working Group meetings between 1988 and 2003. And another eight round of border talks between the Special Representatives of India and China have already taken place since the boundary negotiations were taken to a political level in June 2003. Instead of being agree to define a line of control, Beijing deliberately injected confusion by suggesting to seek an overall border settlement through a package deal and the two countries agreed for the same when Indian Prime Minister Atal Bihari Vajpayee visited Beijing in 2003. This is clearly a clever ploy : If the Chinese are not willing to even define the Actual Line of Control, why should they be willing to resolve the border problem through a package settlement? It is also said that the 1988 and 1993 accords supremely suited Beijing's strategy of seeking to change Indian perception about China without conceding any ground to New Delhi and yet continuing to quietly contain India. In the nearly 54 years since the communists seized power in Beijing, no nation has undermined India's interests more than China.

Initially the problem of Indian settlers in Sri Lanka made no hindrance to India's relations with the island nation. In later years Sri Lanka wished to define its nationhood in terms of Sinhalese race and Buddhist religion had begun to damage that country's political cohesion and national security from the mid-1950s. Sri Lanka's insensitive and heavy-handed handling of Tamil aspirations led to a guerilla war which had serious political impact in the next door Tamil Nadu state of India. Sri Lanka's attempt to seek Pakistani, Israeli, US and British help to combat the insurgency posed a wider national security threat as well to India. It created the situation in which Indian involvement became essential and to protect the unity and integrity of the island nation India and Sri Lanka signed an agreement in July 1987. But the said agreement failed to bring an enduring understanding between the Sri Lankan government and the Liberation Tigers of Tamil Eelam (LTTE). A devastating fighting between the Sri Lankan armed forces and the Tigers of Tamil Eelam continued with intervals in the name of ceasefire agreements. The Sri Lankan government decided to launch a fight to finish war against the Tamil Tigers when Mahinda Rajapaksa took over as the new President of Sri Lanka in November 2005. Having all the constitutional methods failed to convince the Tamil Tigers both sides fought a decisive war from the year 2007 and it came to an end in May 2009 with the defeat and death of LTTE's supremo Prabhakaran. In the war with the Sri Lankan security forces the military capabilities of Tamil Tigers was decimated and a new chapter has been opened in Sri Lanka's multi-ethnic society and politics.

Hectic political developments took place in Nepal with the

emergence of the Maoists as a potent force from the mid-1990s, and it brought in the Himalayan Kingdom a long phase of political instability. As the Indian government remained sympathetic to the anti-Maoist establishment in the kingdom it extended no direct support to the newly born political force in the country. It made both sides apprehensive to each other for a long time to come. Particularly after the death of King Birendra in a Palace shoot-out, the political situation in Nepal in the period of King Gyanendra became out of control who declared emergency in February 2002 and handed over the executive power to a coalition in April 2006. Finally the election of Constituent Assembly was held in April 2008 whose members would also act as a legislature till the new constitution is written. In August 2008 a Maoist-led coalition government was formed and Pushpa Kamal Dahal 'Prachanda' was elected the first Prime Minister of the new federal republic of Nepal who was known for his anti-India stands. A change of guard also took place in the year 2009 in which Prachanda was replaced by Madhav Kumar as the new Prime Minister of Nepal but the political uncertainty and instability are likely to continue in the Himalayan Kingdom. In the circumstances India needed to remain watchful towards the developments in Nepal and pursue a policy suited to country's long-term interests–bilateral, regional and global.

With the partition of the subcontinent in August 1947 the issue of Farakka emerged between India and Pakistan. Later the failure of west Pakistan state to allow adequate political and economic space to its eastern wing and to accommodate the latter's distinctiveness had led to inter-wing conflict which ultimately, with the support of India, gave birth to a new nation in December 1971 named, Bangladesh. Before the emergence of Bangladesh India held several round of talks with united Pakistan without any concrete result. Construction of a barrage at Farakka was initiated by India but Islamabad tried to internationalise the issue by raising it at various international fora. After formation of Bangladesh in December 1971 the new government held talks with the then Government of India and they concluded an interim agreement on the sharing of Ganga Waters at Farakka. The second agreement between the two was signed in November 1977 while the latest one in December 1996. The treaty of 1996 was for the period of thirty years with provision of review after every five years or earlier. Although it is not an issue for the present but deterioration of understanding with Bangladesh may aggravate the problem and pose a threat to good relations between the two neighbouring countries. Other issues of concern to India include use of Bangladeshi territories by Indian insurgent groups, support for terrorist activities and involvement of Bangladeshi nationals in crimes in India. These have been raised with the Bangladesh government, but they can be dealt with effectively only in condition of acceptance of each other's legitimate concerns.

PART ONE
CONTEMPORARY INDIA

1

INDIAN POLITICAL SYSTEM AT WORK

1.1. PARLIAMENTARY DEMOCRACY IN INDIA

The form of government that we have enshrined in our constitution is known as parliamentary democracy. Under it, the people of India was to exercise their sovereignty through a Parliament at the Centre and a Legislature at each state. The final shape of the system was given in Article 79 to 123 in part Vth of the Constitution. It was preferred as it would provide a continual assessment and control of the activities of the Executive by the Legislature, thereby contributing to a more stable and effective government. It however in India's case, failed to give desired results. Our failure lies in the fact that despite adopting a democratic structure of governance, we have not been able to evolve the kind of norms, values, attitudes and style of conduct, conducive to the functioning of a healthy democratic system. Feeling of casteism, communalism, regionalism, etc. still occupy the minds of many of our people vitiating the entire Political process. The anatomy of parliamentary democracy is still a challenge for us because it depends upon habits of consent and compromise which are attributes only of mature political societies.

Origin and Development

Democracy on the basis of its vast history comprises narrow as well as wide meaning. To some it is a form of government, to others a way of social life. The political aspect of democracy found its earliest roots when men protested against systems which upon one ground or another excluded them from a share in power. Oppressive and discriminatory forms of government were opposed by the people because of privileges which were made confined to a narrow range of persons. At the juncture mass of the people sought the extension of such privileges to more people on the ground that limitation was not justifiable. This notion of equality paved the way to the essence of the democratic idea–the effort of men to affirm their own essence and to remove all barriers to that affirmation. The development is therefore the demand for equality, the demand that the system of power be erected upon the similarities and not the differences between men. Time and place played a significant role in determining the substance of the term but with the passage of time its natural character extended to electorate, the relation between government and the people, the absence of wide economic differences between citizens, the refusal to recognise privileges built on birth or wealth, race or creed.[1]

In its larger sphere democracy is not a way of governing whether by majority or otherwise, but primarily a way of determining who shall govern and, broadly, to what ends. The only way in which the people, all the people, can determine who shall govern is by referring the question to public opinion and accepting on each occasion the verdict of the polls.[2] The growth of democracy has always been associated with the free discussion of political issues, with the right to differ concerning them and with the settlement of difference, not by force majeure but by resort to the counting of votes. The right to differ did not end with the victory of the majority but was inherent in the system. It establishes a new and more integral relationship between community and state.

Apart from a specific form of government, the perfect form of democracy also refers to situations and systems. When a person lives in a genuine democracy, he knows it, feels it, and breathes it. A basic principle of democracy is a full recognition of the dignity and worth of the individual. Man's dignity, in the democratic view, is not something conferred on him or legislated into existence. It is part of his birth right as a human being. In a true democracy, money, machines, and systems are important only as they contribute to man's welfare.[3] But in the large states of modern day we can not hope a democratic form of government to be the government "by" the people in the literal sence of the term. With the growing authority of some assembly of the people or of the people's representative, such as the Greek ecclesia, the Roman comitia, the English Parliament, development of representative institutions began to take a definite shape.

Modern Parliament is a representative body through which the democratic ideals are hoped to be served. It is a means rather than an end in itself. Its aim is to achieve the ideals of a mature political society. Earlier the struggle for the attainment of democratic institutions has taken forms as various as the conditions it encountered. The eighteenth century, in particular, popularised three ideas. English experience led to the belief that Parliament is the parent of civil society. The American Revolution made popular the notion that a discontented people has the right to cashier its governors. The French Revolution established the principle that autocracy is the necessary parent of special privilege. All these necessarily increased the rate of progress towards democratic institutions. When in later years representative system was criticized as leaving the members of Parliament the master of the electorate between elections, constitutions began to embody the initiative, the referendum and the recall as the necessary safeguards in a democratic state.[4]

Among political thinkers in ancient and medieval times, marsiglio of Padua with the experience of Italian cities in his mind, William of Ockham and Thomas Aquinas' insistence on an elective monarchy played a very positive role in consolidating the concept of representation. Though ecclesiastical in origin the notion was based on the famous Phrase Quod omnes tangit, ab omnibus approbetur' which showed a sense that the exclusion of an interest may make the representation of a body imperfect. The idea of representation was of seminal importance because it gave those excluded from a share in the organs of government the opportunity of grievance. The cause of representation was further championed by John Locke, Voltaire, Montesquieu and Rousseau who sounded a deeper note and denied the legitimacy of all government in which the general will of all the people was not the effective lawmaking power.

Keeping in view the large number of population, the fact emerged that decisions cannot be taken without government by parties. "Party organisation," as Bagehot said, "is the vital principle of representative government."[5] Without the party system in some form it is impossible to get that concentration of voters for decision which is essential with electorates of the modern size. But parties, inevitable as they are, have brought with them a host of complex problems. The method of choosing candidates, the proper size of a constituency, the prevention of corruption, the exact powers which an elected member should exert, the representation of minorities are only the outstanding issues for which suitable machinery need to be devised. In order to achieve a functional society in effective terms the new democratic theory calls for a thorough overhauling of existing institutions, particularly on the political side.

Adoption in India

Deliberately and after long argument India adopted a constitution based on Parliamentary government. It was the only form of government with which India was familiar when it gained independence because the British had introduced this system in our country through the Acts of 1909, 1919 and 1935. They were conscious enough and Parliamentary government was implemented with lots of changes and safeguards to protect colonial interests but from 1919 till independence we worked Parliamentary government with one type or the other. It is important in India's case because for the first time in its history, Western democratic theory has been confronted by a non-western democratic experience. Introduction of modern education through English medium mixed with the political aspirations of young men who came out from this system of education were moulded by the works of eminent British thinkers like Edmund Burke, Bentham, John Stuart Mill and Macaulay. The fascinating story of the struggle for Parliamentary supremacy carried on in England gave these young men a new hope of some day securing a similar set-up for their own country.[6] It was adopted together with the basic ideas underlying it but with suitable amendments to make it a success. For example, unlike the British constitution it did not provide for a hereditary monarchy rather it provided for an elected President.

It was one of the important questions to be dealt by the Constituent Assembly of India and two committees were set up in 1947, one to determine the 'principles of the Union Constitution,' the other 'the principles of a model Provisional Constitution.' The committees decided that within the framework of a Republic the Executive, both at the Centre and in the States, in relation to the Legislature concerned should function on the Westminister model. In presenting the Report of the Union Committee Sardar Vallabhbhai Patel, the then Deputy Prime Minister, said in the Constituent Assembly, "They come to the conclusion that it would suit the conditions of this country better to adopt the Parliamentary system of constitution, the British type of the constitution, with which we are familiar.[7] The recommendation of the Union Committee was also appropriate in the light of the demand made by M.N. Roy, Motilal Nehru Committee Report, the Socialist Party, the Congress and the Hindu Mahasabha before independence for the introduction of full responsible or Parliamentary government in India.[8] In it there was emphasis on daily as well as periodic responsibility. The cabinet is the repository of all powers and is responsible to Parliament for the daily acts of administration.

At the time of the introduction of Parliamentary democracy, doubts were expressed whether it would succeed in India. It was pointed out by some scholars that there were many hindrances in the way of successful working of democracy. At one time Mahatma Gandhi himself was critic of the institution and called Parliament 'a sterile woman and a prostitute'- sterile woman because she does not do anything 'of its own accord', a prostitute as she is 'under the control' of Prime Ministers who change from time to time.[9] But for Jawaharlal Nehru, the then Prime Minister it is a peaceful method of dealing with problems. It is a method of argument, discussion and decision and of accepting that decision, even though one may not agree with it. He valued the opinion of minority in Parliament and held the view that a majority which ignores the minority is not working in the true spirit of Parliamentary democracy.[10] It has been stated at the outset that the form of government introduced by our Constitution both at the Union and the States is the Parliamentary Government of British type.[11]

As a follow up of the principle of Parliamentary democracy the constitution of India has evolved a complete machinery in which it was hoped that the form of government would function within the framework provided by the fundamental rights guaranteed to the citizens and the Presidential authority responsible for upholding the constitution and security and defence of the country. The distribution of powers between the Centre and the States results in a sort of 'convertible federalism' that is a quasi-federalism which in times of national emergency can enable the President to assume the powers of the state, subject, of course, to Parliamentary control.[12] Introduction of the system effected a harmonious blending of the legislative and executive organs of the state in as much as the executive power is wielded by a group of members of the Legislature who command a majority in the popular Chamber of the Legislature and remain in power so long as they retain that majority. However, it may easily be pointed out that it takes more than a Parliament to make Parliamentary democracy a success.

M.N. Roy on Parliamentary Democracy

The Parliamentary system as adopted in Indian Constitution has been in question for a long time. Several Political Philosophers of our time including Manvendra Nath Roy have disliked Parliamentary democracy, as we too feel it is not suitable particularly for countries who lack a political society. The basic guiding philosophy of Roy's idea is that society and state are instruments created by man to serve his own interest.

He argued that man as a creator, is prior to society and state. There is one of ends and means, the means are justified only in so far as they can promote the end.[13] Society has no interest independent of the interests of individuals who form the society.

With this assumption at the heart, Roy has analyed the pros and cons of Parliamentary democracy in the Indian context. Although he admits that the problem of the relation between the society and the individual is becoming more and more complex, the original purpose of all social organisations, is to help man to develop the potentialities inherent in him as a biological organism. His first objection relates to the concept of democracy itself, in which people elect a few representatives to the legislature and these representatives claim the right to rule the country in the name of the sovereign people. This practice of the delegation is a negation of democracy and considered by him as incompatible with the principle of popular sovereignty[14]. If power is taken from the people, even for the shortest period of time, democracy is killed. Periodic power of electing representative is a thorough negation of people's actual authority. The voting right in election is thus, simply a way to surrender power in favour of a particular candidate. The people exercise their sovereignty by surrendering it from time to time, making it a contradiction of democratic practice.[15]

Parliamentary democracy concentrates political power in the hands of the few representatives through the election and by no means, it can establish a government of the people, for the people and by the people which is the essence of democracy. Under it, if the representatives are inspired by a spirit of popular welfare, they can at best set up a government for the people and the same is not a democratic one. However, in comparison to dictatorship he prefers democracy but considers its practice as inadequate for realising the principles of popular sovereignty.

Roy searched for a new pattern of democratic practice and during 1942-44, prepared two documents; Draft Constitution of Free India, and People's Plan for Economic Development of India. These documents contain his conception of organised democracy in which a government will be based on a network of People's Committee. This organised democracy in which a government will be based on a network of People's Committee. This organized democracy would be the source of all constitutional authority, to be exercised directly through local committees in villages, towns and cities.[16] The draft constitution provided for recall of elected representatives. In political as well as economic sphere

Roy strongly pleaded for decentralisation in place of centralisation as we find in Parliamentary democracy in which intelligence, integrity, wisdom, moral excellence do not count for much. In operation it is full of grave defects. The people are powerless between elections. Political parties with their countrywide organisations and vast financial resources become agents of centralisation. Through decentralisation Roy's political philosophy aims to achieve individual freedom with a view to build a new social order.

Implementation

The framers of our constitution in their wisdom and foresight did not contemplate many of the developments that could take place in the country. Democracy in India has aroused a whole new set of expectations, resulting not only in the aggravation of certain existing conflict situations, and in the creation of new ones, but also, on the positive side, allowing for the emergence of new political classes. The dream of 1947 has soured to a certain extent but apart from being an experiment democracy in India has struck deep roots, and in this process, turned the soil over in several unanticipated ways.[17] On the other hand, the coming of new social segments and rural-based fragmentation have, to a large extent, changed the class character of Indian Parliament. Legislatures the world over, particularly in developed countries, still perform their parliamentary duties and contribute substantially to the making, amending and repealing of laws. In our case mainly on account of the lack of adequate education but mostly on account of social, cultural and political ethos they are brought up in, are not fitted to give of their best. The party machine, the political bosses, outrageously expensive elections, hovering political uncertainties and absence of known and legitimate sources of income, apart from what they earn as members of Parliament, have made elected bodies ineffective instrument of democratic polity.[18]

Following the years of India's independence Jawaharlal Nehru's charm as a statesman and as a thinker laid the foundations of Parliamentary democracy in the country. He viewed four major institutions- the Parliament, the Cabinet, the Congress Party and the bureaucracy as tools of social transformation. He cherished and respected Parliament and paid close attention to his views. He set up consultative committees, in which members of parliament of all political parties had opportunities to discuss and generate new departmental policies. He encouraged debates on important issues and helped create both informed public opinion and consensually- based policies. Despite criticism from the knowledgeable people and the warnings against introducing universal adult franchise, Nehru could not but make Indian democracy as broad-based as possible.[19]

The democratic system so established worked in a satisfactory manner for a number of years. The electorate at least appeared to vote responsibly when it did not throw any substantial part of its strength on the side of extremist, particularist and splinter parties. There were good and stable majorities, as a rule both in the states and the centre. Regional parties declined between the first and second general elections. The constitutional liberties of the subject were substantially assured in practice.[20] It established a fundamental principle relating to India's political authority that operation of the democratic process is the only way and that political power in India flows through the ballot box. The only time since independence when a breach of such a principle was likely to be committed was during the Emergency when Indira Gandhi took upon herself the right to decide whether or not there should be another election.[21] Most Parliamentary conventions and practices were temporarily discarded or abused; the federal system was undermined; the judiciary failed to uphold even the right of habeas corpus; a new cult of leadership was promoted in the democratic tradition of India. But by calling an election, regardless of her motives, even Indira Gandhi ended up by strengthening the fundamental political belief in the country that the only legitimate way of constitutional political authority was by means of an electoral mandate.

Peaceful transfer of power from the Indian National Congress to the Janata Party in March 1977 contributed in the heralding of an effectively functioning democracy in India. It established the basic principle of an orderly change of government. It opened up an era of political self-help for the Indians who, after 1977 never tried to explore other forms of government which might be more suitable. They now realised that the man in office had no inherent right to be there ; that such men were given the mandate to govern only because of their policy commitments and promises at the time of elections. In general elections at the state and national levels have become increasingly competitive and have a occasioned numerous transfers of power in the states and several at the centre.

The parliamentary democracy of India from the very beginning, considered political participation and successive entry of new groups into the electoral/political process as the essential ingredient of the system. Concerning political participation it became evident not only in the high rates of electoral turnout, but in many other forms. With regard to turnout, the figures vary from election to election and from region to region. It ranged from a low of 45.7 per cent in the First General Election in 1952, to a high of 64.1 per cent in 1984; it remained above 55 per cent in every general election conducted after 1962 onwards. Additionally participation of Indians is also extensive and involves rural as well as urban, poor as well as middle-class segments of society.[22] New tactics, devices, methods and symbols are frequently used to mobilize large numbers of people for political causes in the country.

In the First, Second and Third General Elections India did not witness any basic change in traditional vote bank, and their attitude towards political parties and supremacy of the Indian National Congress remained unchallenged. The Fourth General Elections reduced the majority of the Congress in Lok Sabha and Legislative Assemblies of states. High Governmental stability of the fifties was followed by the rapid rise and fall of governments and the first indications of the use of crowds by opposition parties to press their demands for political change in the sixties. As observed by one scholar. 'It was obvious consequence of the 1967 election results, the general contours of the political power structure were undergoing basic changes. The otherwise highly fragmented opposition, saw in the situation an opportunity to capture power at least in some states. Election after election caste groups with large population concentrations in particular regions, districts, and constituencies, whose members previously either did not vote in large numbers or voted for persons from the dominant castes, have produced their own leaders who have given them a voice in the political process and access to political and economic patronage'.[23] In south it took the course of the mobilization of non-Brahman castes while in north India the mobilization of the backward and lower castes became the main plank in coming years.

Despite large scale participation of the people and entry of the new classes in the mainstream of national politics India failed to prevent the wearing down of institutional authority at the peak of which our Parliament rests. Though legislators the world over have to toe the line followed by the executive, the Parliament and state assemblies of India, in particular, have lost much of their sanctity mainly to the behaviour of the members. There is a steep decline in the standard of debates and the proceedings of these bodies are usually characterized by ignorance of or studied indifference to the subjects discussed.[24] Besides every group tries to use the Parliament as a platform for spitting venom against the party in power. The smaller the group, the more raucous it is for lacking strength of number, it compensates it by the incessant use of lung power. Since getting into Parliament does not depend upon the sincerity with which a number takes up ;his duties, he has to make sure that the party bosses should be kept pleased and enough moolal set beside, no matter how made to enter parliament and the assembly again and again.[25] It has led criminalization of politics which is a shocking development and as the dons and the ganglords make their presence felt more and more, parliamentary democracy can not but be degraded and in course of time become a pitiable farce of the democratic process.

The problem of government in India is complex and far from being uniform, it is historically variable and often in contradiction with prediction. The scene witnessed in parliament and in state assemblies have put the entire system of parliamentary government under a crumbling strain. It should be checked and reformed without further delay.

1.2 INDIAN DEMOCRACY IN PRACTICE

Today the people in India are in a mood which comes rarely in the life of a country. They are looking forward starry eyed, to a new direction, a new era, a life. It is time not merely for a new budget or a new licensing policy or a new price structure. It is the moment for shaping and moulding a new society, for giving a new and clear orientation to the nation. The constitution is not a structure of fossils like a coral reef and is not intended merely to enable politicians to play their unending game of power. When a republic comes to birth, it is the leaders who produce the institutions. Later, it is the institutions which produce the leaders. In India's case the established structures failed to give desired results. If the system of Parliamentary democracy had been worked in conformity with the objectives for which it has been established and the obligations and codes of conduct it imposes on politicians, political parties and their mutual relations, it would have constituted a most heart warming feature in finding a way out of the morass and confusion in which we are finding ourselves as a nation. In the words of T.S. Eliot, 'we had the experience, but we missed the meaning'. We the Indians, know it well that our democratic institutions have not been worked in that manner. Our electorate is largely illiterate and not in a position to take an objective or critical view of the promises and performances of different political parties.

System at Stake

Our constitution was framed on the basis that our citizens, including the best, would be willing to take a continuous and considered part in public life. Democracy depends upon habits of consent and compromise which are attributes only of mature political societies. The lawful government by the majority under the rule of abiding law, and with freedom of opposition and dissent is, both geographically and historically, an exceptional human achievement rather than the normal way of organizing nations. Where the spirit of moderation does not prevail society degenerates into divisions and hatred replaces goodwill.

The single criteria for a good government in democracy is progress; and by progress we mean peace, liberty and better life. To quote Gandhi. 'Democracy must in essence mean the art and science of mobilising the entire physical economic and spiritual resources of all the various sections of the people in the service of the common good of all.[26] It is a way of life; it is also a process forever recreating that way of life. In it, each person is important as an individual; his well being is vital in itself. Lord Acton, after a profound examination of historical processes came to the conclusion that the fate of every democracy, of every government based on the sovereignty of the people, depends on the choice it makes between these opposite principles; absolute power on the one hand, and on the other the restraints of legality and the authority of tradition. It must stand or fall according to its choice, whether to give the supremacy to the law or to the will of the people; whether to constitute moral association maintained by duty or physical one kept together by force.[27]

Without doubt, the constitution of India is one of the best ever devised by the ingenuity of men who were engaged in the task. But while piloting the Constitution Bill Dr. Ambedkar said, I feel that, however good the constitution may be it is sure to turn out bad if those called upon to work it happen to be a bad lot. However bad a constitution may be, if those who are called upon to work it happen to be a good lot, it will turn out to be good'. The constitutional structure of the world's newest and largest democracy as held by Sachchidananda Sinha, Provisional Chairman of the Constituent Assembly, that it all may Perish in an hour by the folly, corruption or negligence of its only keepers, 'The People'. These prophetic words came true. The foundations of the constitution have been shaken by the folly of the people, the corruption of our politicians and negligence of the elite. In the last fifty years, we have reduced the noble processes of our constitution to the level of a carnival of claptrap, cowardice and chicanery.[28] Just as it is not enough to import the latest technology if a country lacks the scientific temper and skills to harness it, so the Parliamentary system too can become arid if members of Parliament, on both sides of the political divide, continue to display a lack of democratic temper. The essence of Parliamentary democracy lies in the tolerance of dissent and a willingness to hear and even heed a point of view contrary to one's own.[29]

Nehru Era

The democratic system so established certainly worked well for a number of years. Jawaharlal Nehru's idea on democracy can best be attributed to his submission to the objective laws that led him to realise the direction of the historical process, to understand as an objective and progressive course of events proceeding from the lower to higher. He proceeded to his political work not with the approach of a religious one, but went ahead scientifically, trying to bring it into line with the general objective of course of history and subjugate it to progressive trends. Nehru played a very significant role in order to strengthen political institutions under the framework of the Indian constitution. The adoption of the constitution in its secular spirit during the years of strife and communal tension was itself a dashing step taken under his leadership.[30] He was one of those great democrats who believed in democracy as a political system allowing the peaceful play of power, the adherence by the 'outs' to decisions made by the 'ins' and the recognition by the 'ins' of the rights of the 'outs'.[31] It was an inherent virtue of Nehru that he always gave the opposition an opportunity to express its view. In his opinion, the end of Parliamentary democracy should be the maximum good of the people and to this end, he was opposed to delaying and complicated procedures, since parliamentary institutions reflect the character of the people, he laid emphasis on the purity of means and ends under this system.

In an initial and experimental manner, we have accepted and dealt with this great world-moving force of man-on-the-March, which is democracy. We are aware that such experiment in democracy is sure to bring about revolutionary changes in our individual and social life. However, the founding fathers of the Indian republic, too, had their own fears of the future of democracy, given the backlog of the problems. They grafted a democratic political system on to a society which was in dire need of fundamental reform in the shortest possible time. It was the faith and the hope of the fathers that in India democracy would not only survive but that through it the necessary social changes would also occur.[32] To sustain democratic institutions, in general, what is required, is a political society which shares their underlying values and constantly manifests commitment to them in its own political activities. Only such a political society can ensure the operation and survival of the democratic processes.

Democracy is meaningful only to the extent it leads to the participation of the people. Sensing the dangers of democracy in India, Jayaprakash Narayan felt that unless democratic system involves masses in its working the ideals of freedom, equality and justice could not be achieved. Following the view of Harold Laski, he, in his paper published in 1959 entitled 'The Reconstruction of Indian polity,' held that the worth of democracy must be judged by the amount of voluntary activities within it. It is not the formal institutions like Parliament, assemblies, elected governments which constitute democracy. It must live in the life of the people. Rejecting the theory of parliamentary democracy with multi-Party system, he advanced the system of Partyless democracy of participatory democracy. For practical purpose and in order that the people might participate in the government, the government must be brought as near to the people as possible. This would require a thorough going system of political and economic decentralisation.

Nehru did not confine his opinion to the realm of politics alone but the arena of economy was not out of his reach. He considered that political democracy by itself is not enough except that it may be used to obtain a gradually increasing measure of economic democracy. Nehru believed in industrialisation and a strong industrial base. The Russian five year plans and the progress made in that country had a great impact on the mind of Nehru. Though he was impressed by Russia's economic progress he was against the dictatorial form of rule. Therefore, he was for a mixed economy and a good deal of progress was achieved but during his economic period he invested more in industry. More emphasis was laid on industry than agriculture.

Modernisation as sought by Nehru by its very nature promotes contradictory tendencies. It involves advances and retreats, hope and despair, determination to push forward and desire for escape into the past. Inevitably, India, too has experienced such contradictory pulls. Though it has moved too far on the road to modernisation to turn its back on it, it has marked time again and again. The Indian intelligentsia was full of confidence and believed that the country would industrialise rapidly and move into an era of distributive justice without going through any hardships of primitive accumulation of capital. Nehru in the fifties represented this hope and innocence. He himself was convinced that the Indian economy could reach the take off stage in a decade or two.

The lack of authority, order and discipline can adversely affect economic development as well. And as the economy becomes sophisticated, it becomes highly vulnerable to disruption. Modern agriculture, for example, needs a steady supply of power, diesel, fertilizers and pesticides, an assured market and remunerative prices. In the fifties, we had many eminent men in public life who were every inch a gentleman. In the sixties we had many public figures who were every alternate inch a gentleman. Unfortunately, in the seventies we have an unacceptably large number of politicians who are no inch a gentleman.[33] Therefore, by the end of Nehru era, this economic optimism had begun to give way to serious doubts. The sixties and seventies saw grave economic difficulties. From the mid-sixties onwards, with the 1965 Indo-Pakistan war, the massive IMF – enforced devaluation of the rupee soon after and the terrible drought that ravaged the land, it was clear that the system which had seemed hitherto to be sailing in tranquil waters, had entered a turbulent sea. It was only aroused this time that the rumblings of a system beginning to come under socio-economic stress were first quite clearly heard. Politically the most significant manifestation of this gathering crisis appeared in 1967 elections which saw the once unassailable Congress Party lose out to a motely assemble of opposition parties in a number of northern states.

All this was perhaps too good to last, though it did not last for well over a decade. Despite the scientific temper he had for the country, he was a poor judge of men, and therefore, he could not distinguish between real friends and sycophants. In the later phase of his life he took the support of undesirable elements to remain in power. Though he was popular with the masses he did not take action against vested interest which exploited the masses. He did not mind taking funds from anti – social elements. The Congress Party started accepting black money for elections during his time. Though soft, he was not always straightforward in dealing with his colleagues. The Kamaraj Plan was contrived to ease out some persons he disliked. His 'soft pedaling' of corruption had a disastrous effect on public morals. Nehru admitted the facts of public life then prevailing and said, 'Unhappily during the war and afterwards various types of corruption have grown. Controls have added to them and general standards fallen, both in government servants and in the public. Black marketing in India is not merely an individual offence, but a social evil. There can be no two opinions that adequate measures should be taken to check and end this degradation of our public life.[34]

Post–Nehru Era

Indira Gandhi took over the reigns in this hopeless political and economic situation and soon gave way to hope and confidence. She used morally dubious and politically skillful tactics, nationalised the major Indian banks, abolished the princes privilege and launched a radical sounding populist, peronist style 'garibi hatao' programme. In addition as the Nehru era drew to a close, the Indian intelligentsia had more or less taken shape of the larger society and it was badly divided. As such, its commitment to national integration and a strong central authority had become feeble. Large sections of intelligentsia were opposed to her primarily because she stood for a strong centre which was a dangerous approach. As a result, the elite and the newly displaced groups began to lose confidence in the efficacy of the system. Some individuals and groups attempted to provide leadership to the alienated millions and to meet their need for escape. While some of them advocated a drastic revision of the constitution or brand new constitution as if the constitution had stood in the path of economic progress, others offered populist and radical solutions. They struck a sympathetic chord even in the elite, which though committed to and part of the slow moving democratic process, was looking for quick solutions to complex problems.

The five-fold oil price rise by OPEC countries at the end of 1973 and the energy crisis it precipitated was for the Indian economy the last straw on the camel's back. By then the system was in deep crisis. Industry was in recession, the level of investment had fallen, successive droughts had lowered agricultural productivity, traders had began to cash in on, shortages and the consequent black market in a wide range of commodities from steel and cement to edible oil and food grains. Hard pressed by this array of hostile economic forces, large sections of the population stepped up their demands on the system at the very moment when it was least able to meet them. Since 1947 tremendous social forces with the most far reaching implications had been at work in the cities and in the countryside. Development often means discontent. It is only when relatively stable societies are sought to be changed rapidly and profoundly that they begin to undergo ferment. These forces appeared at the time of agitation over the linguistic reorganisation of states but on relatively limited scale.[35]

The emergency which Mrs. Gandhi imposed on 25 June 1975,

was largely in response to a desperate coalition of dominant groups she represented to and a deep rooted, all pervasive structural crisis. The pre-emergency assumption was that it would give full and free play to demands by diverse groups for the fulfilment of their new found expectations. However, during the emergency social contention was artificially held in abeyance, aspirant groups were inhibited about voicing their claims and social conflict was sought to resolve not by accommodation through the free play of argument but with the iron hand. Not surprisingly, this approach brought rapidly diminishing returns in terms of 'discipline' 'order' and 'stability'. Social conflict could not forever be held in abeyance, public opinion could not forever be manipulated and regulated, popular resentment could not forever be contained.

Unlike many other countries where democracy has fallen by the way side, India's one billion people have increasingly thrown ruler in and out of office. But all is not well with Indian democracy. The panchayat amendments have innovated a unique constitutionally mandate multi-tier federalism which would bring power closer to the people. Indian federalism gives too much power to the union. Exercised around one hundred times, the power to impose President's Rule subverts democracy and has been grossly abused. Communalism, muscle and money power has intruded into the electoral process. Parliamentary governance is threatened by weak coalitions. Floor crossing had not been disciplined by the anti-defection amendments; and likely to increase with 1998 judgement that clothes bribe taking legislators with criminal immunity.

In a democracy based on adult suffrage which means the nose-counting method, the only way to achieve progress is to educate the masses. But we made no attempt to educate our people in the obligations that a democratic system places upon its citizens on the manner in which they represent their needs and grievances or thoughts through representations, dialogues, discussions and non-violent political lobbying but left them to carry on their relations with government on the agitational and confrontationist basis which had been employed in the past against their colonial rulers. Leaders of consequence did not explain to the people that, as democracy provided for periodic elections at which ruling parties and governments could be thrown out of power if they had misbehaved during the inter-election period. There was no recognition of the serious obstacles that illiteracy and lack of civic consciousness places to the efficient functioning of a democratic political system nor was any serious attempt made to wipe out mass illiteracy and lack of understanding of the norms of democratic functioning.

The national conscience has to be roused to such a degree that it would cease to tolerate falsehood and dishonesty in public life. Standards of ethics and decency in public life are less easy to enforce by law than by public opinion. Hence, there must be a nation wide campaign to disseminate correct facts and right ideas among the public at large. The best charity which one can do in India today is to carry knowledge to the people as Abraham Lincoln rightly held that the people would be able to face any crisis, provided only the correct facts were made known to them. The duty of the citizen is not merely to vote but to vote wisely. He must be guided by reason and by reason alone. He must vote for the best man, irrespective of any other consideration and irrespective of the party label. What India today badly needs, and sadly lacks, is not political leadership but moral leadership which can lead to a renaissance of true Indian culture.

1.3 HUMAN VALUES IN INDIAN CONSTITUTION

The framers of Indian Constitution through its preamble and different provisions made it a prime source of human rights and its development. As a follow up of Human Rights from the days of Magna Carta the new Constitution which came into force on 26 January 1950 lays down a set of rules relating to the traditional civil and political rights and the new economic and social rights. Preamble, the heart of the constitution, was itself based on the Objectives Resolution drafted by Jawaharlal Nehru and introduced in the Assembly in its first session on 13 December 1946 and adopted on 22 January 1947. It states that the people of India in the Constituent Assembly made a solemn resolve to secure all citizens, justice, social, economic and political; liberty of thought, expression, belief, faith and worship; equality of status and of opportunity; and to promote among them all, fraternity assuring the dignity of the individual and the unity of the nation.[36] The spirit and the made arrangements were praised by Granville Austin, the constitutional scholar, who opines, probably no other nation's constitution has provided so much impetus towards changing and rebuilding society for the common good.[37] The provisions of Fundamental Rights and Directive Principles are supplementary to each other and hardly confronts at any point. The first is a guarantee against encroachments by the state and second, a set of directives to the state to introduce reforms to make those rights effective.

Human Rights Defined

The concept of human rights, in general, refers to all human beings having universal rights or status to which we are entitled simply by being human.[38] They are inherent in nature and without which we can not live as human being as Harold Laski remarks, 'Rights are those conditions of social life without which no man can seek in general to be himself at the best". Human rights allow us to fully develop and use our human qualities, intelligence, talents and conscience and to satisfy our inner and other needs. In wider or global standards human rights based on subsistence is universally accepted and thus not limited to providing to all human beings with the needs for their physical subsistence but involves a certain degree of minimal comfort beyond merely keeping one's organs working because human subsistence also consists of being able to function.[39]

The very motivations for human rights came from its offer of protection from tyrannical and authoritarian calculations. Repressive measures of an autocratic government may be constrained with the recognition of supreme moral limits on any government's freedom of action. The prime rhetorical benefit of human rights is that they are viewed as being so basic and so fundamental to human existence that they should trump any other consideration. Any conception of rights trumps other claims within a society, human rights may be of a higher order that supersedes even other rights claims within a society. The next attraction of human rights that they are often thought to exist beyond the determination of specific societies. They set a universal standard that can be used to judge any society. At best human rights provide an acceptable bench mark with which individuals or governments from one part of the world may criticize the norms followed by other governments or cultures.

The shape and size of human factor that we have enshrined in our constitution should be considered as an extended idea of freedom struggle fought in India for decades. Among the several streams, the main movement was under the leadership of Mahatma Gandhi who laid emphasis on Swaraj and which was essentially anti-colonial. Our national movement was not anti-feudal, although a number of peasant and tribal struggles at one level and the Dalit movement led by Ambedkar at another level, were the clear manifestation of serious drawbacks of the mainstream movement but they failed to get an all-India character.[40] The neglect of the social and economic development, in due course, posed a challenge for the political process and the system itself. The so called constitutional governance, modelled after liberal ideas with the guaranteed rights, was introduced in a society which was a glaring example of poverty, inequalities and unemployment. The social order, as visioned by the constitution was not backed by the existing state-society relationship and as a result, the idea of human dignity and self-respect became a farce.

Apart from this ideational background of human factor in Indian Constitution, last but not the least important was the Declaration of Universal Human Rights on 10 December 1948 announced by the United Nations. Earlier the Charter of the United Nations which was formed after the Second World War, gave prominence to the aim of promoting Human Rights and freedom. The Preamble of the UN proclaimed, 'We the people of United Nations determined – to reaffirm faith in fundamental Human Rights, dignity and birth of human person in equal rights of men and women and of nation, large and small – have resolved to combine efforts to accomplish these aims.[41] The very first Article of the UN Charter declared that one of the purposes of this organization is the achievement of international cooperation in promoting and encouraging respects for human rights. Likewise, Article 68 of the Charter provides for setting up of several commissions including one for the promotion of Human Rights. Further, going a step ahead, the General Assembly of the UN adopted on December 10, 1948, the Universal Declaration of Human Rights, a report submitted by the Commission of Human Rights. The said Declaration contains 30 Articles pertaining to the common standard of the achievements for all people and the nations. Articles 1 to 21 of the Declarations relate to the traditional so called natural rights and basic freedom and Articles 22 to 28 concern social and economic rights without which there can be no opportunities for the enjoyment of these Natural Rights and basic freedom by the millions of people around the world.[42]

Constitutional Provisions

The Constitution of India was framed during a period of three years (1946-49) by a Constituent Assembly when the country was under severe stress. Following a long tradition of India the framers of the Constitution provided provisions of human rights and their development in the socio-economic perspectives of the country. Especially Part III and IV of the Constitution deal with human Fundamental Rights and Directive Principles of the State Policy respectively which form a total development of human personality. The Constitution-making body gave top priority to these lofty ideals and expressed their commitment to human values as stated by Nehru, 'the first task of this assembly is to free India through a constitution, to feed the starving people, and to cloth the naked masses, and to give every citizen the fullest opportunity to develop himself according to his capacity.[43] Despite pious intentions of the framers of Constitution, the provisions relating to fundamental rights were recognised as justiciable and it was hoped that in due course political process would bring a qualitative change in socio-economic development of the country. Austin, the constitutional expert, called these provisions the 'conscience of the constitution' and was of the opinion that the core of the commitment to the social revolution lies in part III and IV, in the Fundamental Rights and in the Directive Principles of State Policy.

With a view to promote and ensure human values several fundamental rights have been embodied in Part III of the Indian Constitution. These rights are of seven kinds; the right of equality, the right of freedom, the right against exploitation, the right to freedom of religion, cultural and educational rights, the right to property and the right to constitutional remedies. These rights have been incorporated in Articles 12 to 35 of the Constitution and primarily protect individuals and minority groups from arbitrary state action. Among the Articles the most important are 15 and 16 of the Constitution. Article 15 has provided Prohibition of Discrimination on certain grounds in employment; such as religion, race, caste, sex, place of birth or any of them. In the same vein Article 16 of the Constitution guarantees equality of opportunity in matters of public employment for all citizens and is expected to provide a bulwark against consideration of caste, community and religion.[44] The inclusion of fundamental rights in the constitution of India Bill framed in 1895 had contained this concept in embryo, and it had figured prominently in the Motilal Nehru Report of 1928. The freedom movement till the forties also demanded concessions, resulting in the Acts of 1909, 1919 and 1935. The shape of rights was influenced by these acts which were essentially liberal in character. It is one of the important causes for the privileging of civil and political rights which have come to assume the status of fundamental rights.

In Part IV of the Constitution certain Directive Principles of the State Policy has been provided which intend to be a declared fundamental in the governance of the country. These Directive Principles are intended to lay down in general terms the object which the framers of the constitution designed how the government at the centre and states should pursue in guiding the destinies of the Nation. They are in the nature of affirmative instruction to governments to direct their activities to do certain things and thereby promote the realisation of the high ideals set forth in the Preamble of the constitution. The state was to take steps to organise village Panchayats, to improve standards of living and nutrition, provided free legal aid, and promote educational and other interests of Scheduled Castes and Tribes and other weaker sections.[45] It was to protect and improve the environment and safeguard the forests and wild life of the country.

For the full realisation of human values socio-economic rights were viewed as essential by the framers of the Indian Constitution. It was a perplexing question for them........ how to distinguish between those rights that could be granted immediately, such as political rights, and those that should be there as ideals to be reached and could be granted only overtime, such as social and economic rights? The solution was found by borrowing a concept from the Irish Constitution and encoding the socio-economic rights as Directive Principles of State Policy. Among the different provisions, the essence of the Directive Principles has been contained in Article 38 which lays down that 'the state shall strive to promote the welfare of the people by securing and protecting as effectively as it may a social order in which justice, social, economic, and political, shall inform all the institutions of the national life.

The members of the Constituent Assembly while providing for the Fundamental Rights and Directive Principles of the State Policy did not visualise any contradiction and hoped for creating a condition for the building of an egalitarian society in which individual freedoms were secured. The relationship between the individual liberty and social change was rightly envisaged as dynamic. To quote Nehru, 'The Directive Principles of State Policy represent a dynamic move towards a certain objective. The Fundamental Rights represent something static, to preserve certain rights which exist.[46] In later years serious differences of interpretation have arisen many times and it is agreed that till 1971 the courts gave greater importance to Fundamental Rights than to Directive Principles. Two amendments...... 25th and 42nd made in 1971 and 1976 respectively were brought by Indira Gandhi and gave precedence to Directive Principles. It, however, was equated in 1980 when in a landmark judgement in Minerva Mills Limited Vs. Union of India the Supreme Court has held the view that both Fundamental Rights and Directive Principles are equally important and one cannot be sacrificed for the other.

Operational Aspect

The Constitution of India draws extensively from Western legal traditions in its principle of liberal democracy and provided all citizens the opportunities essential for the proper development of human potentials. Even at the time of implementing the constitution, there was a visible gap between the state system and the prevailing society of the period. The ideal hope that political and civil rights would soon create a condition conducive for the socio-economic rights disappeared in coming years. In fact, the unjust and unequal relations between state and the society determined the character of the state in which no agrarian changes, land reforms and changes in rural power structure were initiated in years following the independence. In due course it proved dear and the neglect of social and economic development began to put pressure on political process.

From the late sixties different types of dissent including the violent one appeared on national scene. There were regional and sub-regional agitations, autonomous movements, ethnic assertions, tribal and peasant struggles, and so on. Among them some of the agitations proliferated and took to armed resistance … insurrectionary or insurgent or militant or even terrorist forms. In that kind of situation the established system or state started depending on coercive force, with and without the backing of the law. The political elite who did not command organized cadre and popular consent, approved the use of necessary and unnecessary force and increased the violation of rights, including the right to life.[47] These violations include lawless behaviour, assaulting ordinary people, raiding of the villages, unlawful detention, brutal forms of torture, custodial deaths and also killings of human rights activists. Even after liberalisation of the Indian economy, the market forces driven by self-interest and global pressure would hardly be in a position to produce human values or sustain civil and political rights.

In recent years as the issues relating to human factors received prominence in India and the world around, the Indian Parliament and the Judiciary as well began to deliver certain rules and judgements to promote and ensure human values in the country. The Indian Parliament has enacted legislation regarding ownership of the land, fixing a ceiling, minimum wages for workers, prevention of child labour, and provision of old age pension. Untouchability, the age-old curse of Indian society, has now been made an offence punishable by law. It has also modernized our labour law and improved the conditions of labour by enacting laws.

The latest example in this regard is the Domestic Violence Act 2005 which has come into force from October 26, 2006.

Likewise, in a more asserting and judicious way the Supreme Court of India, through its various decisions, gave an equal legal status to Directive Principles of the State Policy. Right to Education and provisions for free and compulsory education up to the age of 14 years have been granted the status of fundamental rights to do justice to Article 41 and 45 of the Constitution. Other significant decisions that include the free legal aid, protection of environment, prevention of child labour in a hazardous work, protection of working women from sexual harassment which is considered violation of rights of gender equality and right to life are the landmark judgements in making India a country who cares much for human values. The provision of Fundamental Rights and its working with the Directive Principles of State Policy now largely depend on Parliamentary enactments and judicial activism which can be a path-finder. Acting on constitutional provisions a good beginning has been made just to gain the rest which is much more in this regard.

1.4 CHANGE OURSELVES NOT CONSTITUTION

As a follow up of the commitment made in its Election Manifesto, the National Democratic Alliance has constituted a commission to review the constitution of India under the Chairmanship of M.N. Venkatachaliah, a former Chief Justice of the Supreme Court of India. The commission as per its terms of reference was to examine, in the light of the experience of past 50 years as to how far the existing provisions of the constitution are capable of responding to the needs of efficient, smooth and effective system of governance and socio-economic development of modern India and to recommend changes, if any, that are required to be made in the constitution within the framework of Parliamentary Democracy without interfering with the basic structure or basic features of the constitution. Originally, the faith in the words of Abraham Lincoln that the government of the people, for the people and by the people have been embodied in our constitution to which all dignitaries of State Ministers, Judges, Legislators, and others, as well as Members of the Nyaya Panchayats in villages swear allegiance. Although the law presumes that every citizen knows the law yet that presumption is sometimes rudely shaken by the speech or action of executive authorities or officers of state or even of those who are trained in law and who knows it better.

Background of the System

We all know it that the truly serious philosophical problem that has implications for the destiny of all mankind is political. What is the ideal form of government? After the achievement of freedom our national leadership was faced with the task of : (a) stabilising the new state and (b) framing a new constitution for the country. The preamble of the constitution of India defines the ideal philosophy of Indian democracy and its key concepts are laid down as liberty, equality, justice and fraternity. A democracy to be real must be characterised by three features: use of the rational techniques of discussions, negotiations, persuasions, debates and argumentation in place of coercion, intimidation, threats and violence, a belief in and action according to the Kanatian concept that man is an end, not a means and lastly resort to certain institutional procedures for the realisation of individual liberty, for example, remedies for the enforcement of fundamental rights, judicial independence judicial review of legislative and administrative measures, free elections etc.

The adoption of Parliamentary democracy in India was deliberately decided upon by the Constituent Assembly in the context of an illiterate population and underdeveloped economy.[48] The democratic system so established worked well for a number of years. As we are acquainted that democratic institutions are easy to establish but difficult to sustain. They can be formally set up by means of constitutional provisions and their implementations. But to sustain them, and the democratic process in general, what is required is a political society which shares their underlying values and constantly manifests commitment to them in its own political activity. India's social and economic problems are so immense that only political parties and party workers, deeply committed to the goal of the welfare of the common man, can provide the necessary driving force. They can not be solved by means of periodic party eliminating movements.

Parliamentary government, to retain its hold, as maintained by Harold Laski, "must give the promise of great results. Nothing is more dangerous in a democratic state than a condition in which the people is persuaded that the fundamental instruments of its government are not equal to the tasks that are imposed upon them. A habit of lethargy is thereby induced which easily persuades a people to lend a ready air to the siren voices of dictatorship.[49]

Fortunately for us, the most lively minds in India were engaged in the search for the best form of government. All of them have brought out from their shelves dusty volumes of Digly, Bagehot, Harold Laski and Sir Ivor Jennings. Recently, I.K. Gujral, the former Prime Minister of India, recalled that the Indian constitution was framed by a Constituent

Assembly, whose members were elected representatives. Every individual or party had its own idea and many provisions were adopted through consensus instead of majority voting. He added further that the review of the constitution through nominated members defeats the very spirit in which it was originally framed.[50]

On the fiftieth anniversary of the founding of the Indian republic President K.R. Narayanan too, in his address to the nation counted the challenges arising out of imperfect or half hearted implementation of the provisions of the constitution. He charged that we have increasingly become callous and insensitive and have given a raw deal to the weaker sections of society like women, Scheduled Castes and Tribes. Many of the inadequacies of the working of our system and the lapses we have made are obvious to us. In fact, for the first time in its history, western democratic theory has been confronted by a non western democratic experience which has not only questioned some of its underlying assumptions but has also cast doubts on the efficacy of some of its conceptual tools. Such a challenge has come from the Indian democratic experiment. Like most other social and political theories, theories about democracy are deeply grounded in the political history and tradition of the countries of the west, and with the exception of a few scholars working in the field of comparative Government or political development, such a challenge to their universal validity has largely gone unnoticed.[51]

Position as Today

All insights into the constitution are wasted unless we comprehend that it was not built for an ordinary nation state but a complex civilization composed of the most unique cultural diversity the world has ever known. It is not the constitution that has failed us but the people have failed the constitution and so there is a need to change ourselves instead of changing the constitution. Loyalty to the chair is a valuable trait of today while it should be, in any case, to the nation and not to some individuals. A good Prime Minister, to use Winston Churchill's phrase, has to be a good butcher. He or she must get rid of those who fail to perform and, in our context, those who persistently attract adverse attention on moral grounds. Jawaharlal Nehru was not a good butcher, but he did not need to be. He has by and large a good team and challenges he faced were not as difficult to cope with as those of later years. India had ceased to be the stable society that it was in the fifties and the early sixties.

At a later stage, indisputably the standards of public life have declined sharply and unless we watch out we may join the ranks of countries where public life is lucrative business, perhaps the most lucrative of all. It would also be dishonest for anyone to suggest that standards have fallen only in public life. The same story is repeated in almost all other walks of life. Corruption seeps down from the top politicians, businessmen, industrialists and almost the entire ruling elite, think nothing of privately using corrupt means for their ends even while publicly decrying corruption. "Investigation" of corruption against political leaders remains "in process" for years and decades while the leaders continue not only free, enjoying official perks and privileges, but are also active in the ruling echelons.[52] Leading businessmen cheat the government as well as the public on an unprecedented scale. Top lawyers and doctors insist on payment in cash so that they can avoid paying taxes. University authorities make appointments on caste and communal considerations. A majority of professors do not deserve to be junior lecturers. Journalists peddle influence and engage in blackmail. Money and access to power rather than caste and old family reputation have began to determine one's status in the countryside as well.[53]

However, India is a land of contradictions. On the one hand every kind of malpractice prospers and on the other there are honest and competent men in top places who have reached there without pulling or needing to pull wires. In such a country hope is as much in order as despair. But the net result is that the entire system is tending to bend and collapse beneath the weight of injustice, misgovernance, the tyranny of the police and of the petty official, the easy corruptibility of the elite, and improbability and graft in their widest sense. There is a tendency to start fiddling with the nuts and bolts of the system to correct its balance and stand it up. In the circumstances, review of the structure (constitution) would hardly make any difference. A system, a society, a culture, a nation these are collective entities. They are made up of individuals. If the quality of an individual who make up the collective entities is wanting, it is futile to do this.

References

1. Edwin, R.A. Seligman, ed., Encyclopaedia of the Social Sciences Vol.5 (Macmillan, Newyork, 1954), p. 76.
2. R.M. MacIver, The Web of Government (Macmillan, London,1965), pp. 148-149.
3. John T. Reid, 'Democracy', in Sardar Patel Institute of Administration, ed., Administration and politics in Modern Democracies (Chugh, Allahabad, 1976), pp. 4-5.

4. Edwin R.A. Seligman, op.cit., pp. 79-81.
5. Ibid.
6. Dr. K.M. Munshi 'Our Parliamentary Government' in Paras Ram Manwani, compiled, Democracy on the Anvil (Kitab Mahal, Allahabad, 1968), p. 31.
7. Constituent Assembly Debates, Vol. IV, p. 580.
8. R.C. Agarwal, Indian Political System (S. Chand & Company, New Delhi, 1986), pp. 161-162.
9. M.K. Gandhi, Hind Swaraj (International Printing Press, Phoenix, 1910), pp. 22-23.
10. Jawaharlal Nehru's Speeches September 1957- April 1963, Vol. IV (Publication Division, New Delhi, 1964), p. 69.
11. Dr. D.D. Basu, Introduction to the Constitution of India (Wadhwa & Company, Nagpur, 1960), p. 42.
12. Dr. K.M. Munshi, op.cit., pp. 38-43.
13. M.N. Roy, Reason, Romanticism and Revolution, Vol. 1-2 (1952) p. 283.
14. Ibid., Politics, Power and Parties (Renaissance Publishers, Calcutta, 1960), p. 84.
15. Ibid., p. 52.
16. R.M. Pal, 'M.N. Roy's Views on Decentralisation', The Hindustan Times (New Delhi), March 23, 1998.
17. Dipankar Gupta, Political Sociology in India : Contemporary Trends (Orient Longman, Hyderabad, 1996), pp. 75-76.
18. A.B. Mathur, 'The Indian Polity : A Mild Indictment', in Ramesh K. Arora, ed., Administrative Change, Vol.XXIX No. 2 & Vol. XXX No.1, January-December 2002 (Jaipur), p.24.
19. Ibid; 'Nehru the Man and the Statesman' Vol. XXVIII, No. 2 & Vol. XXIX, No.1 January- December, 2001, p.4.
20. V.K.N. Menon, India Since Independence- From the Preamble to the Present (S. Chand & Company, New Delhi, 1970), pp. 39-40.
21. A.H. Somjee, The Democratic Process in a Developing Society (Macmillan, Delhi, 1979), p.139.
22. Paul R. Brass, 'India : Democratic Progress and Problems', in Selig S. Harrison, Paul H. Kreisberg, and Deunis Kux, eds., India and Pakistan, The First Fifty Year (Cambridge, United Kingdom, 1999), p.26.
23. Ibid., pp. 26-27.
24. A.B. Mathur, op.cit., p.23.
25. Ibid ., p.24.

26. Joseph N. Greene, Jr. 'The Goal of Democracy' in Sardar Patel Institute of Administration, ed., Administration and Politics in Modern Democracies (Allahabad, 1976), p. 19.
27. N.A. Palkhivala, We the People-India the Largest Democracy (Bombay, 1984), p. 198.
28. Ibid., p. 41.
29. Inder Malhotra, 'The Changing Face of Parliament', The Times of India, August 17, 1980.
30. Dr. Akhileshwar Singh, Political Leadership of Jawaharlal Nehru (New Delhi, 1986), p. 266.
31. S.M. Lipset, Political Man (Newyork, 1983), p. 1.
32. A.H. Somjee, op.cit. p. 150.
33. Palkhivala, op.cit., p. 44.
34. Jawaharlal Nehru, India's Independence and Social Revolution (New Delhi, 1984), pp. 135-55.
35. A.S. Abraham, 'Decade of Turbulence-System under Growing Stress', The Times of India, December 21, 1979.
36. Bipin Chandra, Mridula Mukherjee and Aditya Mukherjee, eds., India After Independence 1947-2000 (Penguin Books, New Delhi, 2002), pp. 43-44.
37. Granville Austin, The Indian Constitution : A Cornerstone of a Nation (Oxford University Press, New Delhi, 1966), p. 50.
38. Prakash Talwar, Human Rights (Isha Books, Delhi, 2006), pp. 1-7.
39. Ibid.
40. Haragopal and Chandra Shekhar Rao, 'Human Rights: Perspectives and Practices', in G.P. Deshpande and Alka Acharya, India and China 50 Years of Crossing a Bridge of Dreams (Tulika, New Delhi, 2001), p. 190.
41. United Nations Charter (1945).
42. Human Rights Today (UN Publication, 1998), p. 22; See also Universal Declaration of Human Rights.
43. Jawaharlal Nehru in Constituent Assembly Debates 11.3 p. 326.
44. D. D. Basu, Introduction to the Constitution of India (Prentice Hall of India, New Delhi, 1983), pp. 75-80,
45. Ibid., pp. 132-40.
46. Parliamentary Debates, May 16, 1951, Vol. XII, cols. 8820-22.
47. Verghese Koithara, Society, State and Security, The Indian Experience (Sage Publications, New Delhi, 1999), pp. 279-80.
48. V.P. Varma, Modern Indian Political Thought (Educational Publishers, Agra, 1971), pp. 518-19.

49. Sardar Hukum Singh, Democracy Under Asian Conditions, in Paras Ram Manwani op.cit., p. 108.
50. Rajesh Ramchandran, 'And They have Got it', The Hindustan Times, (New Delhi).
51. A.H. Somjee, op.cit., p. 1.
52. Rakshat Puri, 'What the President Didn't Say', The Hindustan Times, February 3, 2000.
53. Girilal Jain, 'Importance of Moral Values' The Times of India (New Delhi), September 17, 1980.

2

INDIAN POLITICAL BASE EXPANDED

2.1 EMPOWERMENT OF WOMEN IN INDIA

Respect for women is a necessary trait of a rising nation. It equally applies to the women in ancient India when they were not a meek, shy and weak creature but were bold, free and strong. In the pre-Aryan period, an average Indian women continued to lead a happy and contended life. In later years Aryans changed from a pastoral people to agriculturists and they became conscious of preserving the purity of their race which made them the victim of growing social evils. The position of women in Indian society deteriorated further by the laws of Manu but improved a little as a result of the advent of Islam because it granted much stronger legal position. Europeans in general and Christians Missionaries in particular ushered India in an entirely new phase of women emancipation and gave birth to a powerful reformist movement led by Raja Ram Mohan Roy, justice Ranade and Swami Dayanand Saraswati and they all agreed that only women's education can solve the problems of Indian women.

Since Independence, there has been a dramatic change in the legal, political, educational and social status of women. Earlier the improvement of the position of women had been at the heart of the social reform movements from the first quarter of the nineteenth century. The Constitution of India ensures gender equality in its preamble as fundamental right with a view to remove black holes of ignorance and orthodoxy. It also undertook the task of modifying/enacting several laws regarding personal laws of Hindus the Special Marriage Act,

Hindu Marriage Act, women labour family planning and educational opportunities for women.

In late eighties and early nineties, due to several constraints the phase of Liberalisation and Globalisation entered in economic affairs of which India became an integral part. In the changed situation the legal-judicial system of India became more responsive rather sensitive to women's needs especially in sphere of empowerment. Now the Government of India has drawn up a National Policy for the empowerment of Women which outlined the legal, institutional and programmatic schemes. Lately 2001 was observed as Women Empowerment Year to create large scale awareness with the active participation of women themselves. Apart from the constitutional guarantee, several schemes and programmes have been planned and executed from time to time to achieve the goal of empowerment and meet the challenges of 21st century.

Position of Women

Empowerment of women in Indian context primarily means that they should be able to turn aspirations into policy and law. They should have control over their lives and livelihood decisions. They should also be able to pursue self-realisation and self-assertion, and live informed, rational, self-interested lives as those in the upper reaches of Indian society.[1] In today's world India occupies a strategic position in Asia being the largest in South Asian countries with a population of over one billion. Women constitute a population of 495.74 million, with 360.52 million in rural areas and 135.22 million in the urban areas. The human development status of women shows wide interstate and intrastate variations, there has been a systematic decline in women's status despite recent advances in their education and economic status. It is also in contrast with the position that women enjoyed in different phases of Indian history.

The worth of a civilization can be judged from the position that it gives to women. A survey of Indian social history reveals the fact that women enjoyed a high dignity and freedom in society. She was adored by parents, cherished by husband and revered by children. In the Rigveda we read the existence of the son and the daughter side by side, the former taking to the profession of the father while the latter inheriting the glory and honour of her mother. The birth of a daughter was endorsed with acclamation in the period of the Upanisads for which certain rituals were prescribed to be performed by the man who wants a learned daughter to be born.[2] At that time Indian society was perhaps matriarchal and men and women enjoyed equal rights. Even in the initial phase of Aryan period the importance of women as mother or wife was recognised not as an auxiliary in the management of the household but the very centre of the domestic world and empress in her home. The husband identified her with his very home, his abiding hearth. A wife, says the great seer Visvamitra." is home and dwelling. She is auspicious, the most auspicious who brings blessings and prosperity of her husband's household.[3]" Thus, she enjoyed a high dignity and freedom in society especially in comparison to Spartan and Athenian position of women where they were treated merely as vegetables. Even in that period the social adjustment of the sex was so perfect that we find no complaint on the part of the women against the authority of the man.

However, at the close of the Rigvedic period various social restrictions were imposed on the freedom of women. This process started when Sakas, Abhiras, Hunas and others, who were also called the non-Aryans, raided the rich plains of India and were lost in the Aryan social fabric. The new comers were enveloped in the Aryan folds and absorbed in the Indian social matrix. In that kind of situation the Aryans strove and struggled to devise means to keep their blood pure and then ran after an unreasonable mirage. They prescribed rules for early marriages and banned freedom of women in deed, speech and even thought. Further women's position in society was also weakened by the laws of Manu and its fundamental assumption that women are completely dependent on men. 'From the cradle to the grave, a woman is dependent on the male, in the childhood on her father, in youth on her husband, in old age on her son.' Manu advocated that married woman could own no property, "their wealth belongs to those whom they belonged".[4] His philosophy regarding women forced them to accept their lot with humility.

Around 1000 A.D. Muslims began invading India and temporary hopes were raised because Islam had granted much stronger legal position than that prevalent in India that time. But unfortunately all that the upper society borrowed from the Muslims was the system of Purdah in order to save Hinduism from the yoke of Islam. The social taboos were tightened and this further deteriorated the position of women. During the Muslim period of history women were deprived of their rights of equality with men. They were compelled to keep themselves within the four walls of their houses with a long veil on their faces. It was natural of the Muslim subjugation of India that woman was relegated to a plaything of man, an ornament to decorate the drawing room. The women members, such as Jodhabai, Nur Jahan and Mumtaz Mahal of the royal household who played an undeniable role in making the majesty can hardly be considered as representatives of the typical Indian women – Hindu or Muslim.[5] An important point in this regard is that this inferior position of women was largely confined to the North, particularly among the upper urban classes. In the South, society was more settled because it was not much influenced by the changes that took place in the North. At large both Muslim and Hindu women in this period remain restricted to the private domain and were expected to be in Purdah or behind a veil.

Emancipation of women in India witnessed a drastic change with the advent of Europeans, especially the Christian Missionaries, who undertook the work of social reforms as an essential part of their programme. Conversions made on behalf of these missionaries invited a criticism and reaction among the Hindus. Religious Hindus and social reformers sprang into leadership to take the initiative in such matters. In the Pre-British Indian society, except in the early periods of the Vedic times, woman was assigned a position subordinate to man. Law and religion did not recognise the equality and equal rights of man and woman. Society permitted man to have rights and freedoms from which woman was excluded. Emergence of the new economic environment, the establishment of the new political system and the spread of modern Western education found expression in the movements initiated in order to liberalise the women of India.[6]

In later years a powerful reformist movement led by Raja Ram Mohan Roy in Bengal, Justice Ranade in Bombay and Swami Dayanand Saraswati in Punjab sprang up. They denounced the disabilities that handicapped women's social advancement and tried to abolish practices such as Sati, early marriage etc, through legal means. With the help of Lord William Bentick in 1829 the system of Sati was abolished followed by the legalisation of the remarriage of widows in 1856. The thought that women's education was the only means to solve all the problems took a definite shape. This was championed and advocated by Swami Vivekanand and Ishwar Chand Vidyasagar in Bengal that paved the way for the furtherance of women's education leading to the formation of Indian Federation of University Women and its seven branches in the state. Emancipation and empowerment of women in India was made a prime objective of the national movement which was being fought under the leadership of Mahatma Gandhi. The reformist and educationist movement continuing in India and as a result of the British influence on Indian culture and civilization the position of women had, once again, undergone a change. They actively participated in the national movement and their warm patriotism and unabashed enthusiasm won for them the love and respect of their fellow countrymen who, after independence, became founding fathers of Indian constitution.

WOMEN AND INDIAN CONSTITUTION

As woman is the pivot of the family, programmes for women's welfare assume primary importance. Women in general can take advantage of different welfare schemes but there are certain categories which call for special care, women suffering from one disability or another, widows with or without children, women who had an unhappy domestic life, deserted, destitute or exploited women.[7] After Independence Dr. B.R. Ambedkar has tried to remove the barriers in the way of advancement of women in India. The first natural attention in this regard was given to securing legal and constitutional rights. The Constitution of India was ahead of its time, not only by the standards of the developing nations but also of many developed countries, in removing every discrimination against women in the legal and public domain of the Republic. It provided complete equality to women and fulfilled the promose made many years ago by the national movement: women got the vote, along with men, without any qualification of education or property or income. A right for which women suffragettes fought long and hard in many western countries was won at one stroke by Indian women.

The principle of equality of women with men enshrined in the Indian Constitution in its preamble, Fundamental Rights, Fundamental Duties and Directive principles. Under the provisions the state is also allowed to adopt measures of positive discrimination in favour of women. For instance Article 14 conferred equal rights and opportunities on men and women in the political, economic and social spheres, Article 15 prohibited discrimination against any citizen on the grounds of sex and Article 15 (3) empowered the State to make affirmative discrimination in favour of women and children. Likewise Article 39 enjoyed upon the State to provide equal means of livelihood and equal pay for equal work and Article 42 directed the State to make provisions for ensuring just and humane conditions of work and also for maternity relief. Article 51(e) imposed a fundamental duty on every citizen to renounce the practices derogatory to the dignity of women.

In the initial phase of independence, the most important step in direction of women's development was the codification of Hindu personal laws. The Government realised that any reform would be possible only by enacting laws. Earlier in 1941 a committee under the Chairmanship of B.N. Rau, the constitutional expert who prepared the first draft of the constitution of India, had already gone into the matter and submitted a draft code in 1944. Another committee, chaired by B.R. Ambedkar, the law minister, after independence submitted a bill which raised the age of consent and marriage, upheld monogamy, gave women the right to divorce, maintenance and inheritance and treated dowry as stridhan, or women's property. It was because of the stiff opposition of the bill from conservative sections of society including President Rajendra Prasad, sections of the bill were passed as four separate acts: The Hindu Marriage Act, the Hindu Succession Act, the Hindu Minority and Guardianship Act and the Hindu Adoption and Maintenance Act. The enacting of legal rights to Hindu women was, although, not sufficient but it was a big step forward.[8] Thus, from the beginning the Government of India tried to give equal status and opportunities of life to women through laws.

The planning strategy of the Government of India regarding women has evolved from welfare to development to empowerment. The approach in the First Five Year Plan (1951-1956) was to provide adequate services to promote the welfare schemes of women so that they can play their legitimate role in the family and the community. In this plan period the Central Social Welfare Board (CSWB) was set up in 1953 to promote voluntary organizations at various levels, especially at the grass roots, to take up welfare related activities for women. The Second, Third, Fourth and Fifth Plans continued the same approach for the welfare of women. The end of the Fourth plan witnessed the release of the monumental report of Committee on Status of Women in India entitled "Towards Equality". It revealed that the dynamics of development had adversely affected a large section of women and created new imbalances and disparities. In 1976 a Women's Welfare and Development Bureau was set up under the Ministry of Social Welfare to initiate necessary policies, programmes and measures for women.

The Sixth Plan (1980-85), for the first time, recognised women as participants of development and not merely as objects of welfare. It adopted a multi-disciplinary approach with a special thrust on the three core sectors of health, education and employment. In 1982 a Women's Employment Programme was introduced with assistance from Norwegian Development Agency (NORDA). The theme of Sixth Plan continued in the Seventh Plan (1985-90) and stressed on generation of both skilled and unskilled employment of women through proper education and vocational training. In this plan period two new schemes – Support to Training and Employment (STEP) and Awareness Generation Programme for Rural and Poor Women (AGP) were introduced.[9] Apart from this several landmark reports namely Sharam Shakti, the Report of the National Commission on Self-Employed Women and Women in Informal Sector, National Perspective Plan on Women (1988-2000) and SAARC guidebook on Women in Development were prepared. These all paved the way for empowerment of women in India, especially in this age of Globalisation.

GLOBALISATION AND INDIAN WOMEN

The concept of global village given by Marshall Mcluhan in the sixties is realising today. There are several things in it – an ideal, a destination to be reached and a conceptualisation of the ongoing transformation in the community. The earth in which we live is an integrated, interpenetrated and interconnected unit. The advances of communications and information technology have made the global village a virtual reality and this has paved the way for evolving frameworks of global governance.[10] In this context Globalisation, Liberalisation and Privatisation is gaining growing attention as a strategy for survival, competition and growth. The exploitation of resources to the detriment of common good has created many imbalances and there is growing awareness to the issues related to sustainable development. In addition to this a new horizon of peace and co-operation of global level opened with the end of cold war that resulted in international changes and diminished competition between the super powers. Earlier excessive military expenditures, including global military expenditures and arms trade or trafficking and investments for arms production and acquisition have reduced the resources available for social development. In this phase, in many developing countries structural adjustment programmes have also been poorly designed and implemented. They have not been designed to minimize their negative effects on vulnerable and disadvantaged groups or on women, nor have they been designed to assure positive effects on those groups by preventing their marginalization in economic and social activities.[11]

With a view to empower the marginalized groups of society and especially the women, in the early nineties the Government of India launched the liberalisation of its economy and expanded social structures to ensure the participation of women in national development. Immediately on assuming office in June 1991 the Government of Narasimha Rao began to unfold new policies in July whose major signpost are Stabilisation, Globalisation or linking up Indian economy with the economies of the world. According to government it was necessary to generate confidence among the countries of the world in

India's economic development and to restore its credit worthiness in the world.[12] The reform package covers a broad spectrum and includes fiscal correction, exchange rate adjustment, monetary targeting with inflation control, a high degree of economic liberalisation and financial sector reforms.[13] The rapid process of change and adjustments in all sectors has also led to increase unemployment and underemployment, with particular impact on women. Recent international economic developments have had in many cases a disproportionate impact on women and children, the majority of whom live in developing countries.

Women play a critical role in the family. The family is the basic unit of society and as such should be strengthened. The world public opinion alongwith the world body the UN have been active in this field and the exhaustive efforts started in 1975. Since then the knowledge of the status of women and men, respectively, has increased and is contributing to further actions aimed at promoting equality between women and men. The year was also proclaimed as the 'International Women's Year by the United Nations General Assembly. The United Nations Decade for Women (1976-1985) was a world-wide effort to examine the status and rights of women and to bring women into decision making at all levels. In 1985, a World Conference was held to review and appraise the achievements of the United Nations Decade for Women and Equality. Development and Peace was adopted at the Nairobi Forward-Looking Strategies for the Advancement of Women to be implemented by the year 2000.

In the circumstances the Government of India in the early nineties decided to bring a policy about the advancement, development and empowerment of women. It was aimed to create an environment through positive economic and social policies for full development of women to enable them to realise their full potential. As a positive development the National Commission for Women was set up by an Act of parliament in 1990 to safeguard the rights and legal entitlements of women. Recognising the role and contribution of women in development, the Eighth Plan (1990-95) adopted the strategy to ensure that benefits of development from different sectors do not bypass women and special programmes are implemented to complement the general development plans. Two new schemes for Women-Mahila Samiridhi Yojana and Indira Mahila Yojana were introduced during this plan period and a National Commission for Women and National Credit and Fund for Women known as Rashtriya Mahila Kosh was set up.

However, the major breakthrough of the Plan period was the

passing of 73rd and 74th Constitutional Amendment Act which Guarantee that all local elected bodies reserve one-third of their seats for women. Passed in 1993 it laid a strong foundation for their participation in decision making at the local levels. Since the creation of the quota system, the local women-the vast majority of them illiterate and poor-have come to occupy as much as 43% of seats, spurring the election of increasing numbers of women at the district, provincial and national levels. Their mass participation through Panchayati Raj Institutions (PRI) have brought about significant changes in the lives of women who have become empowered, and have gained self-confidence, political awareness and affirmation of their own identity.

In continuation the Ninth Plan 1997-2002 made two significant changes in conceptual strategy for women. First 'Empowerment of Women' became one of the nine primary objectives of the plan and the approach was to create an enabling environment where women can freely exercise their rights both within and outside home. Secondly it attempted the convergence of existing services, resource, infrastructure and manpower available in both women-specific and women-related sectors. Likewise the Tenth Five Year Plan (2002-2007) constituted three working Groups : (a) Working Group on Empowerment of Women, (b) Working Group on Child Development and (c) Working Group of Improving Nutritional Status of Population with Special Focus on Vulnerable Groups. Secretaries of the respective Departments would be Chairperson and joint Secretaries would be Convenors of the Groups.[14] Under the Working Groups on Empowerment two sub-groups were constituted, on focusing on Social Empowerment of women and the other on Economic empowerment of Women.

A like globalisation, empowerment of Women is a multidimensional concept. The world opinion is active enough in this regard and the Government of India, in cooperation with the state governments and different non-governmental organizations is doing its level best to empower the women in India.

2.2 GLOBALISATION AND PANCHAYATI RAJ SYSTEM

The need of the hour is to make Panchayati Raj Institutions an engine of growth by devolution of power in true sense of the term. It remained vital in past and is essential in the present as it provides an ideal forum for decentralised planning and implementation of developmental programmes in accordance with the people's necessities and aspirations. In pre and post independence era, the then governments of the time, have tried their level best to get it done but failed due to socio-economic and political factors. Earlier and at the start of British rule the village Panchayat was a unit of local administration but worked under government. Since the 1920s rural development had received priority and as a follow-up action, several programmes and experiments were made in different parts of the country. Such programmes include Tagore's 'Sriniketan Institute of Rural Reconstruction'. Hatch's Martandam experiment in Kerala, Gandhi's Wardha and Sabarmati experiments, Bryne's Gurgaon experiment, Krishnamachari's Baroda experiment and Firka Development Scheme in then Madras. These experiments proved fore-runners and influenced the form and programme of rural development in independent India.

Earlier experiences in this sphere and the feeling that programmes of rural development could not be carried out without the active participation of rural people themselves paved the three-tier Panchayati Raj system in 1958. The Community Development Programme was an innovation which laid emphasis on extension rather than on executive methods' and Government officers were to act as agents and persuaders for change. The central idea of the programme was investment in man through the means of integrated extension service and scientific knowledge and techniques. With these aims and objectives the Five Year Plans initiated a process of transformation of the social and economic life of the rural India. The three-tier system of Panchayats in the form of democratic decentralisation was introduced in 1959 as a supplement to the CDP. This new system was accepted largely by the states but with variations and different models of the constitution of Panchayati Raj bodies. These along with other defects compelled the structure to fail and in conclusion presented a very gloomy picture of rural development even decades after Independence.

Despite 'Not so Good' position of Panchayati Raj institutions and rural development in independent India, several committees asserted the importance of democratic decentralisation. With the passage of the Constitutional Amendment 73rd in 1992, and later the 74th a new spirit has been ushered throughout the length and breadth of the country. Apart from conferring it constitutional recognition the Act has empowered them for their vibrant growth. The most important Article 243G entrusts the Panchayat bodies with powers authority and responsibilities. Now the Panchayats have started transforming the living conditions of rural poor and the marginalised groups of Indian society.

Historical Perspectives

The concept of village Panchayat to solve the problems of local people is not unknown to Indian history and existed frequently in ancient and medieval periods. Various types of local government institutions were found under the Chola, Pallva, Pandya and Vijayanagaram Kingdoms and were known from different names and titles.[15] Their reference may easily be made to the traditions of Panchayats in ancient Village Republics in rural India. The role of these Panchayats was mainly to settle disputes, where caste Panchayats existed quite visibly. The system of Panchayats in earlier periods not only provided a local forum for redressal of people's grievances in rural India but became able to develop a feeling of community life among them. Unlike towns they were closely related in terms of social psychology, social attitudes, and habits. Physical factors such as density of population per acre, organized provision of services and social amenities are important since they have a direct bearing on social psychology and attitudes.[16] All these factors combined build up a sense of community.

The old system of Panchayats deteriorated further during the period of Mughal emperors but was revived under the British rule as a statutory and elected body, responsible for the development of the village in the later part of 19th century. In this period village Panchayats were upgraded as an institution of local self-government and found the favour of the Famine Commission and Ripon's Resolution of 1882. More specific on the issue was Decentralisation Commission Report which emphasised 'it is most desirable, alike in the interests of decentralisation and in order to associate the people with local tasks of administration that an attempt should be made to constitute and develop village Panchayats for the administration of local village affairs.[17] Initially as held by Lord Ripon, the then viceroy and father of local self-government in India, 'the institution of local self-government was not primarily with a view to bring improvement in administration but it was chiefly meant to act as an instrument of political and popular education.[18] However the British administrators who fostered the growth of local self-governing bodies on a statutory pattern in India placed a greater premium on the regulatory rather than autonomous aspects of local government. It was saddled with a complex and comprehensive network of controls circumscribing the operational autonomy of the local bodies in all vital matters.

The decade 1920s was important for rural development through

Panchayati Raj Institutions and otherwise. On the basis of earlier reports regarding decentralisation the Government of India Act 1919 introduced the system of Dyarchy at Provincial level which provided additional span of powers and functions of the local bodies and as a follow up Bombay Village Panchayat Act of 1920 and Madras Village Panchayat Act of 1920 were passed. The formation of popular governments under Dyarchy virtually represented the last opportunity for strengthening local bodies in the pre-Independence era as the next opportunity offered by the Government of India Act 1935 was too short-lived to make a dent on the functioning of village Panchayat.

As the national liberation movement advanced in positive direction it became clear that the efforts of British Government to develop rural India through Panchayati Raj were a major disappointment. It encouraged several visionaries including Mahatma Gandhi, a political agitator and social reformer to undertake the task of rural development and establish the centres of reconstruction in different parts of India. Though they all represented different experiences in sphere of rural development the common among them was the moral and spiritual meaning which, when linked with the cultural traditions of the country, could fire the deepest emotions of the citizens. The efforts of early initiators resulted in the emergence of a Rural Construction department when a Congress Ministry was formed between 1937 and 1939. But the Panchayat system of Gandhi's dream was actualised in the new Constitution of India which came into existence on 26 January 1950.

Constitutional Provisions and Implementation

The framers of Indian Constitution heavily cut short the Gandhian concept of Panchayats and rural development while providing for the different arrangements. Despite the fact that they were not much satisfied with the working of these local bodies as institutions of popular government they simply gave a Directive in Article 40 of the constitution which follow, the state shall take steps to organise village Panchayats and endow them with such powers and authority as may be necessary to enable them for function as units of self-government.[19] Under the heading of Directive Principles of State Policy (Articles 36 to 51) different guidelines of rural development were given to state government with no binding to implement the ideals. In initial years in order to achieve rural development and strengthen Panchayati Raj Institutions the Community Development Programme was launched in the country on a large scale with National Extension Service as an agency through which the social and economic transformation of village life was to be brought about.[20] It was implemented with assistance from the Technical Cooperation Programme Agreement between the Government of India and the US which was signed in May 1952. The Programme was initiated with a great deal of enthusiasm and hope having different in style and orientation of administration, the structure of new development administration and the element of people's participation that was a part of basic assumptions and objectives.[21] Earlier the district and the village levels of local bodies had existed for long but blocks at the intermediate level was the new introduction in the administrative structure of development.

The above arrangements were made in the light of changed circumstances which signalled in post World War II phase. The liberation of many Afro-Asian nations from the clutches of colonial rule has been a catalytic phenomenon in this direction. These countries which were poor and underdeveloped adopted different strategies for their development. Even development which earlier was mainly associated with economic growth, has now acquired broader meaning. Unlike in a technical sense in which development refers to qualitative and structural changes in the state of an economy, the development, in modern sense, refers to a relatively stable long-range increase in real national income that is accompanied by a change in the attitudes of the people, their motivation, institutional set-up, production techniques, etc. From another angle it may also refer to the production and utilisation of material resources or to the development of human resources. Enrichment of human capital refers to the un-economic factors such as the social, political, ethnic or educational background of the people who participate in the development tasks. Thus, the goal of development clearly means the enrichment of the total quality of life and its availability to all sections of the community.[22] Development is not merely the provision of opportunities but also their actual utilisation by the people for whom they are intended and involves the creation of facilities necessary for such utilisation.

Like other Afro-Asian countries the large majority of population live in rural India which became the main thrust of national development effort. Different countries adopted, with a view to develop rural areas different approaches and strategies depending on their ideological orientations of the elite, the structure of political power and the perception of national needs.[23] In India about four-fifths of population live in rural areas as Gandhi rightly says 'that India lives in villages'. In this context India laid particular emphasis on people's institutions because the programmes of development, it is generally agreed, are to be carried out not only by the state bureaucracy but also through effective public participation.[24]

The actual working of Community Development Programme and National Extension Service did not deliver desired results and lack of peoples' participation was considered as the greatest weakness of the system. The need to examine the whole issue in comprehensive detail with a view to evolving a system to enlist peoples participation and make the Panchayats more effective was felt which resulted in the formation of a study team in 1956 under the chairmanship of Balwantray Mehta. The report of the team contained a three-tier scheme of democratic decentralisation and it was endorsed by the National Development Council in 1958, which followed its implementation by several states in one form or another. The Village Panchayat, Panchayat Samiti and Zila Parishad constituted the three tier of Panchayati Raj, located at the village, the block and the district levels respectively. Since the scheme of decentralisation was conceived as a means to facilitate programmes of development, the middle tier of Panchayat Samiti at the block level was to be the basic institution in the entire scheme of Panchayati Raj. The establishment of a three-tier system of local self-government with full powers to assume responsibility for local development was the core of the Mehta Committee recommendation.

The new pattern and practice of Panchayati Raj witnessed a substantial transfer of power into local hands but this revolution was not accompanied by any social or economic revolution. The process of its decline was started after the mid-sixties and it continued for almost the next two decades. In fact the non-devolution of the sources of revenue proved to be the greatest stumbling block in the performance of Panchayati Raj bodies. The PR institutions were not regarded either as a political means to bring about change in rural India, or as part of the overall political process in the country or as institutions reflecting social divisions in society. Indian politics in the 1970s showed a shift towards centralisation of power on the one hand, and on the other hand, an effort on the part of the central leadership to reach out to the people directly.[25] The first non-congress government of Janata Party was formed in 1977 who appointed a high power committee under the chairmanship of Ashok Mehta to examine the whole issue and make suitable recommendations. Its report represented a landmark because it treated the PR as an extension of democracy, it declared the need of providing constitutional sanction of Panchyati Raj and suggested to transfer substantial quantum of powers from the State Government to the local bodies. The major thrust of the report was on decentralisation.

At a later stage during the period of 1985-92 some serious thinking was done at the national level in favour of giving constitutional status to Panchayati Raj Institutions. In the regime of Rajiv Gandhi it was considered necessary to further the organisation of these local units by inserting specific provisions in the Constitution itself on the basis of which the Legislatures of the various States might enact detailed laws according to the guidelines provided by the constitutional provisions. Simultaneously the phase of Globalisation and Liberalisation came in the world and India as well which made the Constitutional Amendment regarding Panchayati Raj institution an essential factor for the development of rural India.

Globalisation and Panchayati Raj System

The premiership of Rajiv Gandhi provided life blood to the dying institutions of Panchayati Raj. He had always taken special care to project an image of a dynamic young man interested in futuristic techno-economic policies inspired by modern technology in such fields as computers, telecommunications and bio-technology. Under him India's quest for techno-economic and socio-cultural modernity gave rise to the necessity of a series of inventions amongst which the idea of democratic decentralisation and its institutional manifestation in the form of Panchayati Raj Institutions deserves to be ranked very high. To revitalise the PRIs Prime Minister himself took initiatives and five workshops were organised between December 1987 and June 1988 at different places in the country on the broad theme of 'Responsive Administration'. He laid special emphasis on the development of rural India and a Committee on Administrative Arrangements for Rural Development (CAARD) was constituted on 31 March 1985 with G.V.K. Rao as its chairman. The Committee, in its report, pointed out that the decline of PRIs may be attributed to the reluctance of political leadership at the state level to share powers with district leadership. Another committee was also set-up in June 1986 headed by L.M. Singhvi to prepare a concept paper on the revitalisation of the Panchayati Raj Institutions. After exhaustive preparations it took the form of 64th Constitutional Amendment Bill which could not be enacted due to the lack of support in the Rajya Sabha.

In a fresh general election the congress party again came to power with P.V.Narasimha Rao as the new Prime Minister. He spelled out in May 1991 the new economic agenda of privatisation, liberalisation and globalisation of Indian economy. Globalisation may be broadly seen as a process that widens the extent and form of cross-border transactions among people's assets, goods and services that deepens economic interdependence between and among globalising entities. True economic globalistion involves a qualitative shift towards a system based on a consolidated global market place for production distribution and consumption rather than on autonomous national economies.[26] The emerging implications of the liberalisation process which had begun in the early 1990s, are far more evident in terms of the resultant of new economic policy and change in the historical – ideological orientation of our political economy. Though considerable progress has been achieved in terms of higher growth rate and GDP, the basic needs and the crucial concerns of the core sectors of Indian economy such as agriculture and textiles affected millions of people pose a challenge to the successive governments.[27] Developed countries erect obstacles to trade in particular, barriers to trade in agricultural products and textiles. The West, under the guise of globalisation, pushes the developing countries to open their markets. But they raise barriers of entry into their markets. Globalisation the way it is practiced, encourages an unequal distribution of power and wealth among the countries of the world.[28]

In the world-wide atmosphere of globalisation India enacted the Constitution Seventy–third Amendment Act in 1992 and having got president's assent it came into effect from 24th of April 1993. The necessity of its passing arose in view of the ineffectiveness of the PRIs which failed to gain the status and dignity of liable and responsive people's bodies. The new amendment, has, accordingly provided for the constitution and composition of the Panchayats at various levels, reservation of seats for weaker sections, regular elections, devolution of power, authority and responsibilities, constitution of Finance Commission to review financial position and regular audits of Panchayats, etc. The Provision of the Act can be broadly classified into two heads – the provisions which are mandatory for the states and the areas which have been left for the state legislatures to take decisions keeping in view the socio-economic conditions and other factors of their state. The two amendments – 73rd and 74th have the rich potential to transform the character of democracy from a representative to a participatory one. Regarding devolution of power the amendments are aimed to transfer the power from the dominant group to the weak and the meek. It is a power shift from men to women, from the upper caste to the Dalits.[29]

Negative aspects of globalisation pose a challenge and danger as well for the Panchayati Raj Institutions at large in rural areas where people are unable to understand the complexities of globalisation. Grassroot leaders are not aware of the implications of the process of globalisation and Panchayats are victims of the globalisation process. On water mining, sand mining and many other issues, the Panchayats are not able to do anything. If Panchayat representatives have sufficient knowledge about globalisation, they will take steps to avoid threats, if any and at the same time, they will make use of the opportunity if any.[30] In addition there is a wide gap between globalisation and devolution of power at rural level. Globalisation works for the rich and decentralisation works for the poor and at this stage a mass movement is needed for decentralisation.

The Indian agriculture and its related work force has also been adversely affected by the spread of globalisation. Like India in many traditional societies agriculture is not considered merely as an occupation but a major source of livelihood and for the vast majority a way of life. The traditional relationship between the people, land and agriculture has emotive overtones and any careless tampering with this delicate subject could unleash waves of violence and social disruption. Its direct result is the increase of insecurity of individuals, groups and nations in various domains-economic, financial, culture, employment, legal, social, health care, ecological, political and personal. And this is why the concept of globalisation is encountering resistance from various interest groups-environmentalists, labour leaders, cultural traditionalists, religious leaders of different persuasions and non-government officers.[31] In rural areas it has put intense downward pressure on the wages of the unskilled and less skilled labours making the gap between the rich and the poor wide. To get the best out of globalisation, nations must learn to govern better along with the nations of the world as it does not aim just about the growth in GDP but about sustainable, democratic and equitable development.

Today even in rural areas technology has made a significant impact on the lives of consumers. With television and the internet extending their reach to rural India, People are better informed and their aspirations have changed. The changing face of Indian society is bringing with it new challenges and opportunities.[32] In the circumstances, decentralisation the heart of Panchayati Raj system, will work effectively and to the best of our hope if I. there is a strong presence of a middle class; II. land reform is done; III. larger pressure of civil society organisations is ensured; IV. high literacy rate is ensured; and V. adequate powers and finances are with the grassroots, institutions. In India a new proposition is emerging in this direction and we hope it to be a success in the shortest possible span of time.

2.3 PANCHAYATI RAJ AND RURAL DEVELOPMENT

Development of land resources through the Panchayati Raj Institutions (PRIs) in the age of globalisation is a problem and challenge for the developing world in general and countries like India in particular. Since the days of independence the Government of India had adopted several measures to develop land resources it, however, laid less emphasis in doing this through PRIs. The Panchayati Raj Institutions are the product of a committee report headed by Balwant Roy Mehta at the close of the fifties when the Community Development Programme of earlier failed to give desired results due to certain bureaucratic bankruptcy and financial shortcomings. The Panchayati Raj Institutions,though implemented in various degrees and proportions were considered as an engine of growth by devolution of power in true sense of the term. It remained vital in past and is essential in the present as it provides an ideal forum for decentralisedplanningandimplementationofdevelopmentalprogrammes in accordance with the people's necessities and aspirations.

As we live on land we also perform our economic activities on land and therefore, it is a natural resource of utmost importance. It supports natural vegetation, wild life, human life, economic activities, transport and communication systems. The use of land resources largely depend on physical factors such as topography, climate, soil types as well as human factors such as population density, technological capability and culture and tradition. In this context we need a balance between availability of land resources as well as its proper conservation.

Today in the era of globalisation a major challenge has been imposed on panchayati Raj Institutions which work largely in rural areas where people are unable to understand the complexities of this new concept. Grassroot leaders are not aware of the implications of the process of globalisation and our panchayats are the easy victims of globalisation process. In the circumstances proper and maximum use of land resources through the planning and implementation of panchayats can save us from the devastating situation. It however, needs a careful planning at each and every stage.

Panchayati Raj An Engine of Growth

In modern federal countries local government is part of the state government and Panchayati Raj Institutions (PRIs) which deal mainly with local affairs, administered by authorities are subordinate to the provincial government. The local authorities which we refer as PRIs may be elected independently of the state authority by qualified residents or they may consist of partly elected and partly nominated or wholly nominated members. State government and the PRIs both derive its powers from a portion of the same electorate but local authorities are the creatures of the State legislature. They can not do many things without the explicit sanction of the State government. In independent India it was felt in general that democracy can not be realised as a human and political ideal, nor can a stable and competent democratic state be built in practice, unless there is active participation by the citizen in the process of government and the electorate itself is educated in the exercise of political responsibility. All levels of government must be accessible for popular participation[33].

Before the conquest of India by the British in ancient and medieval periods the system of local self government in the form of Panchayats were more widespread, more real and more successful. The powers and functions of the local bodies varied from time to time and from one to another. Generally, they were concerned with municipal functions, such as the acquisition and disposal of lands, grant of lands, collection of taxes for local purposes and the administration of justice etc. Almost every village in the country had a self – governing body of its own. Like today a vast majority of the people live in villages, and about all the people enjoyed the advantages of local self-government. In that period there was a community feeling. Tradition and custom strengthened this spirit. As a result there were no group rivalries and the administration of the village went on smoothly. Mahatma Gandhi had elaborated these things for the present when he says, 'every village will be a republic or Panchayat having full powers self – sustained and capable of managing its affairs. In this structure composed of innumerable villages there will be ever- widening, never ascending circles, life will not be a pyramid with the apex sustained by the bottom. But it will be an oceanic circle whose center will be the individual always ready to perish for the village, the latter ready to perish for the circle of villages, till at last the whole becomes one life composed of individuals'.[34]

Independent India's search for a permeated local society with multifarious agencies of development and political mobilisation needed an elaborate machinery of consultation, investigation and decision-making in order to cover the gap between tradition and modernity on the one and different political cultures on the other. The result has been the

Panchayati Raj , an integrated system of local self – government with the twin objectives of democratic decentralisation and local participation in planned programmes[35]. The doubt and cynicism perceived by the administrative and intellectual circles were rejected by both Mahatma Gandhi and Jawaharlal Nehru who were firm believers in the scheme of Panchayati Raj.

The Panchayat system of Gandhi's dream was actualised in the new constitution of India which came into existence on 26 January 1950. In spite of the fact that the framers of Indian Constitution were not much satisfied with the working of these local bodies as institutions of popular government they gave a Directive in Article 40 of the Constitution which follow, 'the state shall take steps to organize village Panchayats and endow them with such power and authority as may be necessary to enable them for function as units of self- government[36]. Under the heading of Directive Principles of State Policy (Article 36 to 51) different guidelines of rural development were given to state government with no binding to implement the ideals. In initial years in order to achieve rural development and strengthen Panchayati Raj Institutions the Community Development Programme was launched in the country on a large scale with National Extension Service as an agency through which the social and economic transformation of village life was to be brought about[37]. It was initiated with enthusiasm and hope having different in style and orientation of administration, the structure of new development administration, and the elements of people's participation that was a part of basic assumptions and objectives.[38] Apart from India it was a demand and need as well of other Afro-Asian nations who were getting liberation from the clutches of their colonial masters.

Soon after the implementation the Community Development Programme and National Extension Service signalled several weaknesses in the system and the schemes failed to deliver desired results due to lack of people's participation[39]. The system was questioned from various quarters and as a result the need to go into comprehensive detail was necessitated with a view to evolve a system, to ensure people's participation and make the Panchayats more effective.In 1956 under the chairmanship of Balwant Roy Mehta a study team on the issue was formed whose report contained a three-tier scheme of democratic decentralisation. Its recommendations were endorsed by the National Development Council in 1958 which followed its implementation in several states in one form or another–the Village Panchayat , Panchayat Samiti and Zila Parishad located at the village, the block and the district levels respectively. However this new pattern and practice failed to bring a revolution in social and political life of the country and a high powered committee was constituted in 1977 under the chairmanship of Ashok Mehta to examine the whole issue and make recommendations. It treated the Panchayati Raj as an extension of democracy and declared the need of providing constitutional sanction in Panchayati Raj. Making the major thrust on decentralization it suggested to transfer substantial quantum of power from the State Government to the local bodies.

In the light of recommendations and deteriorating condition of PRIs some serious thinking was done at the national level in favour of giving constitutional status to Panchayati Raj Institutions. Especially during the premiership of Rajiv Gandhi several workshops were organised at different places in the country on 'Responsive Administration' in order to revitalise the PRIs. Later on in between the ideas of liberalisation and globalisation India enacted the Constitution Seventy-third Amendment Act in 1992 and having got president's assent it came into effect from 24th of April 1993. It provided for the constitution and composition of the Panchayats at various levels, reservation of seats for weaker sections, regular elections, devolution of power, authority and responsibility, constitution of Finance Commission to review the financial position and regular audits of Panchayats etc. The two Constitutional Amendments 73rd and 74th have the rich potential to transform the character of democracy from a representative to participatory one.

Now in the age of globalisation the Panchayati Raj Institutions face a variety of challenges in rural areas where people are unable to understand the complexities of globalisation. Grass root leaders are not aware of the implications of the process of globalisation and panchayats are victims of the globalisation process. On water mining, sand mining and many other issues, the Panchayats are not able to do anything. If Panchayat representatives have sufficient knowledge about globalisation, they will take steps to avoid threats, if any and at the sametime, they will make use of opportunity if any[40]. In addition there is a wide gap between globalisation and devolution of Power at rural level. Globalisation works for the rich and decentralization works for the poor and at this stage a mass movement is needed for decentralisation.

The Indian agriculture and its related work force has also been adversely affected by the spread of globalisation. Like India in many traditional societies agriculture is not considered merely as an occupation but a major source of livelihood and for the vast majority a way of life. The traditional relationship between the people, land and agriculture has emotive overtones and any careless tampering with this delicate subject could unleash waves of violence and social disruption. Its direct result is the increase of insecurity of individuals, groups, and nations in various domains – economic, financial, culture, employment, legal, social, healthcare, ecological, political and personal. And this is why the concept of globalisation is encountering resistance from various interest groups-environmentalists, labour leaders, cultural traditionalists, religious leaders of different persuasions and non- government officers.

Dimensions of Land Resource

In broader sense use or tilling of land implies a conscious and determined effort on the part of man to utilize the soil for his benefit. It is used to describe human uses of land, or immediate actions modifying or converting land cover. Starting with dawn of the civilization until the eighteenth century one could not find any record of environmental degradation. Great civilizations in Greece, Rome Mesopotamia, China or Indus achieved great heights in learning, culture and philosophy without any record of such incidents as air pollution or water pollution. The starting point of this problem is industrial revolution and subsequent advancement in science and technology that led to mass production of industrial consumer goods and massive increase in food production due to the evolution of modern agriculture as well as explosive growth in population due to greater access to modern health care. In fact there exists a natural clean up mechanism in the environment and wastes are biologically or chemically processed by the environment. The problem arises only when the volume of wastes released to the environment exceeds the capacity of the nature to clean it up.

The changes that are taking place in the environment are directly related to our land use and methods of agriculture. In agriculture the methods of farming and the amount of yield varies from place to place depending upon a number of geo-economic factors which may be grouped as climate, soil and topography. Temperature and precipitation are the chief elements which are fundamental to the growth of plants. Plants require sufficient heat for their growth and the places having a maximum temperature of less than 10'C are generally unsuited for the growth of plants. In tropical regions, where temperature can be carried on in summer as well as in winter, while in higher latitudes where winter temperature are too low for the growth of crops agriculture is carried on only in summer[41]. Water is also very essential for the growth of plants. The moisture requirements of the plants, however, vary according to temperatures. In lower latitudes where temperatures are always high, plants require a minimum of 75 to 100 cm of rainfall, while in higher latitudes, where the summers are not very hot or where the winds are not dry, even 50 cm of rainfall is sufficient for the growth of plants.

Today we all have accepted that our climate is changing at unprecedented levels. Human and natural drivers of climate change include changes in the abundance of greenhouse gases, gases that trap heat and prevent it from radiating out into space, and aerosols in our atmosphere, changes in solar radiation and in the properties of the land surface largely caused by human actions. Another related distressing call is from heating of the oceans which absorbed nearly 80 per cent of the heat. The warmer sea water expands and this contributes enormously to rising sea levels. Sea levels have been rising at an average of 1.8 mm per year between 1961 and 2003 and at a much faster rate between 1993 and 2003 with no sign of slowing down[42]. Changes in climate have led to widespread variations in patterns of rainfall, wind, ocean salinity and extreme weather including heat waves, drought, intensity of tropical cyclones and heavy rainfalls. Agriculture has been most affected by the increasing unpredictability of the climate. Coastal lands and the people living there are being constantly affected with the rise in sea levels. As a global community, all of us need to take very effective, immediate and sustained actions to halt and hopefully reverse the human contributions to climate change.

Soil is another important requirement for successful cultivation of land and if it is rich in fertile it serves two purposes: it supports the plant and acts as the main medium whereby water and all plant food, except carbon dioxide is brought to the roots of the plant. Generally soils differ from one another in respect of physical and chemical contents. Physically soils also differ from one another in the condition of their particles .They may be coarse or fine, porous or compact and tenacious. The chemical composition of the soil determines its fertility. Soils having a variety of chemicals are more fertile and suitable for the growth of a variety of crops. In addition there are transported soils which may be categorized as loess: transported by the wind, alluvial: transported by river water and gravel: transported by glaciers.

People before the advent of modern techniques, use their land for cultivation and kept fertility of the soil maintained through traditional methods failing which soil soon becomes barren and useless for the growth of plants. The first method is the cultivation of land in every alternate year. This method is wasteful as it reduces the land under cultivation by fifty per cent and is practised only where either the land is abundant or the population is meagre. The second is the rotation of crops which is based upon the principle that different crops require different types of plant food and the soil regains the lost fertility when different type of crop is planted. In India the main crops are alternated with pulses and oilseeds. Crop rotation also helps in checking the soil erosion and eradicating the weeds. Today, the best method of maintaining and improving the fertility of soil is the application of manures in the form of commercial fertilizers, such as, phosphate, nitrate and ammonium sulphate for maintaining and improving the fertility of the soil.[43] It, however, requires a high degree of skill and knowledge on the part of the farmers so that they may use the right type of manure.

The recent research on land and its productivity has proved that soil organic carbon is the source of energy to fuel biological activities in the soil, which in turn control the availability of nutrients for plant growth as well as soil water availability. Its result in the soil are three- fold—a reduction in atmospheric carbon level, increased crops yields and more income for farmers. This new discovery is advantageous especially for dry farming where rainfall is scanty and the irrigation facilities are either absent or very little. In this area farmers make special efforts to conserve soil moisture and to make the maximum use of the limited rain water. This method is practised in the western part of the USA and Canada, in the drier highlands of Mexico and Central America in South-West Brazil, in South Africa, in West Australia, Israel, Lebnon, Syria and Turkey[44] etc. Although there is much attention and support being given to irrigated agriculture, dry lands occupy 80 per cent of agricultural land and generate 58 per cent of the world's staple foods. In fact most of the food for poor in the developing countries is produced in dry land and rain fed areas.

Several research institutes including world's top research centre for dry land agriculture, the International Crops Research Institute for the Semi Arid Tropics (ICRISAT) in Andhra Pradesh is working on increasing the organic carbon level in the soil through increased accumulation from the environment the center's research has shown that legumes in general and pigeon pea in particular have the ability to sequester more carbon in tropical soils. It also suggested that the adoption of improved water soil and crop management options carbon sequestration in legume base systems can be improved further. The application is advantageous even for the productivity of rain fed agriculture. In recent years major emphasis has been given towards increasing agricultural production through technological developments augmentation of agricultural research and greater use of fertilizers and mechanisation of agriculture[45].

In the age of globalisation which is seen as a process that widens the extent and form of cross-border transactions among peoples assets, goods and services that deepens economic interdependence between and among globalising entities. True economic globalisation involves a qualitative shift towards a system based on a consolidated global market place for production, distribution and consumption rather than on autonomous national economies[46]. The concept itself is not an automatic remedy for all economic maladies.While the country has achieved remarkable progress in terms of bio, space and information technologies, the quality of a majority of rural masses has not improved much. Illiteracy, unemployment, poverty, lack of basic amenities such as drinking water, shelter, food security and higher rate population growth still challenge the planners. Several structural changes have been made in the Panchayati Raj Institutions (PRIs) in order to meet the challenges posed by globalisation and make acquainted the rural masses ready for the best utilization and conservation of land resources. In the changing global scenario, modernization is inescapable but rational and selective approach to technology is essential to prevent careless degradation of environment which is closely related to the harnessing of land resources.

2.4 DISASTER MANAGEMENT IN INDIA

The word 'Disaster' is defined as a serious disruption of the functioning of a society, causing widespread human, material, or environmental losses which exceeds the ability of the affected society to cope using its own resources. It is among the many shocks and surprises that human history has witnessed since its inception and is a product of hazards which is considered a dangerous condition or events that threaten or have the potential for causing injury to life or damage to property or the environment. Without hazards there is no disaster. Hazards, itself on the basis of its origin, has been basically grouped in two broad headings – natural and unnatural. The first is closely related to meteorological, geological or even biological aspects, while the second is with human-cause or advancement of technology.

Another component of disaster is vulnerability which is an extent, a community, structure, service, or geographic area is likely to be damaged or disrupted by the impact of particular hazard, on account of their nature, construction and proximity to hazardous terrain or a disaster prone area.[47] Thus, a disaster occurs when hazard and vulnerability meet. A disaster minus hazards is a natural phenomena. For example, a massive earthquake in an unpopulated region is a natural phenomena, but when it interacts with the man made environment or fragile areas and causes widespread damage, becomes a hazard.

To some extent social and economic conditions determine the vulnerability of a society. It has been observed that human losses in disasters in developing countries like India tend to be high when compared to developed countries where material losses predominate. While no country in the world is entirely safe, lack of capacity to limit the impact of hazards remains a major burden for developing countries. According to an estimate 97 per cent of natural disaster related deaths each year occur in developing countries. In developed countries the absolute cost of physical damage increases, but its relative cost decreases; and the number of lives lost also declines. The rise in the cost of disasters reflects increase in the quality and quantity of property and infrastructure. Wealthier countries can also afford increasingly sophisticated early warning and communications systems, allowing people more time to move to safe places and resulting in fewer deaths and injuries.

Causes

Vulnerability plays a key role in natural and unnatural disasters. Mainly it is a human factor, liable to be affected from a number of other considerations. In the case of natural disaster hazards, location of the hazards, exposure that includes various types of structures and lifeline systems such as water supply, communication network, transportation network etc and finally, vulnerability of the exposed structures and system are badly affected. In a developing country like India what make any area vulnerable to the disaster are increased demographic pressures and escalated environmental degradation.[48] Environmental factor increases the impact of any hazard and caused by deforestation, which causes erosion and clogs rivers, siltation of riverbeds etc.

All disasters bring with themselves a lot of sufferings and pain to the people of the affected area. The accelerated, and often uncontrolled growth of cities has contributed to the ecological transformation of their immediate surroundings. In addition, the lack of appropriate drainage systems and sealing increase the volume and speed of rainfall. Recent studies have highlighted that a poor understanding by decision makers of seismic related risk and tendency of some builders to use the cheapest designs and construction materials, increase the risk during catastrophic earthquakes.[49]

As to the unnatural disaster which has a much larger spectrum includes epidemics, industrial accidents, communal violence, terrorism, nuclear weapons and biological bombs etc. They cause mainly to the unhealthy social, economic and environmental conditions. Reports of outbreaks of communicable diseases are due to poverty which is one of the major factors contributing to the vulnerability.

Economic and Social Effects

Often in an affected area there ensues a period of economic and social instability characterized by fluctuating prices, shift of class lines and movement of population. The shock of disaster always produces unusual or extreme types of human behaviour.[50] Normally financial impacts of a disaster are calculated on the basis of damage to homes, hospitals, schools, factories, infrastructure and crops. It does not include less quantifiable effects such as the loss of personal belongings or jobs, widening trade or government budget deficits, or the increasing scale and depth of poverty. The degree of severity largely depends on the type of hazard, the size of the economy and its economic structure and the sectors affected by the disaster. For instance, droughts do not damage buildings or physical structures but their lengthy duration creates other problems. However, in contrast, sudden-onset disasters such as floods or earthquakes have a direct impact on infrastructure and productive facilities and resources.[51]

Traditionally, it was the pacific region that was supposed to be prone to tsunami, which usually occur because of earthquakes on the ocean floors 70 kilometers deep. But in the case of recent tsunami, the deep was just 30 kilometers and that too close to the Asian landmass.[52] There are large parts of the earth where the potential hazards are likely to occur and the problems may result of an event. India is highly prone to almost all the disasters. Out of 35 states and Union Territories, 25 are officially considered disaster prone. More than half the country is in a seismically active zone.[53]

The economic costs of disasters, in a broader view, can be of three types - direct, indirect and secondary. The direct costs relate to the capital cost of assets such as buildings, other physical structures, raw materials and losses of crops. The indirect costs pertain to the flow of goods and services and include lower output from factories, loss of sales income and the costs associated with having to purchase more expensive materials.

The last, the secondary effects concern the short and long-term impacts of a disaster on overall economic performance and include deterioration in external trade and government budget balances, the reallocation of planned government spending and increased indebtedness.

All disasters, proportionately limit the economic development and seriously affect the household livelihoods and push already vulnerable groups to poverty. The loss of income earners through death or injury, the interruption of production or access to markets and the destruction of productive assets affect local and household economies.

Every natural disaster to the degree of its severity, makes damages to the economic structures of the affected areas which has a direct bearing on population of the region. With the destruction of health or education infrastructure and personnel, death, disablement or migration of key social actors, social development becomes limited, leading to an erosion of social capital. In addition to the loss of social assets, there are many examples of disaster events destroying the gains of the health, sanitation, drinking water, housing and education sectors that underpin social development. The Kutch-Bhuj earthquake in 2001, completely damaged district hospital, 992 primary schools and 18 secondary schools. The cyclone that hit Orissa in 1999 led to the contamination of drinking water wells and damaged many schools in the direct impact of a single event.

Institutional Arrangements

As natural disaster is not a new phenomena, institutional arrangements for carrying out response, relief and rehabilitation have been well-established since independence. We can not deny the role of institutional set up of governments, and responsibilities of different levels of government in achieving emerging national disaster risk management systems. However, the time has come to expand the structures beyond traditional response such as relief and rehabilitation. The changed policy mandates a priority to pre-disaster aspects of mitigations, prevention and preparedness. In the light of this new approach new institutional mechanisms are being put in place at Central, State and Local levels to meet the potential challenges.

Although the primary responsibility for disaster management is of the concerned State Governments, the Central Government plays a key role for providing financial and logistic support in case of major disasters. At Central level Cabinet Secretary is the highest executive officer who heads the National Crisis Management Committee (NCMC). Its members are all secretaries of the concerned Ministries/ Departments and Organisations. The NCMC gives direction to the Crisis Management Group and to any Ministry, Department and Organisation for specific action needed for meeting the crisis situation. The Central Relief Commissioner in the Ministry of Home Affairs is the Chairman of the Crisis Management Group. In the event of disaster, the CMG meets frequently to review the relief operations and extend all possible assistance required by the affected States to overcome the situation effectively.

At the level of state it has been asked to set up Disaster Management Authorities under the Chief Minister with Ministers of relevant Departments as members. Eleven States and Union Territories – Tamil Nadu, Arunachal Pradesh, Uttaranchal, Orissa, Gujarat Kerala, Nagaland, Rajasthan, Delhi, Andaman and Nicobar Administration and Chandigarh Administration have notified the constitution of the authority.

On the otherhand, in some states the work of the Department of Relief and Rehabilitation has been restructured. The Government of India is working with the State Governments to restructure the Department into Departments of Disaster Management with an enhanced area of responsibility to include mitigation and preparedness. The changeover has already been made in 11 States including Union Territories - Andhra Pradesh, Arunachal Pradesh, Bihar, Himachal Pradesh, Rajasthan, Tamil Nadu, Uttaranchal, Nagaland, Andaman and Nicobar Administration, Sikkim and Lakshadweep. The States have also been advised to make four groups of the officers and staff within the Department with a view to manage the definite functions of hazard mitigation, preparedness and capacity building, relief and resources, and administration and finance, respectively.

The disaster management has also its structures at district, block and village levels. The District Coordination and Relief Committee is being redesigned into Disaster Management Committee with officers from relevant departments being added as members. At the district level, the District Magistrate, who is the chief coordinator, is the focal point for coordinating all activities relating to prevention, mitigation and preparedness. The District Disaster Management Committee have already been constituted in 256 districts in the country and are in the process of being constituted in the remaining districts.

Similarly, efforts have also been made to constitute the Disaster

Management Committees at sub-divisional, block and village levels. At the village level both - Disaster Management Committees and Disaster Management Teams are being constituted. The DMC will consist of elected representatives at the village level, local authorities; government functionaries including doctors, paramedics of primary health centres located in the village, primary school teachers etc. The Disaster Management Teams at the village level will consist of members of youth organisations like Nehru Yuva Kendra Sanghathan (NYKS) and National Service Scheme (NSS) and other non-governmental organizations.

Management and Mitigation

The disaster management and mitigation falls under global trends of causing policy makers to think in terms of risk reduction. The term 'Management' can be defined as the body of policy and administrative decisions and operational activities which pertain to the various stages of a disaster at all levels. Mitigation includes hazard mapping, hazard and vulnerability assessment, structural and non-structural measures. It embraces all measures taken to reduce both the effect of the hazard itself and the vulnerable conditions to it in order to reduce the scale of a future disaster.

In wider perspective disaster management can be divided into two situations pre-disaster and post-disaster. Under the purview of disaster management, there are three key stages of activity-before a disaster strikes, during the disaster and after a disaster. The first one is precautionary and involves all activities taken to reduce human and property losses caused by the hazard and ensure that these losses are minimized when the disaster strikes. They are called mitigation and preparedness activities.

In course of disaster occurrence some activities are done to ensure that the needs and provisions of victims are met and suffering is minimized. They are also called emergency response activities. The activities taken after a disaster are called response and recovery activities. In the post-disaster phase best results can be achieved by mobilising youth from affected communities themselves, and training them as psycho-social counsellors. Experiences in Orissa and Gujarat have shown that these young people, frequently from working class backgrounds, have remarkably helped people heal emotionally, to come to terms with their profound grief and loss and to gather the resolve to pick up the threads of life once again.[54]

Only honest efforts involving institutional reforms, improved analytical and methodological capabilities, education, awareness, financial planning and political commitment will reduce the risk and vulnerability of natural disaster. In order to minimize the effects of disasters, we need to coordinate and cooperate the entire system of management and mitigation, not just from the government of the country but from the whole of the world community. Let us hope and try our best to make a world free of disasters, natural and unnatural.

2.5 PERSPECTIVES ON HUMAN SECURITY

Like human nature the idea of human security is not static and has to be adjusted in order to promote human development in a ever-changing society. In the classical formulation security is about how states use force to manage threats to their territorial integrity. Now it is no longer confined to the military or territorial threats to a state but also considers non-military threats. The emphasis has shifted on the internal source of threats emanating from within the boundaries of the state, such as, coercive diplomacy, economic and, psychological warfare, political subversion, defamatory propaganda, terrorism and political violence. The central question – how safe and free are we as individual is the result of the growing dissatisfaction with prevailing notions of development and security in the 1960s, 1970s and 1980s. The reports of various commissions on security and the United Nations Development Programme (UNDP) have focussed a lot the cause of human security. This article is an attempt to analyse and evaluate the basic dimensions of human security.

Themes of Human Security

While discussing the themes of human security the classical concept, which refers to the security of territorial state, has been criticized on grounds more than one. It laid too much emphasis on force in a world where there were weapons of mass destruction and interdependence is knitting nations together willy-nilly. In the circumstances security cannot be restricted to military threats as rival states may also deploy other kinds of threats against each other's territorial integrity and domestic political order. There may also be various non-state actors and even natural catastrophes. However a large and more fundamental critics of security go further to suggest that security cannot be restricted to the well-being of the state. But in this context what is central or should be central – is the protection and welfare of the individual citizen or human being.[55] A concept of security that is centred above all on the sanctity of the individual may be called human security.

The basic themes of human security have been elaborated in a series of reports prepared by multinational independent commissions composed of prominent leaders, intellectuals and academics. In the early years of 1970s the Club of Rome groups produced a series of volumes on the 'World problematique' which narrated "a complex of problems troubling men of all nations: poverty; degradation of the environment; loss of faith in institutions; uncontrolled urban spread; insecurity of employment; alienation of youth; rejection of traditional values; and inflation and other monetary and economic disruptions"[56]. The said report further laid stress on a state of global equilibrium to be designed so that the basic material needs of each person are satisfied, and each person has an equal opportunity to realize his individual human potential'.

In line, the 1980s witnessed two independent commissions in order to change thinking on development and security. The first was the Independent Commission on International Development Issues chaired by Willy Brandt and second, the Independent Commission on Disarmament and Security Issues, chaired by Olof Palme. The first Commission issued the North-South report in 1980 and in its introduction, it noted that the heart of the matter was the "will to overcome dangerous tensions and to produce significant and useful results for nations and regions- but first and foremost, for human beings- in all parts of the world".[57] It also argued the necessity of a North-South engagement for development. The second Commission authored the famous Common Security report which drew attention towards alternative ways of thinking about peace and security. Apart from focussing on military issues and the staples of national security, it acknowledged that in the Third World security was also threatened by "poverty, deprivation, and economic inequality".[58]

A new thinking in matters of human security began to grow rapidly with the end of Cold War in the first part of the 1990s. First the Stockholm Initiative on Global Security and Governance issued a call for "Common Responsibility in the 1990s". It referred to challenges to security other than political rivalry and armaments and dealt also with threats that stem from failures in development, environmental degradation, excessive population growth and movement, and lack of progress towards democracy.[59] Four years later its sentiments were echoed in the Commission on Global Governance's report, "Our Global Neighbourhood" which maintained that the concept of global security must be broadened from the traditional focus on the security of states to include the security of people and the security of the planet.[60] These reports were the precursors to human security thinking which led us to an explicitly human security perspective with some vigour.

Human Security in Perspective

In the context of human security two concepts- human rights and human development need to be analysed first. Basically human rights refer to all human beings having universal or status to which we are entitled simply by being human.[61] It is not limited to providing all human beings with the needs for their physical subsistence but involves a certain degree of minimal comfort beyond merely keeping one's organs working because human subsistence also consists of being able to function. Having grown out of the liberal traditions of the 18th century Europe, the concept had roots in the philosophical traditions of most civilizations which ranges for over two thousand years. The main idea of Aristotle that like should be treated alike remained a motivating factor in the history of human existence.

Typically human rights are categorized as two–negative human rights and positive human rights. The concept of negative human rights denotes actions that a government should not take as it follow mainly the Anglo-American tradition. It was codified in the United States Bill of Rights, the English Bill of Rights and the Canadian Charter of Rights and Freedom and freedom of speech, religion and assembly. On the other positive human rights denote rights that the state is obliged to protect and provide. It follows mainly the Rousseauian Continental European legal tradition and is codified in the Universal Declaration of Human Rights and in many constitutions of contemporary world. Examples of such rights include: the right to education, to a livelihood, and to legal equality. The legal concept of human rights is itself the product of a specific process of history. In Europe it emerged as a consequence of the political and legal values gained from 16th century renaissance and 18th century enlightenment.[62] In later centuries even the legal frameworks also began to be based on liberal and Marxist Philosophies. While the liberal philosophers from Locke to Rawls thought of individual rights in terms of personal freedom, Marx considered rights in a bourgeois framework as constraints on human freedom. Further these two schools of thought also differ in their analysis of the relation between the individual and the collective.[63] While liberals have always interpreted this relation in terms of the private and the public, the logic of Marxists has always been to create the conditions for greater human solidarity through resolution of tensions rooted in the structures of dominance, the power and property, in particular.

The concept of human security and human rights is incomplete without human development. Generally, while analysing human development, three approaches are used to measure the well-being of the people. The first one is, physical quality of life index which contains three indicators–adult literacy rate, infant mortality and life expectancy. The second approach is basic needs approach which argues that the basic needs of adequate nutrition, primary education, health sanitation, water supply and housing available to the poorest to a reasonable extent. The last, being the human development index approach, is the most widely used index.[64] According to the Human Development Report 2005, published by the UNDP, all the 177 countries in total are categorized into three broad groups: High Human Development, Medium Human Development and Low Human Development. In this report India is placed in the Medium Human Development countries and ranks at 127 among them.[65]

Important Contributors

In last one decade the cause of human security has been championed by the prevailing schools or approaches. In between Mahbub ul Haq and UNDP, there exists the Canadian-led middle powers', approach which tries to seek a compromising point. All these approaches make an attempt to answer the four key questions: Security for whom? Security of which values? Security from what threats? And security by what means?

In the history of human security 1994 was an important year. In it, Haq's approach to human security was outlined in his paper "New Imperatives of Human Security", which answered the question 'security for whom. He says simply 'Human security is not about states and nations but about individuals and people'. Elsewhere he wrote normatively, 'we need to fashion a new concept of human security that is reflected in the lives of our people, not in the weapons of our country. In answer to the question what values will we seek to protect, he clearly counts that individual safety and well-being in the broad sense are the prime values. He laid especial emphasis on how can human security be achieved?[66] In the same year (1994), the UNDP's Human Development Report was published which included a section on human security. It insists as Haq did, that the contextual object of human security is individual or people. The Report also cited the founding document of the UN and its original delineation of security as 'freedom from fear', 'freedom from want' and the equal weight to territories and to people.

In response to Mahbub ul Haq's paper and UNDP's report on human security, Canada had made two statements of its position (1997 and 1999) and along with Norway organized a middle powers 'conference in Lysoen in Norway (1999). Like the UNDP, for Canada human security implies security for the individual as Lloyd Axworthy, the Foreign Minister of Canada, argued in his 1997 paper' a people-centred view of security includes security against economic privation, an acceptable quality of life, and a guarantee of fundamental human rights.[67] Canada, in its later paper presented in 1999 referred to the dangers posed by civil conflicts, large-scale atrocities and genocide. It also amplified the 1997 approach by listing six broader principles that might guide actions. Inspite of having similar on several aspects relating to human security, the Canadian approach considers security of the state as an important element for individual or human security.

In nutshell, human security relates directly to the protection of every individual simply by being a human. In Post-Cold War phase a clear cut thinking and action as well have taken a concrete shape in this regard which have focussed, in place of classical notion of state security, the safety of individual and its values thereof. Though in sphere of ideational and institutional frameworks and issues, they both are different but successes in human and national security areas have become mutually supportive and failure in either will reciprocally weaken the other.

References

1. Verghese Koithara, Society State and Security – The Indian Experience (Sage Publications, New Delhi, 1999), p. 268.
2. B.S. Upadhyaya, Women in Rigveda, (S. Chand and Co., New Delhi, 1974), p. 42.
3. Ibid., p. 136.
4. Mala Singh, 'Women of India, the Old Order Changeth-But only for a Few', The Illustrated Weekly of India, August 9, 1970, p. 8.
5. Sugata Bose and Ayesha Jalal, Modern South Asia- History, Culture, Political Economy (Oxford University Press, New Delhi, 2004), pp. 35-36.
6. A.R. Desai, Social Background of Indian Nationalism (Popular Prakashan, Bombay, 1948), pp. 273-76.
7. Plan and Prospects of Social Welfare in India, 1951-61, p. 14.
8. Bipin Chandra, Mridula Mukherjee and Aditya Mukherjee, India

After Independence 1947-2000 (Penguin Books, New Delhi, 2002), pp. 451-52.

9. Dr. Priyanka Tomar, Indian Women (Shree Publishers, New Delhi, 2006), pp. 216-18.
10. B. Ramesh Babu, 'The Liberal Capitalist West as the New Global State', Bansidhar Pradhan, ed., International Studies, Journal of the School of International Studies, Jawaharlal Nehru University, Vol. 43, No. 3, July-September 2006 (Sage Publications, New Delhi, 2006), p. 291.
11. Gurkirat Kaur, Women and Law (Shree Publishers, New Delhi, 2005), pp. 227-30.
12. Vijaya Nambiar, Liberalisation and Development – Agenda for Economic Reforms (Commonwealth Publishers, New Delhi, 2003), pp. 101-2.
13. G.S. Batra and R.C. Dangwal, Liberalisation, Globalisation and International Business (Deep and Deep Publications, New Delhi, 2006), pp. 97-98.
14. Dr. Priyanka Tomar, op.cit., pp. 219-22.
15. V. Venkata Rao and Niru Hazarika, Local Self-Government in India (S. Chand & Company, New Delhi, 1980), p.1.
16. Chetakar Jha, Indian Local Self-Government (Novelty & Co., Patna, 1953), pp.1-2.
17. S.N. Jha 'Introduction' in S.N. Jha, P.C. Mathur, eds., Decentralisation and Local Politics (Sage Publications, New Delhi, 1999), pp. 17-18.
18. Ashok Bajpai, M.S.Verma, Panchayati Raj in India –A New Thrust, Vol. 1 (Sahitya Prakashan, Delhi, 1995), pp. 1-2.
19. Durga Das Basu, Introduction to the Constitution of India (Wadhwa & Company, Nagpur, 1997), p. 267.
20. S.N. Mishra, Rural Development and Panchayati Raj (Concept Publishing Company, New Delhi, 1981), p. 36.
21. S.C. Dube, 'Communication, Innovation and Planned Change in India' in Lerner and Schramn, Communication and Change in Developing Countries (East-West Centre Press, Honolulu, 1967), p. 159.
22. V.K.R.V. Rao, 'Integrated Rural Development', Janata, Vol. XXXII, No. 35, October 9, 1977, p. 9.
23. V. Sivalinga Prasad, Panchayats and Development (Light & Life Publishers, New Delhi, 1981), p.3.
24. Ibid., p. 4.

25. S.N. Jha, op.cit., pp. 22-24.
26. J.C. Mohanty, 'WTO and Implications for Indian Agriculture', in Ramesh K. Arora, ed., Administrative Change, A Journal on Political and Administrative Development, Vol. XXX, No. 1 & Vol. XXXI, No. 2, January – December 2002 (Jaipur, 2002), p.67.
27. Dr. R. Balasubramanian, 'Indian Polity in Transition', Presidential Address 53rd Annual Conference of Indian Political Science Association, University of Rajasthan, Jaipur, 27-29th December 2006, p.2.
28. C. Sheela Reddy, 'Globalisation – A Human Rights Perspective' Dr. Subhash C. Kashyap, ed. South Asia Politics, Vol. 5, No. 2, March 2007 (New Delhi, 2007), pp. 39-40.
29. G. Palanithurai & V. Ragupathy, 'Critical Issues in Democratic Decentralization of Power in India', in Ibid., Vol. 6, No. 1, May 2007, p. 27.
30. Ibid., pp. 28-29.
31. Ibid., pp. 41-42.
32. The Hindu (Madras), July 2, 2007.
33. V. Venkata Rao and Niru Hazarika, op.cit., pp. 10-14.
34. Ruchi Tyagi, 'The Relevance of Gandhi's Economic Swaraj in the Era of 21st Century Globalization' Dr. Subhash C. Kashyap, ed., South Asia Politics, Vol.6, No.6, October 2007 (New Delhi, 2007), p.18.
35. Rajni Kothari, Politics in India (Orient Longman, New Delhi, 1970), p.134.
36. Durga Das Basu, op.cit., p. 267.
37. S.N. Mishra, op.cit., p. 36.
38. S.C. Dube, op.cit., p. 159.
39. S.N. Jha, op.cit., pp.17-18.
40. G. Palanithurai and V. Ragupathy, op.cit., pp. 41-42.
41. Abha Lakshmi Singh and Shahab Fazal, Agriculture and Rural Development (B.R. Publishing Corporation, Delhi, 1998), pp.61-62.
42. The Hindu, October 26, 2007.
43. Abha Lakshmi Singh and Shahab Fazal , op. cit., pp.63-64.
44. Ibid., p. 71.
45. Vijay Bahadur Singh, Land Development Banking in India (Commonwealth Publishers, New Delhi, 1990), p.27.
46. J.C Mohanty, op.cit., p. 67.
47. A Primer for Parliamentarian, Document prepared by Anand S.

Arya, Anup Karanth and Ankush Agarwal under the UNDP Disaster Risk Management Programme, pp. 5-6.

48. Ibid., pp. 51-52.
49. Ibid.
50. Edwin R.A. Seligman, ed., Encyclopaedia of the Social Sciences, Vol. 5 (The Macmillan Company, Newyork, 1954), p. 162.
51. A Primer for Parliamentarian, op.cit., p. 53.
52. The Hindustan Times (editorial), December 28, 2004.
53. Manoj Joshi, 'The Tsunami as Metaphor', Ibid., December 29, 2004.
54. Harsh Mander. 'Out of Sight, Not Out of Mind', Ibid., January 13, 2005.
55. Kanti Bajpai, 'The Idea of Human Security', Bansidhar Pradhan, ed., International Studies, Jawaharlal Nehru University, Vol. 40, No. 3, July-September 2003 (Sage Publications, New Delhi, 2006), pp. 196-97.
56. Donella H. Meadows, Dennis L. Meadows, Jorgen Randers and William W.Behrens III, The Limits to Growth (Universal Books, Newyork, 1972), p.10.
57. The Independent Commission on International Development Issues, North-South: A programme for Survival (The MIT Press, Cambridge, 1980), p. 9.
58. The Independent Commission on Disarmament and Security Issues, Common Security: A Blueprint for Survival (Simon and Schuster, Newyork, 1982), P.15.
59. 'The Stockholm Initiative on Global Security and Governance' 'Common Responsibility in the 1990s', The Prime Minister's Office (Government of Sweden, Stockholm, 1991), pp. 17-18.
60. The Commission on Global Governance, Our Global Neighbourhood (Oxford University Press, Newyork, 1995), p.338.
61. Prakash Talwar, Human Rights (Isha Books, Delhi, 2006), pp. 1-7.
62. Mahua Sarkar, 'Human Rights and Environment: A Case Study of Colonial India', in Proceedings of the Indian History Congress, 65th Session, Baraeilly, 2004, Indian History Congress (Delhi, 2005-06), pp.1218-19.
63. G. Haragopal and B.Chandra Shekhar Rao, 'Human Rights Perspectives and Practices' in G.P. Deshpanda and Alka Acharya, eds., 50 Years of India-China-Crossing a Bridge of Dreams (Tulika, New Delhi, 2002), pp. 189-90.
64. K. Muthalagu and Dr. K. Vijayarani, 'Perspectives on Human

Development in India', Babuddin Khan, ed., Third Concept, Vol. 20, No. 235, September 2006 (New Delhi, 2006), p. 38.

65. Ibid.
66. Mahbub ul Haq, New Imperatives of Human Security, Rajiv Gandhi Institute for Contemporary Studies (Rajiv Gandhi Foundation, New Delhi, 1994), p.1.
67. The Canadian Foreign Minister in an address to the Fifty-first UN General Assembly (1996) first broached the idea of human security on behalf of his government. See Lloyd Axworthy, 'Canada and Human Security', p. 184.

3

INDIA AND THE WORLD AROUND

3.1 INDIA'S POLICY OF NON- ALIGNMENT AT PRESENT

At the close of the century India's understanding with the US touched a new height which demoted India to the status of a camp follower. The US foreign Policy under George William Bush was felt by the world with difference. Bill Clinton's vision of a brave new world is being supplanted by Bush's dangerous new world. His belief was that with the cold war over, the world could get together and agree not to do certain nasty things – test or build nuclear weapons, block trade and investment. Clinton's liberal world view was left behind by George Bush who announced on January 29, 2002, "I will not wait events while dangers gather. I will not stand by as peril draws closer and closer. The US will not permit the world's most dangerous regimes to threaten us with the world's most destructive weapons.[1] Although the statement was made in the background of terrorist attack on World Trade Center in September 2001, we can not overlook US plan of implementing National Missile Defence (NMD) and Threat Missile Defence (TMD) which is bound to add to India's problems. If NMD is seen to work, the United States could extend a "Missile Umbrella" to its allies the way it presently holds out a nuclear umbrella. The US Ballistic Missile Defence Organisation is of the view that such a globally – expansive missile defence system would help safeguard unipolarity, providing the impetus to other nations to enhance their military arrangements with the US.

Terrorism, no doubt, is a new threat to international system which aims to smash all principles and norms of the day. But the shift in US foreign policy under George Bush indicates more than fight against terrorism and one can not reduce the problems of the world to the single dimension of the fight against terrorism however vital that might be. The US now threatens a virtually unending, unilateral war on terrorism which has presence in 70 countries. This war will comprehensively violate the principle of peaceful settlement of disputes through diplomacy and legitimise the rule of brute force in world politics. It will burn to a cinder every principle of international relations for which India has a strong commitment not just during Nehru's idealistic period, but even under more pragmatic leaders like Narasimha Rao and I.K. Gujral. With such a unilateralism India is now mindlessly building a strategic partnership with the US simply to isolate Pakistan and stalling any negotiations on Kashmir. India supported uncritically the war in Afghanistan, violating its own commitment to multilateralism and the UN. It is more loyal than many US allies in welcoming US missile defence plans that ultimately plans to reshape the world order violently to ensure its total domination. Indian diplomacy would need to re-orient itself in major way if it is to cope with the emerging world that is not only globalising but is also becoming deeply demanding in multi-disciplinary terms.[2]

A new international system is still being formed with unprecedented changes having taken place in recent years. The collapse of the Soviet Union which led to the fall of Communist rule in Eastern Europe and the disintegration of the Warsaw pact have affected the entire international system. The Soviet Union lost its former superpower status, paving the way for increasing US influence in world politics. In the changed circumstances the United States of America liked to balance its interests in South Asian region and its improving relations with India is understandable. The speculation that India is going to emerge as one of the six major military power in foreseeable future allured Washington most because it viewed New Delhi essential for the crisis management in world politics. The increasing influence of Islamic fundamentalism was also considered as the extremely dangerous development in which India can act as regional stabiliser.

On the part of India, despite its adherence to the policy of Non-alignment, emerged the more compelling reasons to seek a close alliance with Washington in order to strengthen its position in the international system. It was hoped that strong relations with the US would help India increase its bargaining position vis-à-vis Pakistan, act as a restraint on China and also end its over – dependence on Moscow. Keeping these all in view, India has recently supported the US on several international issues relating to the Gulf war, Israel and Libya. It established diplomatic relations with Israel, a move encouraged by the US. It has also introduced a free-market economic policy following the advice of the International Monetary Fund (IMF) and the World Bank.

Political Diplomacy

At independence the policy of Non-alignment was adopted as a tool of political diplomacy in international politics which meant, from the very beginning, to keep away from bipolarity, the cold war, ideological crusades, the arms race and military blocs which were the chief characteristics of the era following the second world war.[3] The unique configuration of world Politics after the second world war admirably suited the establishment of India's non-alignment and gave it greater significance than it would have had in other circumstances. The balance of power diplomacy of the pre-war years disappeared and the entire developed world was divided into two opposing nuclear-armed blocs, each with an integrated politico-military structure. As a result of the cold war the Third World countries, which were gaining independence became a surrogate area for superpower competition. The Soviet Union, though a nuclear armed, was essentially a territorial power at that stage. It possessed neither economic nor military capability to influence the countries emerging from colonial rule. Political alignment with the Communist bloc was also not a viable option for India which was not prepared for a revolution. Therefore, the drive to incorporate the new countries into its strategic structure came almost entirely from the West. Alignment with the West was economically attractive but perceived by most of the newly independent nations as likely to prevent self-reliant growth.

The concept of non-alignment had negative as well as positive elements. The negative element envisaged a course of refusal to take side in any military line-up of the world powers. The most important positive element of it was the preservation and promotion of national interest. The elements of national interest itself change with variations in national and international circumstances and enable the leaders of respective country to take an enlightened and a broader view of their national interest. India was the first nation to design and articulate a new non-aligned foreign policy framework. It was also an attractive model for most developing countries who wanted both peace and progress at a time.

India generally perceived herself as a major actor to play an international role. Unlike domestic politics, playing a role in international system broadly refers to the wish and capacity of a nation to push the movement of international events in a given direction or to influence the behaviour of other states, or to manage a crisis through a series of mediatory initiatives, or even to project herself as a model for others to emulate. A visible or impactful role in the international system can be of two types. The first pertains to the utilisation of force or pressure through which a nation can modify a given situation or through which it can change the behaviour of a nation or a group of playing pertains to the utilisation of respect, confidence and the moral authority that the state may have as nations. However, material capacity and the appropriate political determination to do so is the obvious precondition for the successful achievement of such an objective. The second type of role acquired to peacefully wield influence on nations or situations. At the time of independence, India did not have the necessary military power to forcefully play a regional or global role. But on the otherhand, there appeared a fairly large consensus that India had some moral authority in terms of philosophy and religion.[4]

It was this policy of non-alignment which became the most characteristic and abiding feature of India's foreign policy. However, until 1950 India's non-alignment appeared to have a pro-Western orientation. From 1951 to 1956 it moved from a Western oriented non-alignment towards a more strictly middle of the road position. During this period India's relations with both the Soviet Union and with China improved, with the US deteriorated and those with Britain showed some considerable fluctuations. India's consistent disapproval of all Western alliances helped India improve its relations with the Communist powers and by the end of 1956 India's policy had inclined in favour of the Soviet bloc.[5] But things did not work smoothly any more and the closing years of Nehru era witnessed a slow erosion of his policy's framework. Factors responsible for this decline include border disputes with China, a humiliating defeat in October 1962 and evolution of a global situation in which there was no scope for mediation to manage international crisis.

In the post-Nehru era, India's role playing deteriorated under his successors, never to rise again. The positive and dynamic aspects of non alignment, expressive of a desire for active participation in the grand affairs of world politics, gave way to more humble preoccupation with saving India from predatory neighbours and staying out of other nation's complicated affairs. Many Indians expressed their convictions that it would be more important for India to take care of immediate national interests than of the world's moral welfare.[6] The principal thrust of India's foreign policy was thus more power and region oriented than one of seeking out a new global role for itself. However, Indira Gandhi after her second mandate in 1980, sought out a role in world politics when India had attained the status of a regional power and was internationally recognised as such. But her initiatives and declarations did not lead to the establishment of a real framework as she abruptly disappeared from the political scene of the country.

The changes which were visualised in world order at the close of the eighties began to take a concrete shape in the opening years of the coming decade. The main components of the structural change that has already been affected relate to the revolution of 1989 in Eastern Europe, the reunification of Germany, the collapse of the Warsaw pact, the structuring of NATO, the historic signing of the 1987 International Nuclear Forces Treaty, the outgoing US – Russian talks for further strategic arms reduction, the end of cold war and above all, the Soviet State's changing role in world affairs. With the end of the cold war, the US and the Russian States no longer appeared in confrontationist roles in South Asia. This had relevance for both the 1959 bilateral treaty of alliance between the US and Pakistan, and the Indo-Soviet Treaty of 1971.

The ever – changing international milieu and internal situation of the country are going to pose major challenges to both foreign policy making and diplomatic practice. The old domestic consensus on country's foreign policy framework has crumbled. There are now substantial differences of view on how the US, China and Pakistan should be handled. So are they on the positions to be taken at the various international fora dealing with economic political and security issues. Secondly, the mode of engagement with the external environment has changed. Even at the government to government level, India would have to negotiate much more multilaterally than before. In today's complex world marked by fluidity and uncertainty, India needs to cultivate close relations not only with just one or two powers but with several. Promotion of various interests requires a multiplicity of engagement and different formations of partnership.

Security Dilemma

Security, essentially a negative term, implies the absence of real or perceived threat whether stemming from external sources or internal troubles or incumbent, economic disparities and inequalities of certain coveted values.[7] To cope with perceived threats, nations tend to seek power hoping that power alone may generate the desired level of security.

One nation's ability to attain an adequate level of security may, in turn, breed insecurity for the other. Insecurity would compel the other nation to acquire more power in order to tilt the scale in its favour. Such a process often results not only in regional arms race but also invariably introduces the extra-regional actors into regional conflicts. In India's case, security is the basic framework of the policy of non-alignment and it aims to keep the great powers out of the subcontinent. The concept in the post – world war II era include three types of eventualities. The first a traditional concept is security against external threats. Whatever may be the level of their development, the nature of their geographical location, the choice of their social system, and the viability of their governmental structures, all of them, implicitly or explicitly, have always taken into account this dimension while designing the broad security framework of their foreign policy.

The second aspect, a relatively more recent is the internal dimension. It has through the years, been broadened to include a wide array of domestic factors, situations, forces and so on, that could challenge the core national values. The increasing fear of domestic socio-political destabilisation has brought to the fore this aspect of national security. The third, is the strategic environment in which nations live. For countries that are dimensional in size, endemic political instability on the periphery or the undue presence of their adversial powers in the neighbouring countries may be considered a security threat.

At independence, India had neither the power nor the political inclination, nor the military expertise to pursue a century old national security policy designed by Great Britain. With the departure of the British from the subcontinent, a new class of political leadership emerged at the helm of affairs who considered that the country did not have the means to do. Poverty stricken and problem ridden India had, in their view, other priorities to judiciously use her unexploited resources. But on the other they had a different political goal, which was to contribute to the promotion of peace and welfare of mankind certainly a commendable goal without having any resemblance with the British imperial strategy of pursuing a forward policy. The new defence strategy, in Nehru's view, had to be political. Military power did not feature in his foreign policy calculus. He envisaged a free India secure against attack either by its geo-strategic position, its size or the balance of power. Immediately after the partition of the subcontinent, he made it clear that India did not need a defence policy since we foresee no military threats and since the police are good enough to meet our security needs.[8]

At the regional level, Nehru's strategy on national security was to seek out political solutions to situations of conflict. In his view there was no other alternative for a country like ours who was ambitious to play a definite role in the international system. This broad strategic thinking on foreign policy pushed him to avoid any confrontation even in case of Pakistan. The Indian decision to take the Kashmir question to the United Nations after the 1947-48 Indo-Pak war, for example, illustrated India's approval to conflictual situations. Security was sought through non-alignment, the UN, Panchsheel and moral suasion.[9] At the global level where the threat could have emanated from the politics of the cold war and the resulting superpower pressures, Nehru's perception led him to the conclusion that the existing balance of power in the international system would guarantee India's security.

In the post-Nehru era the combination of defence and diplomacy was a major development in India's foreign policy. It served India well during the serventies and eighties. The successful conclusion of Indo-Soviet Treaty of 1971 deterred the United States of America and China from preventing Indian intervention in East Pakistan on the one hand and made it possible to detach the area from Pakistan on the other. It also helped India became a pre-dominant force in South Asia. However, this alliance system with Moscow became irrelevant in the nineties. Politically the world was no longer what it had been for decades. The Soviet Union, as a superpower ceased to exist and the protection that India had received from Moscow evaporated. The Russian Federation was neither willing nor capable of continuing the Soviet alliance policy vis-à-vis India.

During the current unipolar phase the US has been blantly misusing the UN Charter's Article 51 for individual and collective self defence to serve its national purpose under a UN cloak. In 1997, 73 countries were under one or another kind of US sanctions. The status of superpower has become rooted in the American psyche. The cold war victory has added to that psychological baggage. In the changed circumstances, India and the US can help each other in a big way. But while building closer links with the United States, the world's pre-eminent power, India can not neglect Russia. Despite Russia's present fragility, its importance for India has not declined. Rather the growing imbalance of power in Asia has only reinforced the value of a close Indo-Russian partnership for

Asian stability.

The US under George Bush is on the move. Both the defence systems TMD and NMD are good enough to provide the world a US – sponsored security umbrella. They would add India's problems rather indirectly. Aimed to challenge the deterrent posture of China, the rest of Beijing's arsenal consists of weapons can threat only the security of its neighbours like India. The rapid Chinese build-up will underent India's modest deterrent capabilities, New Delhi will be compelled to divert more of its resources to new nuclear missile projects. Apart from this, a stepped-up Chinese build-up would mean increased transfer of no-longer needed technologies to Pakistan by Beijing. China's filching of advanced US nuclear and missile blueprints had already set the stage for larger transfer of older technologies to Islamabad. It would also have a commercial motivations to recover some of its costs through such transfers. Cosequently, as capabilities of its own two hand-in-glove neighbours grow, India would come under greater strategic pressure.

Economic Diplomacy

The original development strategy for India was based on the broadest national consensus within the country. For a country like ours, international trade could hardly be an engine of growth. Viewing with its large size, vast population, natural resources, and so on, there could be no other viable economic option than to meet most of the growing needs of the country domestically with the heavy involvement of the state. Soon after independence India faced with a dilemma. While on the one hand, she had opted for the development of a solid and autonomous economic base of her own, she had on the other hand, realised that this was not possible without the imports of goods as well as capital under the circumstances, India had decided to obtain official external assistance on favourable terms that would be concessionary. India's policy of non-alignment proved very useful by non-controversial participation in international system.

In seventies the worsening of the economic conditions made governance difficult and a new thinking in India's economic sector was building up. Efforts to promote growth through a different approach began during 1977-79. In the 1980's the approach got predicted on substantially increased borrowing, both internal and external. The failure to raise productivity and competitiveness with borrowed money shook the macro-economic stability of the country. Under Indira Gandhi signs of some change were discernible and a number of initiatives were taken to improve the situation. Rajiv Gandhi also talked of "strategic control" over the economy with a view to move towards greater flexibility for both the private and public sectors.[10]

The overall economic situation did not seem to improve and compelled the Government of Narasimha Rao to take clear steps towards the globalisation of the Indian economy. The decision was followed by the depreciation of the Indian rupee by 20 per cent; decreased the fiscal deficit from 8.5 per cent to 6.5 per cent; cleared the way for foreign trading houses to function in India, increased the limit of foreign equity to 51 per cent in many priority areas etc.[11] However, the obvious reason for the new economic policy was not the recognition of the path but because India's economy was running out of time and was on the verge of default[12] with foreign reserves as low as Rs. 25 billion. It was introduced half heartedly and without any political preparation. In terms of reforms India is only at the base camp with a mountain still to climb. This is reflected in the continuous increase of capital intensity that has been needed to raise growth rates. In the factors contributing to competitiveness, according to a survey conducted in 1997, out of 53 countries, India was placed 51st in openness, 48th in infrastructure, 23rd in government 38th in finance, 36th in technology, 38th in management, 13th in labour and 30th in civil institution.[13]

In today's world, with the economic well being of citizens at large, the supranational organisations that produce general economic benefit, are becoming more acceptable, even though they contribute to the erosion of state authority. The General Agreement on Tarrif and Trade (GATT) and World Trade Organisation (WTO) are undoubtedly, a global organisation which cover much wider field, but India's agriculture has suffered a great due to the rules set by the WTO. Its Agreement on Agriculture (AoA), which forms a part of the final act showed no respect for the realities of India's economy. Apart from this, the policies pursued by the developed countries have done considerable damage to agriculture in the developing countries, particularly in India. The developed countries, especially the United States, have jealously protected their interests while neglecting the interests of the developing nations.[14]

The damage done to Indian agriculture on account of US attitude is immense and can not be viewed in isolation. It has its own impact on the agro-industries, particularly the small-scale industries. Elaborating its negative impacts the Minister of State for Commerce and Industry, in reply to a question in the Rajya Sabha on March 13, 2000, stated that 306, 221 small scale units were rendered sick by March 1999, displacing vast sections of labour in the small scale sector. Thus, the result of the WTO agreement has been the ruination of agriculture, closing down of small-scale industrial units, growing unemployment and accentuation of poverty. It is a sad state of affair in a country like India where 70 per cent of the population depends on agriculture and allied activities.

3.2 SAARC, INDIA AND SOUTH ASIA

The region South Asia which comprises eight countries of the globe covers India, Pakistan, Bangladesh, Sri Lanka, Bhutan, Nepal, Maldives and Afghanistan. It is a fact that the major countries of South Asia share a common historical past in the form of the British colonial rule, in terms of political stability, economic regeneration and socio-cultural change they remained poles apart in Post-Independence period with the exception that they cooperated each other both at the bilateral as well as multilateral levels under the umbrella of forums, such as Economic and Social Commission for Asia and Pacific (ESCAP), Non-Aligned Movement and Commonwealth. Years following their independence were full of internal characteristics of the polities comprising the region ranged widely from democratic, federal and parliamentary to monarchical and unitary. Over the decades, they have restructured, developed and maintained altogether different political traditions and with certainty none of the member states has fully succeeded in evolving in a 'nation state'. The earlier quest for autonomy, rivalry, autonomy of the region and sovereign rights had produced adverse effects on integration and interdependence and prevented, in particular, the evolution and growth of regional cooperation in diverse fields.

The concept of regional cooperation emerged late in South Asia and it was only during the seventies that various political and economic factors created congenial environment. As a result of the long deliberations among the member countries of the region the South Asian Association for Regional Cooperation (SAARC) came into existence on 8 December 1985 with its first summit meeting of the Heads of States in Dhaka. The basic aim of it is to accelerate the process of economic and social development in the member states through joint action in certain agreed areas of cooperation. It is a manifestation of the determination of the peoples of South Asia to cooperate regionally, to work together towards finding solutions to their common problems in a spirit of friendship, trust and understanding and to create an order based on mutual respect, equity and shared benefits. Like other regional bodies of the world the SAARC has also developed an institutional framework within which different level meetings take place at regular intervals, and within which a wide array of institutions, working groups, and so on, have been set up to discuss the feasibility and modalities of cooperation among the member countries. Over a dozen of summits have been held so far and adhering strictly to its basic objectives it has promoted regional cooperation through active collaboration and mutual assistance in the economic, social, cultural, technical and scientific fields. However, for enhancing the effectiveness of SAARC attempts at all levels should be made to resolve various bilateral and tri-lateral issues which slow down the processes of regional cooperation in several areas.

Inheritance of South Asia

The Indian subcontinent or South Asia ıncompasses today eight very diverse sovereign states of very different sizes: India, Pakistan Bangladesh, Sri Lanka, Nepal, Bhutan, Maldives and Afghanistan. The terms South Asia and India refer, in the first instance, to a vast geographical space stretching from the Himalayan mountain ranges in the north to the Indian Ocean in the south and from the valley of the Indus in the west to the plains of the Brahmaputra in the east. The subcontinent carries the weight not only of its people but also of their ancient history, stretching back five millennia, and a modern history incompassing the experience of British colonialism compressed in tumultuous developments within the past couple of centuries.[15] It has 3 per cent of the world's area, 23 per cent of its population and 2 per cent of its GDP. Within that, India has 72 per cent of the area, 77 per cent of the population and 75 per cent of the GDP.[16] The geographical boundaries drawn by the highest mountain ranges in the world and encircling seas and oceans set the whole of the subcontinent apart from the rest of the world.

The region South Asia and its peoples present a picture of diversity in unity, indeed of immense diversity within a very broad contour of unity. Among them there is great diversity in natural attributes–imposing hills and mountains, lush green river plains, arid deserts and brown plateaus. The South Asian societies are marked by their plural character in terms of languages, cultures, regions and religions. The peoples of South Asia speak at least twenty major languages and if we include the more important dialects, the count rises to over two hundred. The very diverse languages and language families of South Asia have made enormous contributions to world literature from ancient to modern times. In a broad historical and cultural sense all states of the region may be viewed to be belonging to the Indian family of nations.

Culture, as Spengler and Toynbee used the word, is the product of long tradition, of shared habits among people living together over generations; it reflects a particular way of life and a particular view of the world. Its characteristic is spontaneity, and it is often said that it cannot be exported or imported.[17] Likewise the region South Asia share certain things in common and they are the religious–cultural heritage of the ancient and medieval times and the administrative, political, educational, economic institutions.[18] Adherents of major world religions, Hinduism, Islam, and Buddhism are found in the subcontinent. Hinduism with its ancient roots, modern transformation and multiple interpretations plays a vital part in the culture and politics of the subcontinent. The greatest cultural and political achievements of Islam have taken place in the subcontinent, where more than 400 million of the world's 1.3 billion Muslims live today. Each of the three most populous countries of South Asia–India, Bangladesh and Pakistan has nearly 140 million Muslims, next only to Indonesia as the largest Muslim countries in the world.[19] Buddhism, apart from the formal adherents in the land of its birth, continues to flourish in Sri Lanka and the Himalayas as well as in East and Southeast Asia. South Asia has also significant number of Jain, Zoroastrian, Christian and Sikh minorities.

In spheres of culture, economy, politics and society the modern South Asian history witnessed a number of significant changes in which pivotal role was played by the intermediate social groups in the construction and continuation of British raj. As a result of this social group the colonial state succeeded in intervening the earlier communal and caste categories. They also refashioned the social relations of class by the linking of Indian economic regions to wider capitalist system and thus created a new group in subcontinent's society for their benefit. The states of South Asia emerged as sovereign entities after their prolonged struggle against colonialism. In the Post-Colonial era, nation building became an arduous task. It was all the more challenging for multicultural states to blend the diverse religious, linguistic and ethno-cultural groups into a national mould.[20] Majority of these states devised the mechanism of a secular democratic order to achieve this objective. But lack of popular participation or the inadequacy of participation have, rather, contributed to political fragmentation. The absence of a political mechanism to settle who will get what and how has given rise to conflicts among ethnic groups.[21]

The withdrawal of empire leaves a legacy of uncertain frontiers and other disputes among the legatee states. It was complicated further by the lack of self-confidence in the leadership elites of the new nations who frequently direct the fears of their citizens against neighbouring nations in a mistaken belief that this will strengthen the spirit of nationalism and inspire internal cohesion.[22] Real problems among neighbours do exist and in the South Asian System we can easily discern two types of dialectical struggles that have in the past influenced the nature of ties in the region. One type of struggle is by India for a regional role of dominance, maturing into, either a sphere of influence or a hegemonic order. Another is primarily influenced by India's ambitious role, is the struggle by Pakistan and others for autonomy, independence and sovereign existence.[23] Alongwith autonomy security perceptions of the South Asian States remained at the top they, however, have developed stronger economic links with the countries outside the region.

Formation of SAARC

Establishment of the South Asian Association for Regional Cooperation (SAARC) in December 1985 was backed by the concept of regional integration which has been defined by Earnest Hass as the "process whereby political actors in several distinct national settings are persuaded to shift their loyalties, expectations and political activities towards a new larger centre whose institutions possess or demand jurisdiction over pre-existing nation-states". In Post-World War II phase several unsuccessful attempts were made by India and others to stimulate regional identity and consciousness in Asia and create a basis for cooperation among Asian countries.[24] Initially, South Asia did not have powerful economic incentives to offer to the global forces of market exploitation and coordination. It lacked natural resources and primary products potential for quick, easy and wholesome profits to attract investments from the outside world. For long thirty years regionalism could neither be imposed from the global hegemonic forces on South Asia, nor could it be evolved through autonomous initiatives from within the region. In contrast, the regional politics of South Asia was encouraged to feed on conflict and poverty, but, in fact it presents a case of economic parity as Gunnar Myrdal had put it in 1968, "There is a similarity in the basic economic conditions of the South Asian countries. All are very poor in general, the largest are the poorest...... All have endured a long period of stagnation ...... and the levels of living of the masses are either lower or not substantially higher today than they were before the Second World War."[25]

The Charter of the United Nations as contained in Article 52, permits, "the existence of regional arrangements or agencies for dealing with such matters relating to the maintenance of international peace and security as are appropriate for regional action ....", provided they are consistent with the purposes and principles of the United Nations. Though no any criteria was set regarding behaviour among the member countries, in general, any feasible plan promoting the birth of a regional cooperative organisation must satisfy two basic criteria: (a) it must conform to the interests of participating states and (b) it must respect the sovereignty of the member countries.[26] If any member country perceives a threat from other regional states or feels that its economic interests are unlikely to be promoted, the prospects of regional cooperative ventures are diminished and the ongoing process is often effectively slowed down.

In case of South Asia the earlier quest for autonomy against dominance proved fatal for region's integration and interdependence and it prevented, on the other, the evolution and growth of regional economic cooperation.[27] As demanded by the changed situation and pressing needs of the public at large, countries of the region felt the urgency to initiate and institutionalise economic cooperation in South Asia. For the first time an attempt was made to isolate economic cooperation issues stemming from the traditionally dominant factor of political antagonism. Thus, formation of the SAARC is premised on three assumptions. First, the promotion and satisfaction of economic goals through cooperative measures will establish the salience of economic issues in intra-regional relations.Second, the realisation of equitable distribution of benefits from the expansion of cooperation in areas of commercial and industrial activity will reduce the severity of hitherto unresolved disputes to a manageable level. Lastly, dialogue through the SAARC forum and enhanced transactions will effect a positive change in the attitudes of leadership and help bring about consensus on peaceful means of resolution of conflict. Several regional organisations in different parts of the world had already come into existence before SAARC and were working fairly and satisfactorily. These included the Arab League established in 1945, Organisation of American States OAS 1948, the Association of South-East Asian Nations ASEAN 1967, and the European Union, EU, 1993. The last one is evolved from the six-nation European Coal and Steel Community created in 1952. It is now a 15-member union and is the most perfect and effective of all regional organisations.

The first initiative for establishing a regional cooperation association was taken in 1977 by Zia-ur-Rehman, the then president of Bangladesh." It was with the yearning to bring some measure of stability and peace, and to inprove the subhuman conditions of eternal poverty and misery" of new born Bangladesh that President had mooted the idea of regional cooperation in the immediate surroundings. Inspired by the idea the President had also toured India, Pakistan, Nepal and Sri Lanka in 1977, the Government of Bangladesh circulated a working paper in 1980 titled" Regional Cooperation in South Asia" and advocated regional cooperation in economic, technical, scientific, social, cultural and educational fields. It also suggested that meetings at Foreign Secretary-level should examine prospects of regional cooperation.[28] Consultative and preparatory in this direction had been done between 1977-1981 and proposal was formally submitted to the concerned government in May 1980 by President Rehman. It was formally initiated in April 1981 when a meeting of the foreign secretaries of seven South Asian States was held in Colombo. Six more such meetings were held in other capitals.

The second breakthrough in this regard was made in August 1983 in a Foreign Minister's meeting in New Delhi. It adopted an Integrated Programme of Action and it was announced through the New Delhi Declaration. The development elevated the process from the official to the political level. It was followed by the Foreign Minister's meetings held at Male in July 1984, and Thimpu in May 1985. During negotiations, it was agreed that the SAARC would actively try for greater regional cooperation on the basis of sovereign equality of States, protection on the basis of territorial integrity, and non-interference in the internal affairs of each other. The cooperation was likely to grow in the economic social and cultural spheres. In the final phase, the Heads of State or Government met at the first SAARC Summit in Dhaka on 7-8 December 1985 and decided to establish the South Asian Association for Regional Cooperation. It was a historic event and signified the culmination of the process that began as early as 1978-1979 with the consultations of late President Zia-Ur-Rehman of Bangladesh.

Formation of SAARC is an expression of efforts to not only cement ties among South Asian States in diplomatic, social, economic and other fields but also to promote collective self-reliance and to improve the quality of the life for the South Asians.[29] The principles behind this regional organisation, as defined in its Charter are: (a) Regional cooperation through SAARC shall be based on mutual respect for the principles of sovereign equality, territorial integrity, political independence, non-interference in internal affairs of other states and mutual benefit; (b) Such cooperation shall not be a substitute for bilateral and multilateral cooperation but, shall complement them; and (c) Such cooperation shall not be inconsistent with bilateral and multi-lateral obligations. As per the principles several objectives have been enshrined in the Charter of the SAARC.[30] To attain these objectives, seven countries of South Asia decided to launch a cooperative regional organisation and soon developed an understanding to apply to a step-by-step collaborative approach.

Like other bodies, the SAARC has also established an institutional framework within which different level meetings take place at regular intervals, and within which a wide array of institutions, working groups, and so on, have been set up to discuss the feasibility and modalities of cooperation among the member states. Institutionalisation of SAARC would definitely strengthen the regional identity of South Asia and promote community formation. Contacts and transaction envisaged under its programmes would also contribute to the development of the South Asian System. Economic development, which is the heart of the SAARC, would primarily be a step-by-step and incremental process for two reasons. Firstly, the smaller states need to carefully study the impact of extended economic cooperation with India both on their economic structures as well as on their political autonomy. Secondly, smaller states in the system wish to institutionalise cooperation based on consensus as a principle and guide to their regional economic diplomacy.[31]

The institutional involvement of SAARC is based on direct involvement of heads of states or governments, foreign ministers and foreign secretaries of all the Member-Nations. It has developed among the South Asian states, mutual understanding and tolerance. It would also help reduce tensions and a overall character of the system would emerge in the process. In the first ten years of its formation the SAARC has made considerable progress in terms of institutionalisation. Rules governing its working procedures have been laid down systematically and its various meetings at the levels of expert committees, secretaries, ministers and summits have taken place fairly regularly. Though an elaborated programme of action has been chalked out to advance regional cooperation in various areas, not much has been achieved except in the area of trade.

Initially the activities of the SAARC were limited to areas such as health, population, meteorology, telecommunication, sports, culture etc. A significant development in this field was made at its summit held in December 1988 in Islamabad. It emphasised the need for concrete and result-oriented activities within the framework of SAARC to include trade. Further at its sixth summit held in Colombo in December 1991, Heads of State declared their commitment to the liberalization of trade in the region through a step-by-step approach in such a manner that countries in the region share benefits of trade expansion equitably. An Agreement on SAARC Preferential Trading Arrangement (SAPTA) was signed in Dhaka in April 1993. It envisaged the creation of a Preferential Trading Area among the SAARC members and also provided a legal framework for liberalization. Some achievements were noticed in 1998 when as a result of the third round of negotiations tariff concessions were offered on 3456 tariff lines. It, however, failed to pick up intra-regional trade in South Asia as done in other regional economic groupings.[32]

In order to promote the trade among member-states the SAARC Council of Ministers met in New Delhi in December 1995 and emphasised that expression of political will by member states was imperative for the realization of South Asian Free Trade Area (SAFTA). The Framework Agreement on it was signed at the twelfth Summit held in Islamabad. The Government of India, in the last week of December 2005, approved the SAFTA and paved a way for its formal launching on 1 January 2006. Now it can be hoped that tariffs would be reduced within the stipulated timeframe of 2016 by all the participating countries. Especially openness to trade and investment would lead to development and reduce poverty and backwardness.

Evaluation

A systematic analysis and historial perspective of South Asia indicate that it is a region without regional cooperation or a region without regionalism.[33] Before the sentiments for SAARC, two generation's attempts were identified at Asian regionalism. The first one was pursued during several conferences held in Asia between 1947 and 1955. The main thrust of these attempts was characterised as having been dominated by politico-strategic considerations. The second generation's attempt was started in the late sixties and early seventies who were motivated by a different thrust, basically being oriented towards greater economic cooperation in Asia. Interestingly, both generations aimed at regionalism encompassing as much of the overall Asian region as possible. It was only in late 1979/ early 1980 that another attempt was made, this time focussing exclusively on the region which is now known as South Asia. In its latest design, the countries of the region resumed the theme to promote peace and stability on the one hand and to encourage economic development on the other.

While evaluating the entire system of SAARC we should focus the three latest sources of conflict: (a) the involvement in one another's domestic conflicts, (b) the uncontrolled transfer of arms and weapons to the region from external arms suppliers, and (c) the probability of a nuclear arms race between India and Pakistan. One of the basics of internal involvement is the multifaceted issue of ethnic mobilisation, its tendency to escalate to separatist movements and its potential to spill over at the regional level. It is a new conflict and in principle, dates back to colonial times. It works in both ways: it may support regional cooperation and at the same time, is likely to hamper it. While demographic and ethnic problems tend to cause disharmony, they also work in a positive way by contributing to building regional cooperation and consciousness among the South Asian states.

Emergence of bipolarity and cold war tensions between East and West were successfully exploited by the regional antagonists to augment their power, which they used against each other. In general the success of any endeavour to contain a threat within the region from an extra-regional component would depend much on the identity of interests. This identity of interests may not necessarily be related to the regional sub-system but it gains strength from a common strategic outlook. The competitive globalism of the great powers motivated them to establish an influence relationship with the local powers in various sub-systems of the world. Like others the need for security against neighbours and economic aid for development strengthened the multidimensional relations with the Western powers. Extra-regional orientations caused the new states of South Asia in ways. The first was the disintegration of pre-colonial and colonial interdependece among the regional communities and second was the significant reduction of autonomy of the region. The US rivalry with the Soviet Union primarily influenced its interests and policy toward South Asia and on the other it also initiated the uncontrolled transfer of arms and weapons to the area.

In South Asia the rivalry between India and Pakistan in nuclear and other spheres must be viewed in the background of old legacies of colonialism, repercussions on the search for a national indentity and the lack of adequate control mechanism. Broadly, it can be categorised, as five on the basis of the nature of contentious issues; (a) issues resulting from colonial legacies; (b) issues of political and ideological character; (c) issues of strategic conflict and military balance; (d) issues arising from the spill over of internal conflicts and turmoil; and (e) issues related to resource and developmental conflicts. With other countries of the region, India's giantism is the most real obstacle in the way of regional cooperation. The second is India's major political problems with all the countries of the region, with the possible exception of the Maldives. Bilateral cooperation among the states of the region should also be considered as ingredient of the whole system as the King of Bhutan has put it, 'As long as we do not have good bilateral relations, it will be very difficult to have a good regional relationship.'[34]

In fact the South Asian Association for Regional Cooperation or SAARC is falling short of gaining a similar significance as is attached to the economic and diplomatic achievements of the ASEAN group. If we compare various regional groupings in a ranking order, the European Community, on account of its high degree of integration as well as economic and political cooperation, would be on the top. At the present stage the SAARC would only be placed at the bottom; But there is also an optimistic approach. If we take into account the central problem of South Asian politics alongwith India's relationship with its neighbours and the resulting contentious issues, the SAARC has offered an opportunity for introducing Confidence-Building Measures (CBMs) on the higher level and has succeeded in reducing regional tensions. In spite of the many obstacles caused by the regional power and economic structure, the anaemic infant SAARC not only survived but even grew slowly broadening its scope, especially in sphere of trade, build an institutional framework and generate a climate for regional cooperation.

3.3 INDIA UPDATED WITH SAARC

For long SAARC has been hostage to negative trends in India-Pakistan relationship. Since April 2003, this has been successfully reversed and there is definitely a more relaxed approach to the relationship. Nearly 25 years after its formation, South Asia remains one of the most underdeveloped parts of the world, where glaring poverty continues to haunt millions of people. Today, the leadership of the principal nations in SAARC have felt the need of a major push forward towards creating more jobs, increasing trade, and facilitating the movement of people and goods for implementing concrete projects.

Background, Aims and Objects

The countries of the South Asian Association for Regional Cooperation (SAARC) represents 1.47 billion people, which is around 25 per cent of the world population. The inspiring and unique aspects of SAARC countries are: high intensity of bio-diversity in the region; largest population of youth in the world; combined purchasing power that has the potential to be the highest in the world; a civilisational heritage that goes back thousands of years.[35] The regional organisation SAARC originally comprises Bangladesh, Bhutan, India, Maldives, Nepal, Pakistan and Sri Lanka, it however, has included Afghanistan formally in April 2007 as the eighth member which is in turmoil due to its relations with Pakistan. The initial phase evolution of SAARC involved the Foreign Secretaries and senior officials of the region in an effort to agree on a basic framework of regional cooperation. It started with the first meeting of the Foreign Secretaries held in Colombo in April 1981 and extended up to March 1983. The beginning of the second phase was marked by the convening of the meeting of the Foreign Ministers in New Delhi in August 1983 which elevated the process from the official to the political level. In the third and final phase the historic event came when the Heads of State or Government met at the first SAARC Summit in Dhaka in December 1985 and decided to establish the South Asian Association for Regional Cooperation.[36] Further the policy-level meetings, well supported by the reports and recommendations of the technical bodies, have in fact led to a continuous process of expansion, at least in the non-controversial areas of cooperation.

Earlier the pre-independence pattern of externality of interaction had gained strength and prevented the evolution and growth of regional economic cooperation. It has made both the process of community formation and the promotion of a common regional identity more difficult and complex.[37] But when the South Asian countries attained a reasonable degree of mutual trust and a common interest in peaceful change, attempts to initiate and institutionalise economic cooperation began to emerge in early Eighties. In the circumstances fostering of economic cooperation was premised on three assumptions. First, the promotion and satisfaction of economic goals through cooperative measures would establish the salience of economic issues in intra-regional relations. Second, the realisation of equitable distribution of benefits from the expansion of cooperation in areas of commercial and industrial activity would reduce the severity of hitherto unresolved disputes to a manageable level. And finally, dialogue through the SAARC forum and enhanced transactions would affect a positive change in the attitudes of leadership and help bring about consensus on peaceful means of resolution of conflicts.[38] In other words regional cooperation is important in both economic and security terms. Multiplying interdependence through trade, investments, and technology cooperation generally leads to a better alignment of security perceptions and a pacification of historical enmities.

Cooperation among states is promoted by common factors which may be geographic, ethnic, linguistic, religious, civilizational, politico-historical or socio-economic. The greater the interaction, the better are the chances of success of cooperative endeavours. The South Asian region certainly has commonality of several factors with minor variations in their distinct origins or puritanic patents which are neither distinguishable nor material. The entwining communication technology would suffice in times to come to psychologically further integrate the peoples of this region.[39] In today's world satellite beamed images, internet trade, electronic money transfer, foreign investment, multinational businesses, tourism, electricity grids, energy pipelines and a host of other factors are enlarging the interface of persons and nations with their counterparts abroad. Political borders are becoming more porous-economically, technologically, culturally and environmentally.[40]

In the light of fast changing and upward global scenario, the regional organisation SAARC had set its main objective to provide a platform for the peoples of South Asia to work together in a spirit of friendship, trust, and understanding for accelerating the process of economic and social development of member states. The countries of SAARC have several core competencies and every country has a vision to become a developed nation in a time-bound manner. One of its stated objectives is to promote regional cooperation through active collaboration and mutual assistance[41] in unanimously chosen programmes in the economic, social, cultural, technical and scientific fields. In the context the SAARC has two sets of clearly defined goals. The overt and immediate goals are non-political in nature, stressing national development through regional socio-economic and cultural cooperation. The underlying and long-term goals are, however, political in nature, aiming at the ultimate creation of a durable, stable and peaceful regional order.

Needed Expansion

About a decade after the formation of SAARC the world got more interconnected economically. As a result the actual forging of links began to take place at the micro-levels of business and people; the macro-level relationships also witnessed between countries and their aggregates became visible. The growing international economic links were seen in a variety of arenas–trade, investment and money market. In the changed world the spreading web of economic ties appeared creating a global state system that is less discrete and more interlocked than before. The need to balance national interests and global interests was a challenge for the countries of region.[42] Initially the founder members of the SAARC also agreed in the Dhaka Declaration of 7 December 1985 to liberalise trade as early as possible through a step-by-step approach and to prevent marginalisation of South Asia's trade in the larger global interests.[43] In the first decade, SAARC, made considerable progress in terms of institutionalisation. Rules governing its working procedures have been laid down systematically and its various meetings at the level of experts, committees, secretaries, ministers and summits have taken place fairly regularly. But in larger interest of the region SAARC did not remain unaffected by the post–cold war directions of regionalism. The member-countries vigorously initiated programmes of economic reforms and liberalisation with the view to integrate their respective economies with world economy. They felt that now a broad consensus among them to strengthen SAARC in this new direction can no longer be ignored.

The year 1995 was significant in SAARC's life from the view point of its expansion in programme and influence as well. On lines of European Free Trade Area (EFTA) and North American Free Trade Area (NAFTA), the concept of preferential trading within a group of countries emphasised which emerged in the creation of South Asian Preferential Trade Agreement (SAPTA) in 1995. The SAPTA was established in the hope that by the first decade of 21st century a South Asian Free Trade Area (SAFTA) would become a reality. A document to set up SAPTA was signed by the ministers of member countries on April 11, 1993 during a summit at Dhaka. It allowed member states to import commodities from one another with a 10 per cent lower tariff than those imposed on items from non-SAARC countries.[44] P.V. Narasimha Rao, the then Prime Minister of India (1995) also said that there would be zero-custom trading in South Asia. Further with the setting up of World Trade Organisation (1995) the countries of the region were likely to face difficulty in having access to the developed world, which had been major trading partners of these countries. Keeping in view the upcoming challenges the SAPTA countries at their New Delhi meeting in December 1995 also exhanged lists of commodities for preferential trading in which India offered a list of 106 items, Pakistan 35 items, Nepal 14 items, Maldives 17 items, Bhutan 7 and Bangladesh 12 items for trade on concessional rates.

About the period not only SAARC's working areas expanded but it also established links with extra regional actors. It officially reiterated its resolve to encourage and strengthen cooperation with other regions. The New Delhi Summit of 30 April 1995 underlying the resolve listed the progress made by the institution in establishing contacts and strenghening cooperation with the European Union (EU), ASEAN and

Asian Development Bank (ADB). The Summit had felt the need that SAARC should explore the possibility of establishing cooperation with APEC, and keep itself abreast of developments regarding the Association of Indian Ocean Rim Countries (AIORC).[45] In addition a large number of non-governmental institutions and networks have emerged. Among the most promising is the South Asia Regional Initiative / Energy (SARI/E), a $ 50 million project funded by USAID to enable energy cooperation between Bangladesh, India, and Nepal. Others include specific arrangements for furthering climate change initiatives, gender and human rights, the development of law, association of media, disaster management coordination, and business.[46] Further the year 2005 has been fixed as a target to convert the preferential arrangement into one of free trade area.

Spirit Required

Structural arrangements and institutional networking apart, the countries of SAARC have felt in recent Summits that to become a true regional bloc it has to focus on two things; security and economic development of the whole region. There is an impression among the people of South Asian nations that we have yet to make a distinctive contribution that can make a difference to lives of the people of the region. Security can not be effectively felt unless the region is free from terrorist and extremist activities. India is the most severely affected victim of terrorism as countries that are the hot bed of terrorist bases, Pakistan, Bangladesh and Nepal, surrounded it. It is putting pressures on the military and non-military resources of India. On the other despite efforts the intra-regional trade among SAARC countries is less than five per cent of the total trade while in comparison it is more than 20 per cent in East Asian countries. The main obstacle is security related but partly due to the fear that hangs over the minds of the SAARC countries that the Indian companies would dominate their domestic industries if the trade were made totally free. In today's world NAFTA, EU and ASEAN are the three strongest and successful regional blocks furthering prosperity and providing security to their people.

An important challenge for the countries of SAARC are the upliftment of rural people. As more than one billion citizens of SAARC countries live in villages, there is an urgency for all of us to improve the conditions of rural life through better physical connectivity, electronic connectivity, knowledge connectivity, which together will lead to comprehensive economic connectivity. The issue of connectivity was emphasised by the Indian Prime Minister Manmohan Singh at the 13th summit in Dhaka in November 2005 when he said, "Let us agree, at this summit, that all South Asian countries would provide to each other, reciprocally, transit facilities to third countries, not only connecting one another, but also connecting to the larger Asian neighbourhood, in the Gulf, Central Asia and in the South East Asia. India, which borders each of the members of the South Asia is willing to do so"[47] Earlier when Atal Bihari Vajpayee, the Prime Minister of India, met with Musharraf during the January 2004 SAARC meeting in Islamabad, they held out the promise of expanded road, rail, and air contacts, people-to-people exchanges, a new look at regional economic cooperation and even a discussion on Kashmir.[48] There is need of greater understanding and appreciation of each country's problems, accelerate economic growth and enhance self reliance and work to promote the welfare of the people of South Asia.

The latest and 14th Summit of SAARC held at New Delhi in April 2007 was the first after entering into the third decade of its existence and with the inclusion of Afghanistan as the 8th member of the organisation. Unlike the Dhaka Summit of 2005 it was significant because of the absence of acrimony, it however, witnessed a rigid attitude of Pakistani Prime Minister Aziz on the sidelines of SAARC. In the Summit, like earlier, India gave a positive signal and offered in the opening address of accepting asymmetrical responsibilities, opening her markets to her South Asian neighbours without insisting on reciprocity. It was because New Delhi had firm belief that time had come to move from a declaratory phase to action and implementation. The Indian Prime Minister also promised Zero duty access to India before the end of the year to our South Asian neighbours who are least developed countries and further reduce the sensitive list in respect of these countries.[49]

The leaders at the Summit decided to make tangible progress in the next six months on four issues that affect their people's daily lives-water, energy, food and environment. During the meet two agreements-one on setting up a South Asian University in India and forming a regional food bank were signed in the presence of SAARC leaders.[50] The declaration issued on the occasion emphasised the need at an early date, to develop a roadmap for a South Asian Custom Union and a South Asian Economic Union in a planned and phased manner. It wanted the implementation of the South Asian Free Trade Area (SAFTA) agreement launched earlier in January 2006, in letter and spirit. They were of the opinion that successful implementation of SAFTA will catalyse other areas of regional economic cooperation.[51] On the occasion Li Zhaoxing, the Chinese Foreign Minister, who was attending the Summit in the capacity of an observer also hoped that all countries in the region would live in harmony and the regional grouping would play a bigger role in regional and world affairs. He also expressed China's readiness to discuss with SAARC the establishment of a cooperative mechanism to alleviate poverty and carry out a comparative study on poverty reduction models.[52] Apart from China other observers of the Summit the United States, Japan, South Korea and European Union have welcomed the decision taken at the summit to promote regional cooperation in diverse fields.

However, above the deliberations and decisions are the universal truth that good words are not going to help create a healthy trend among the countries of the region. Essential is an effort to develop connectivity and promotion of linkages so that all the countries are well linked in all its manifestations-physical, economic, telecommunication, energy and people to-people contacts. That only will bring prosperity to all.

3.4 INTERNATIONAL TERRORISM IN SOUTH ASIAN CONTEXT

The term 'Terrorism' has not been a new one. At an early stage it was used as a method or theory whereby an organised group or party seeks to achieve its avowed aims chiefly through the systematic use of violence. It is multi-dimensional but the political terrorism, to which we are particularly concerned, is entirely different. It imposes the punishment meted out by the organisation upon those who are considered guilty or who are held to interfere with the revolutionary programme.[53] It essentially differs from mob violence which is ordinarily unplanned and uncontrolled brought into action by some immediate and not necessarily rational motivation and follows no precise programme.

'International Terrorism', in its latest manifestation, has appeared to owe allegiance to a form of religious fundamentalism that aims at subjugating members of their respective communities to conservative norms and practices, selectively excerpted from their traditional religious scriptures and systems on the plea of restoring the fundamental purity of their respective religions. It often enjoy various degrees of popular support – prompted at times by admiration, at other times by fear – ranging from those who see terrorism as mere retaliation against the states' oppression, to those who support it as a means of achieving independence.[54]

Stages of its Development

The first expression of terrorism was as a means of achieving national emancipation. Its chief objective was to be relieved from any kind of domination, exploitation or any other oppressive system of individual or group of individuals. The so-called Anglo-Irish war fought between 1919 and 1921 had its objective to eradicate English control in Ireland and to establish Irish unity. Terrorism in this particular time bordered on guerilla warfare and it was based upon the expectation that the non-combatant population would fall into line with the victorious side. It was largely related to the right of the Irish people to national self-determination and the terroristic practices appeared as retaliatory action against the British reign of terror in Ireland.

With the change of time, Terrorism began to be recognised as a technique of revolution. The writings of Anarchists like Bakunin, Kropotkin, Brousse and others laid emphasis on the idea of the 'propaganda of the deed'. The theory had gained momentum in Germany, France, Spain, Italy, United States and in Latin American countries due to the publicity and value of acts of terrorism. The fullest expression of the theory and practice of terrorism was found in the functioning of the Russian Revolutionary Organisation formed in 1879 against the atrocities of Czar. However, the value of terrorism declined when Socialist Revolutionary Party came into existence and social change seemed visible. As a means of social change, terrorism was replaced by mass movement, industrial strike, rise of working class and changing international milieu. Again it was tried in Russia after 1917 but terrorism as a complete tactic never attained real success.

Terrorism spread rapidly after 1945 particularly in Japan, Germany, France, Greece, Iraq, Syria and Saudi Arabia. It gained a world-wide network adamant to help each other with arms and explosive materials. In this period the concept of state-sponsored terrorism was introduced by the Western countries. They trained their armies in terrorist activities and send them to a destinated place. By that time it had also attained an additional dimension of drug-trafficking which added fuel to the fire and provided funds for terrorist activities all over the world. To get money for the terrorists even USA and USSR had procured funds from drug trafficking. Other countries which had a leading role, were, Columbia, Peru, Ireland, Scotland, Burma, Vietnam etc.

In today's context it is not out of place to underline the factors which overhaul Muslim mind and in general, they feel scandalised. Memory of the recent past, intellectual stagnation and interference of the Western countries in Muslim world are the most important among them. It was Islam who dominated the world in Middle-Ages. Three hundred years ago the three biggest empires in the world – India, Persia and Turkey were Muslims. Even China and Russia were ruled by Mongol Khans. At the time of Napoleon they were powerful. In modern times their power and reach witnessed a substantive decline.[55]

Intellectual stagnation has hurt Islam more than anything else. Despite the fact that the tradition of intolerance is common to both Islam and Christianity, misfortune of the former is that it never passed through 'Reformation and Renaissance'. According to Aurobindo, this situation in Islam should be corrected, they should remodel the religion and change the stamp of their temperament. In Christianity The New Testament is a revised version of The Old Testament which was written centuries ago. Jesus Christ was their first reformer and when it again degenerated in the sixteenth century, Martin Luther King was at hand to redress the shortcomings. Even Hinduism was redressed by Kabir, Chaitanya in earlier phase and by Rammohan Roy and Ranade at the later stage. But in Islam it was only Kemal Ataturk who challenged and modified it. Today all the Muslim countries are trying to refashion their society in accordance with the ideas of a thousand years ago. They are moving towards tyranny while rest of the world towards more and more democratic, Efforts should be made to replace theocracy with democracy, rather to attempt to mould a country's social and political life in accordance with the ancient Islamic tenets.[56]

Last but not the least important, was the interference of Western countries. The West has given science, technology, concept of democracy and human rights. But they have also imposed civilization upon India, China and Muslim world. Many Muslim countries were occupied even after independence. Their governments were either toppled or turned into puppet governments. Oil-rich country's revenues were diverted to the West. Neghbouring countries are encouraged and armed to fight each other. These have contributed to develop a feeling of anger towards the West.

Bases in South Asia

Cultivation of opium in Afghanistan provided a fertile land there to flourish drug-trafficking in the region. The Government of Pakistan and its army had been encouraging this business with a view to take maximum advantage. Afghan Mujahideens with the active co-operation of drug smugglers of Islamabad, Pakistani Government and its army began to spread the drug-trafficking in the area and contacted the terrorists of Punjab and Jammu and Kashmir. The innocent citizens of state had been the softest target of terrorist as well as of the state repression, leaving many among them particularly the youth to go underground and join the insurgents – either for protection or for revenge.

The Soviet intervention in Afghanistan took place on 27 December 1979. It posed not only a serious threat to India's security but to the entire South Asian region. The United States of America took the intervention seriously and went with the single minded purpose of teaching Russia the lesson of its life. For ten years beginning from 1979 Pakistan became the most important ally of USA in this part of the world and the weapons for Afghan Mujahideens were passed on through Pakistan. It also enabled Pakistan to receive substantive military aid as well as quiet acceptance of its indulgence in nuclear technology extended by China. The prevailing global geo-political ambience is neither unipolarity, bipolarity or multipolarity but unashamed opportunism in the pursuit of national interest.[57]

Next to the Soviet intervention in Afghanistan, was the illegal occupation of Kuwait by Iraq which cast a deep shadow on the growth of terrorism. On 17 January 1991, multi-national armies attacked on Iraq to get the Kuwait vacated. It was in that kind of situation that president Saddam Hussain called upon the Muslim world to do terrorist activities at large against the countries involved in bombardment on Iraq. He declared that the multi-national armies had insulted Islam and they must be punished. Iraq had been preparing for terrorism in yester years and had purchased weapons for this from Western countries. Purchased items included electronic detonator, radio control, light machine guns, plastic bombs and other explosive materials. Apart from all these, he organised the terrorists of the world and recruited them in his team. In nutshell, he tried his level best to erect terrorism as a second line of war in which he did not get complete success. Before this innovation, terrorism had been used as a means of protest, revenge, pressure on government etc. Saddam Hussain gave terrorism a new meaning that was to be used in future.

As a Factor in Indo-Pak Relations

For decades, terrorism had been and, continues to plague Indo-Pak relations. India is facing a kind of proxy war imposed by Islamabad – sponsored terrorists. It was the war of 1965 which made Pakistan realised that Kashmir could be gained only through internal rebellions and not through external aggression. Funds were poured in to spread disaffection through proliferating madrassas. Over a period of a decade-and-a-half this achieved a substantial impact. According to an estimate during 1988-94, over 50,000 Kashmiri youth have been trained in Pakistan. Terrorist incidents went up from 400 in 1988 to 5,000 in 1993, and deaths from 30 to 2,600. Mujahideens, freed from the Afghan conflict were sent to Kashmir and their numbers peaked at about 1,600 in 1994.[58]

On the otherhand, it is difficult to overcome terrorism because India had not displayed in the past the level of anti-terrorist intelligence capability and operational competence that many advanced countries have shown. There is little reason to believe that the country would be able to upgrade those capabilities quickly. India's approach to dealing with terrorism has been predicted primarily on providing overwhelming physical security to high profile targets.[59] The effectiveness of such an approach will get degraded as the targets to be protected proliferate and the technological skills of Indian terrorists improved.

The Soviet takeover in Afghanistan ended in February 1989, marked the end of an era. The supply of US arms which were given to Afghan rebels to fight against the Soviet army and, Pakistan to protect itself from Soviet influences were suddenly came to a halt. The US was not in favour of establishing the kind of government in Kabul that Afghan rebels wanted. The pro-US elements in Kabul also suffered a set back on account of Gulf crisis that prevented them to be famous internationally but, more to Soviet disintegration which marked the end of cold war between the two superpowers and made US least interested in Afghan affairs. In the changed circumstances, US interest would directly mean the interference in internal affairs of a country.

The Government of Pakistan exploited the changing situation in its favour to a large extent and tactfully turned the face of Afghan rebels and others towards Kashmir. They shook hands with misguided youths of Kashmir, virtually puppets in the hands of Islamabad. The pace of terrorist activities increased suddenly in Jammu and Kashmir and along the line of control. Gradually and knowingly the entire social spectrum was converted to the point where violence and terror began to be considered a justified means of communication.[60] The overall environment and even state institutions sustained terror in which collection of funds, setting up of training camps, free movement of arms and drug-trafficking was not uncommon. It is a threat to the new international order which largely believes in progress through peace and non-violence. A country who considers terrorism a legitimate tool of diplomacy and neighbourhood behaviour should be nipped in the bud.

The battle against terrorism has gained momentum after its attack on World Trade Center on 11 September 2001, followed by an attack on Indian Parliament on 13 December, the same year. The US bombing of Taliban's hideouts in Afghanistan led to the establishment of a government which is not friendly to them (Talibans). But because Fundamentalism and Terrorism did not begin with Osama bin-Laden, they are not likely to end with him. Bombing Taliban bases in Afghanistan is one thing but smoking out terrorists from hideouts in different countries is a daunting task. It would take a long time and much covert activity to finally overwhelm the evil.

The first difficulty in the fight against terrorism is American psychology which appears determined to dominate and dictate it in accordance with the strategy to establish a unipolar world. It wanted to restore the tarnished image of September 11, 2001. The second possibility that goes against the move is that the countries which are not suffering from terrorism like India, would express sympathy on the one hand but would concentrate on opposing US drive to establish eminence as the sole superpower, on the other.

Further, in the background of close defence, economic and political relations between Islamabad and Washington, it is difficult to assume that America would help and cooperate India beyond a point. Even it can not compel Pakistan to stop proxy war against India. Here is a lesson for India to take that in US strategy still Pakistan ranks No. 1, and the present state of affairs is a situational change that can not last long.

At the juncture, India needs to move with caution. A world dominated and dictated by the US does not suit Indian interests at large but in Washington's fight against terrorism we are with them. As an additional effort, New Delhi should also activate the UN beyond passing resolution and making NAM to take steps to weaken the terrorists. The real positive gain in this direction would be to get a condition in which terrorism would no longer be a threat. It is a common enemy of ours which badly needs a strategy, based upon consensus of the world community.

3.5 NUCLEAR DETERRENCE IN WORLD POLITICS

The emergence of atomic and, later of thermo nuclear weapons of huge destructive power made it clear to mankind that a new world war would cause incredible devastation. From then, peace among nations has become a necessary condition for mankind's survival. It is true that there has been no world war since 1945; it is also true that nuclear weapons have been developed and deployed in part to deter such a conflict. Nuclear revolution, in post-world war II phase, has forced great powers to behave in a careful and restrained manner and to accept a compromise which in prenuclear times would surely have been unacceptable. It has even changed the modes of thinking about warfare as asserted by Albert Einstein in 1946, 'the unleashed power of the atom has changed everything save our modes of thinking, and thus we drift towards unparalleled catastrophe.[61] Obviously, the catastrophe Einstein envisaged has not occurred, the experience of Hiroshima and Nagasaki was more than sufficient to prevent all the nations possessing this new technology from any actual use of it under any circumstances. Nuclear weapons made deterrence work across national and ideological boundaries : they taught Capitalists and Communists alike the virtues of a commitment to the status quo. Despite their revolutionary character, they showed that even revolutionaries can become members of a club.

Deterrence Explained

'Nuclear Deterrence; as a theory means – the threatened use of nuclear weapons, to keep someone else from actually doing what they may be contemplating doing. The possibility of an adversary possessing such weapons influence the perception of nuclear weapon threat by a country. The estimation of the probability of war with the country concerned, and of the probability of that country using or threatening to use nuclear weapons in such a war, play important roles in the development of threat perception.[62] It happened for the first time in the history of international relations that the very existence of a weapons system devised to enhance the security of great powers had become sufficiently threatening to those powers to provide them with a persistent and strong incentive to settle their differences, rather than to risk getting into situations where they might be forced to use the means of warfare they themselves had devised. This was, then, a new kind of international order – imposed not by design or by principle, but by fear.

Nuclear strategy, as a whole, can be regarded as a complex of pseudo-problem of which deterrence is a part. Since the aim of deterrence is to instil caution without raising tensions, there is always a very fine balancing act between making the opponent fear the negative consequences of his own aggression and reassuring him that there is nothing to fear as long as he stays on a peaceful course. However, in military perspective, this balancing act becomes more delicate than ever because of their tremendous destructiveness and closely related advantage of striking first if all-out war appears imminent. Advocates of nuclear deterrence argue that offensive measures are necessary to make the deterrence credible in a period of rough strategic parity. The basic idea is that military capability will enhance stability only to the extent that you are able to convince your opponent that you are better prepared than him to fight even if you are less inclined to start the fighting. The problem, of course, is that the things you do to deter the otherside may also make him suspicious about your intentions. Obviously, continuation of the regime of deterrence depends largely on how the contending powers calculate their gains and loss but with equal rationality and efficiency which is rarely found in today's international politics.

Closely related to it is the aspect that whether the deterrence has worked in the past or not. Looking ahead begins by looking back. If the deterrence has not worked in the past it can not work in future. Its past working can be known in two ways – by knowing facts from archives and files which were planned but not implemented due to deterrence and second, by explaining conflict behaviour of the powers which, in fact, vary from power to power and is totally unpredictable. The core of the deterrence theory seems eminently reasonable, and even self-evident. If the expected punishment exceeds the gain, the opponents will be deterred. The claim of nuclear deterrence is inherent in the claim itself, for it is seeking to explain something that did not happen – a non-event in the literal sense.[63] Because the deterrence is a pseudo-problem and it can not be solved, may be the reason for continuing to discuss and research. At most it should be respected as a necessary category of intellectual discourse. Its discussion does not end but merely punctuate. It often demands sweeping arguments and wide ranging perspective, while conclusions are highly circumscribed.

Cold War Period

An unstable regional security, the drive for international prestige, the nuclear-weapons option as a bargaining chip and aggressive political intentions may be counted as important incentives for a state to acquire nuclear weapons. In case of the United States of America who happened to be the first in order, willingness and ability to play so large an international role, particularly on the Eurasian continent was the prime. Immediately after the second world war the USA was not in a position to challenge Soviet Union on political or strategic issues and it considered the bomb as a counter-weight to the massive Soviet military establishment. Being aware of bomb's destructive capabilities and its unique potential as an influence towards world peace, US president Harry S. Truman linked it directly to the political characteristics of the states possessing it, and, equally important, of the international system to which they belonged. Besides deterring military aggression, this new kind of superiority was also thought to be essential for resisting Soviet attempts at intimidating the vulnerable West European democracies; keeping conventional military spending within reasonable bounds and maintaining US leadership in the emerging Western alliance.

The US monopoly over this new technology or its unilateral deterrence did not last long; The former Soviet Union was the most concerned, who put all its resources available to break US monopoly as told by Stalin that this technology has shaken the whole world and destroyed the balance as well. It feared attack on Soviet camp and expected the Americans to use their exclusive possession of atomic bombs to impose their political and economic schemes in Europe. The first Soviet explosion witnessed in August 1949 and it gained retaliatory capability in mid-fifties. Thus, in the first decade of the cold war, both the US and Soviet leadership developed what we might call a defensive nuclear ideology. They felt that nuclear weapons were essential to prevent both political blackmail and large-scale military attack by the other side. Despite repeated call for nuclear disarmament, both clung to their nuclear deterrents as their best hope of maintaining peace.

The proliferation of nuclear weapons technology to other great powers and later on to the Third World countries was a cause of concern for the US. In its view, to ensure its usefulness and to hinder that it should instead become a destroyer of mankind it was first of all necessary to prevent the secrets of the new weapon from falling into the wrong hands. From that time onwards, US policy has been guided by the premise that, in an anarchic world with expansionist and nuclear-armed enemies, there is no better way to preserve the peace than possessing a superior nuclear force – either in quantitative terms, as in the 1950s and 1960s, or in qualitative terms, as in the 1970s, 1980s and, 1990s. Because of the delicacy of the balance of terror, US decision-makers saw marginal strategic superiority as a necessary condition for a credible US deterrent against Soviet aggression.

Successful nuclear deterrence turned out to be in cold war years 1945-1989. It was an exceptional period of stability in great power relations. While there have been many disputes since the war, neither power has had agrievance so essential as to make a world war whether nuclear or not. In fact, the cold war rivals were no longer deterred by the threat of nuclear retaliation of their opponent, but by the shared risk of a common danger they faced whenever they actively pursued their competition. They did not deter each other, they were jointly deterred by a force external to both. This force is best called common deterrence. It served as a functional equivalent to a monopoly of violence at the global level. The rivals were like siamese twins that die when they are separated.[64] Consequently, beginning with the limited test ban and the hot-line agreement they became entangled in security co-operation with arms control. Even the term 'cold war' lost its meaning after the beginning of security co-operation but it was because the rivalry between them continued for political and economic advantage; for military superiority; for protection of allies and spheres of influence. Things apart, the long peace between the United States and former Soviet Union was also due to non-nuclear factors, such as , the absence of territorial disputes, tolerance of the status-quo, the raising of the provocation threshold by the experience of the two world wars, the creation of the rule of game, crisis management and arms control etc.

Post Cold War

At the close of 1980s cold war rivalry between USA and USSR came to an end. Perhaps, it was the common deterrence which inspired Mikhail Gorbachev to abandon the prenuclear Soviet strategy of the offence, based on conventional superiority. It occurred when nuclear revolution and its proliferation made any kind of war impossible. With the end of hegemonic rivalry in real sense of the term, the Soviet leadership wanted to preserve great-power status for the country by a combination of domestic economic reform and a transformation of the rivalry with the United States into a shared world leadership. This sea change in Soviet policy was totally unexpected but not abrupt as Francis Fukuyama observed, the role of ideology in defining Soviet foreign policy objectives and in providing political instruments for expansion has been steadly declining in the post war period and Gorbachev further accelerated that decline.[65] From 1985 onwards, he, through his several speeches, emphasised that today we face a different world from which we must seek a different road to the future. The change was so visible and forceful that The Newyork Times proclaimed on 2 April 1989, 'the Soviet leaders have for all intents and purposes given up the ideological struggle and have retreated from the basic doctrine of international class struggle – the doctrine that gave rise to the cold war in the first place'. Thus, the key in the demise of the cold war derived from changes in idea.

The United States of America responded favourably over the changes that were taking place in USSR. Ronald Regan, the then President of the USA, gave hint about this in his Presidential Press Conference when said, 'if it can be definitely established that they no longer are following the expansionary policy that was instituted in the Communist revolution, that their goal must be a one-world Communist State they might want to join the family of nations and join them with the idea of bringing about or establishing peace.[66] As a result of the large measures, conditions began to change rapidly and dependence of Western security on nuclear weapons first eased. In 1989 the Soviet Union's grip on Eastern European empires began to relax, and in 1990 the satellite nations had been freed. The Warsaw Pact dissolved. In 1990-91 the Soviet Union itself dissolved into constituent states. Russia itself was weakened and for all intents and purposes the nuclear confrontations of the cold war were now over.

A country buys arms because its leaders espy a threat or opportunity which requires them to arm. But as tensions in post-cold war period relaxed, arms relaxation seemed desirable. According to a survey, published by International Institute for Strategic Studies in 1997, the international trade in armament, which was about $75 billion in 1985, came down to $40 billion in 1996. The US share in 1996 was 43 per cent, the UK's 22 per cent, France's 14 per cent, Russia's 9 per cent, Germany's 2 per cent and China's 2 per cent. The main loser has been Russia, which, as USSR had a share of 36 per cent in 1988. Because of vastly reduced defence spending, the global military procurement came down by 45 per cent in real terms during 1985-95. Consequently, the defence industry world-wide is undergoing a huge restructuring.[67] With the military force downsizing almost everywhere, several trends are manifesting in the international defence trade.

In the similar manners, the weapons that had been built up by the United States of America and Soviet Union during a later cold war period began to seem burdensome as tensions eased. The Soviet Union was under especially severe economic pressure to reduce its arms expenditures and Gorbachev announced that he was going to do so unilaterally. His declaration made it harder for Western government justify large sums for military machines. They began to consider that big armies are expensive, inconvenient and perhaps irrelevant in the present context. At first they both reduced cautiously but after the failure of Soviet hardline coup in August 1991 and ratification of a nuclear arms reduction treaty by the US Senate in 1992, both sides moved further to reduce arms. Even nuclear competition has become irrelevant after the demise of hegemonic rivalry. A common nuclear regime should, therefore, be formed for all relationships together based on the lessons and experience of the bipolar relations. The utility of nuclear weapons is decreasing not only in military terms, but also in political terms and depends largely upon the basic health of a country's society and economy.

After its post-cold war ascendance to the status of the sole superpower, the US has been seeking to establish its right to stop the proliferation of nuclear weapons by the use of force, if other forms of discouragement failed. It is trying hard gradually to mould international public opinion to accept that position.[68] Today, the world is no longer bipolar, but there has not been a revival of multipolar great power rivalry; there is no power as yet to challenge the position of the United States. In the context of nuclear revolution, five powers possessed sophisticated facilities with second-strike capability. Mutual Assured Disagreement (MAD), and common deterrence now extend to all five of them despite their differences in strength. If common deterrence obtains between all the full nuclear power, a future 'great war' has an extremely small probability. Powers that would have become rivals in prenuclear times now have a strong common interest in forging a regime of nuclear deterrence, based on co-operation.

References

1. Praful Bidwai, 'Praxis of Evil', The Hindustan Times, February 22, 2002.
2. Verghese Koithara, Society, State and Security : The Indian Experience (Sage Publications, New Delhi, 1999), p. 325.
3. Author's book, India's Foreign Policy : The First Study in Continuity and Change (New Delhi, 2001), p. 4.
4. Harish Kapur, India's Foreign Policy 1947-92 : Shadow and Substance (New Delhi, 1994), pp. 122-24.
5. Bimal Prasad ed., India's Foreign Policy : Studies in Continuity and Change (New Delhi, 1979), pp. 497-98.
6. Harish Kapur, op.cit., p. 130.
7. Shelton U. Kodikara ed., External Compulsions of South Asian politics, (New Delhi, 1993), p. 42.
8. D.K. Palit, War in the High Himalayas : India in Crisis, 1962 (New Delhi, 1991), p. 20.
9. Koithara, op.cit., pp. 96-97.
10. Rajiv Gandhi's interview to Business India, April 30, 1988, p. 15.

11. I. Gopalakrishnan, 'Reform and Scandal Shake the Economy', India Abroad, January 1, 1993.
12. India Today, December 31, 1990, p. 21.
13. Koithara, op.cit., p. 238.
14. The Hindustan Times, September 26, 2000.
15. Sugata Bose, Ayesha Jalal, Modern South Asia-History, Culture, Political Economy (Oxford University Press, New Delhi, 2004), pp. 3-4.
16. Verghese Koithara, op.cit., pp. 180-181.
17. Geoffrey Barraclough, Turning Points in World History (Thames and Hudson, U.K., 1977), p. 80.
18. D.N. Mallik, Postwar International Politics – A Quadripartite Survey, (Veena Mandir Publishers, Muzaffarpur, 1973), pp 594-95.
19. Bose and Jalal, op.cit., p. 4.
20. The Hindustan Times, August 4, 1988.
21. Tahir Amin, Ethno-National Movements of Pakistan: Domestic and International Factors (Institute of Policy Studies, Islamabad, 1988).
22. Eric Gonsalves and Nancy Jetly, eds., The Dynamics of South Asia Regional Cooperation and SAARC (Sage Publications, New Delhi, 1999), p. 11.
23. Shelton U. Kodikara, ed., pp. 24-25.
24. Sisir Gupta, India and Regional Interaction in Asia (Asia Publishing House, Bombay, 1964).
25. Gunnar Myrdal, Asian Drama (1968), p. 46.
26. Pervaiz Cheema Iqbal, 'SAARC Needs Revamping' in Eric Gonsalves and Nancy Jetly, eds., op.cit., p. 90.
27. Satish Kumar and Leo E. Rose, 'South Asia', in Werner J. Feld and Gavin Boyd, eds., Comparative Regional System (Pergamon Press, Newyork, 1980).
28. V.N. Khanna, Foreign Policy of India (Vikas Publishing House, New Delhi, 2001), pp. 234-35.
29. Pervaiz Cheema, op.cit., p. 95.
30. V.N. Khanna, op.cit., pp. 235-36.
31. Rasul B. Rais, 'South Asia and the Global System: Continuity and Change' in Shelton U. Kodikara, op.cit., p. 28.
32. B. Ambrose, 'Trading Among SAARC Countries : Problems and Prospects', Babuddin Khan, ed., Third Concept, Vol. 20, No. 235 (New Delhi, 2006), pp. 7-9.
33. V.M. Hewitt, The International politics of South Asia (Manchester, 1992), p. 75.

34. Harish Kapur, op.cit., p. 117.
35. A.P.J. Abdul Kalam, 'Realising the Uniqueness of SAARC', The Hindu, April 7, 2007.
36. Ross Masood Hussain, 'SAARC 1985-1995 : A Review and Analysis of Progress', in Eric Gonsalves and Nancy Jetly, eds., pp. 21-22.
37. Rasul B. Rais, Shelton U. Kodikara, ed., op.cit., p. 27.
38. IBID., p. 28.
39. V.N. Khanna, op.cit., pp. 232-33.
40. Verghese Koithara, op.cit., p. 143.
41. Charter of the South Asian Association for Regional Cooperation (Dhaka), December 8, 1985.
42. Verghese Koithara, op.cit., p. 147.
43. The Pakistan Times, September 26, 1995.
44. IBID.
45. S.D. Muni, 'South Asia Outside SAARC', in Eric Gonsalves and Nancy Jetly, eds., op.cit., pp. 118-19.
46. Stephen Philip Cohen, ' Indo-Pak Track II Diplomacy : Building Peace or Wasting Time ?' in P.R. Kumaraswamy, ed., Security Beyond Survival (Sage Publications, New Delhi, 2004), p. 201.
47. Amit Baruah, 'The Best Chance Ever for SAARC', The Hindu, March 31, 2007.
48. The Financial Times, January 16, 2004.
49. Y.C. Halan, 'SAARC, Security and Stability', Subhash C. Kashyap, ed., South Asia Politics, Vol. 6, No. 1, May 2007 (New Delhi, 2007), pp. 5-8.
50. The Hindu, April 5, 2007.
51. IBID.
52. IBID., April 4, 2007.
53. Edwin R.A. Seligman, ed., Encyclopaedia of the Social Sciences, Vol. 13-14 (Newyork, 1954), pp. 575-77.
54. Sumanta Banerjee, 'The Politics of Violence in the Indian State and Society', in Kumar Rupesinghe and Khawar Mumtaz, eds., Internal Conflicts in South Asia (London, 1996), p.87.
55. K.R. Malkani, 'Inside the Muslim Mind', The Hindustan Times, October 13, 2001.
56. Amulya Ganguli, 'Image of Islam', Ibid., October 1, 2001.
57. For detail see author's book, op.cit., pp. 190-91.
58. Verghese Koithara, op.cit., p. 113.
59. IBID., p.253.
60. Manvendra Singh, 'Threshold of Patience', The Hindustan Times,

January 15, 2002.
61. The Newyork Times, May 25, 1946.
62. Verghese Koithara, op.cit., pp. 259-60.
63. Dan Smith, 'The Uselessness and the Role of Nuclear Weapons : An Exercise in Pseudo-Problems and Disconnection' in Jorn Gjelstad and Olav Njolstad, eds., Nuclear Rivalry and International Order (London, 1996), pp. 86-87.
64. Godfried Van Benthem Van den Bergh, 'The Nuclear Revolution into its Second Phase', in Ibid., p. 27.
65. Francis Fukuyama, 'Pattern of Soviet Third World Policy', Problems of Communism, Vol. 36, No. 5 (September – October) 1987., pp. 1-13.
66. The Newyork Times, December 9, 1988.
67. The Economist, June 14, 1997.
68. Koithara, op.cit., p. 261.

PART-TWO
CONTROVERSIAL NEIGHBOUR

4

INDIA, PAKISTAN AND KASHMIR

4.1 PLEBISCITE IN KASHMIR : FACES OF TRAGEDY

The Problem of Kashmir continues to be a perennial cause for military conflicts in South Asia. The dispute, being a 'core issue' for Pakistan, has acquired capability to trigger of a nuclear confrontation between India and Pakistan. Both have also lost interest and relevance in holding a plebiscite[1] or providing Kashmiris right to self-determination as a possible solution to the issue. The nuclear tests of 1998 conducted by India and Pakistan have introduced a new sense of urgency and unfortunately refocussed attention on Kashmir. In the changed circumstances the world opinion in general and great powers in particular demand that India and Pakistan either denuclearised themselves or settle the Kashmir dispute. Pakistan's efforts to involve third party as a mediator or guarantor has been frustrated times without number by India, however, at some future date, even this likelihood can not be ruled out.

The British Paramountcy over the Indian states ceased to exist on 15 August 1947, as the Indian Independence Act came into force, which released the states from the obligations of the Crown and had made them independent– technically and legally. Most of the princely states were geographically situated in such a way that they could not make a link with the dominion of Pakistan and the only alternative left to them was to make a link with the dominion of India. After independence the State of Jammu and Kashmir was free to accede to either of the dominions, India and Pakistan. With a view to compel the Maharaja Pakistan had organizsed a tribal invasion on the State of Jammu and Kashmir and captured thirty six per cent of the state.[2] Several developments of immense importance took place in October 1947, and in a very difficult situation created by Pakistan, the Maharaja of the state decided to accede to the Union of India.[3] Lord Mountbatten, the then Governor-General of India, at the time of acceptance of the Instrument of Accession wrote a separate letter to the Maharaja which provided that in consistent with the policy of the Government of India, where the question of accession has been the subject of dispute : it should be decided in accordance with the wishes of the people of the state. As soon as law and order have been restored in Kashmir and her soil cleared of the invaders, the question of state's accession should be settled by a reference to the people.

The accession of the State of Jammu and Kashmir to India was contested by Pakistan and declared it to be based on fraud, violence and conspiracy.[4] Pakistan took the stand that the predominantly Muslim population of Kashmir was not consulted in Maharaja's decision and that because the majority in the Kashmir Valley are the followers of Islam, they and the region occupied by them must automatically come to Pakistan. Right since the beginning Pakistan called it a 'dispute' and had repeatedly asserted that there could be no peace in the Indian subcontinent until the Kashmir problem was resolved.[5] While India is of the view that the Instrument of Accession was just like a treaty concluded between two states. After the cessation of British authority over princely states, the decision of the King or Prince, as the head of the state, was final. Both signitaries were competent to sign the Instrument. All the principles of International law applicable to treaties were to apply to the Instrument of Accession and even no ratification was required.

As the issue of Kashmir's plebiscite is pending at the United Nations and no solution to the satisfaction of India, Pakistan and people of the state is in sight, three arguments are usually cited by the Indian side.[6] The first, that Pakistani forces failed to fulfil the pre-conditions mentioned in the United Nations' resolution to vacate those parts of Jammu and Kashmir under their control. The second, that the territory's lawful ruler had acceded to India, thereby automatically confirming the validity of such accession. The third contention is that Kashmir is 'an integral part of India'. This holds the argument that the people of Jammu and Kashmir acting through their democratically elected representatives, have repeatedly and freely ratified the moral and legal validity of accession to India.[7] In the light of its experiences at various international fora, India had realised that the UN resolutions passed from 1948 onwards have no relevance for resolving problems related to Kashmir because the entire situation in that state has undergone a profound constitutional and political change in terms of its integration with India. At present, India is in great disappointment at the partisan manner in which important powers dealt with the Kashmir issue in the UN and in their interaction with India and Pakistan. The article is a modest attempt to analyse the developments which led to such a sorry state of affairs pertaining to the issue of plebiscite in Kashmir.

Rolling at the United Nations

Having initial attempts of India failed to settle the disputes through negotiations it decided, on the suggestion of Lord Mountbatten, to place the issue before the Security Council and Pakistan was conveyed accordingly.[8] On 1 January 1948, P.P. Pillai, the representative of India to the UN, in a letter addressed to the President of the Security Council under Article 35 of the Charter, which clearly stipulates that any member of the United Nations may bring any dispute, or any situation of the nature referred to in Article 34 to the attention of the Security Council or the General Assembly. In his letter, pillai, stating the situation existed between India and Pakistan as a result of the raids by Pakistani nationals and tribesmen, requested :

- To prevent Pakistan Government Personnel, military and civil, from participating in or assisting in the invasion of Jammu and Kashmir;
- to call upon other Pakistan nationals to desist from taking any part in the fighting in the Jammu and Kashmir state ;
- to deny the invaders, (i) access to and use of its territory for operations against Kashmir, (ii) military and other supplies; (iii) all other kinds of aid that might tend to prolong the present struggle.[9]

Pakistan, on the otherhand, denied the charges levelled by India and lodged a series of counter charges covering the whole range of India-Pakistan relations. It also appealed to the Council to take up its complaint in toto and not to consider only the Kashmir issue. It, however, stated that some independent tribesmen and persons from Pakistan might have taken part in Kashmir episode.[10] The Security Council met to discuss the issue on January 15, 1948, and Gopalaswami Ayyangar, the Indian representative, explained the circumstances under which the troops were sent to Kashmir after the Instrument of Accession was signed by the Maharaja in favour of the Government of India. He also laid down that the Government of India has accepted the accession on the understanding that the will of the people regarding it could be made clear in a plebiscite or referendum when law and order had been restored. In order to ensure complete impartiality in this regard, it might be held under international supervision.[11] The Indian explanation was meant to impress upon the Security Council that there was neither territorial dispute between the two nor any question regarding the accession of the state into India.

Sir Zafrullah Khan, the representative of Pakistan, replied the Indian contentions and denied all the charges brought by India against Pakistan.[12] He told the Security Council that India had obtained the accession of the state of Jammu and Kashmir by fraud and violence and, as such, Pakistan refused to recognise it. The charges and countercharges levelled by both sides made it clear that the two states basically differed from each other in relation to Jammu and Kashmir. In the circumstances, it became the duty of the Security Council to examine the complaints and find out way to solve them peacefully and restore peace in the region.

In May 1948, a UN Commission on Jammu and Kashmir was formed. A series of mediators were appointed one after the other during 1949-51 - General Mc Naughton of Canada, Owen Dixon of Australia and Frank Graham of the United States. The thrust of the proposals of all mediators was the demilitarization of the state, to be followed by a plebiscite.[13] The most important among the recommendations of the Security Council was one prepared by a United Nations Commission for India and Pakistan (UNCIP) constituted in accordance with the resolution of the Council of April 21, 1948. Its resolution was adopted by the Security Council on August 13, 1948, which was divided into three parts - covering wide range of the subject concerned.[14] Part I of the resolution called for a cease-fire order to apply to all forces under the control of India and Pakistan. Part II has three sub-paras A. B & C. They clearly spell out that the entire portion occupied by Pakistan, called by whatever name, organised or unorganised, must be totally vacated. Part II B specifies that on this vacation the territory must be passed on to the local administration as prevailed before. It also specifies that it shall be the duty of the Government of India to restore normalcy. And only when the conditions of these two parts I & II are satisfied can the opinion of the people be ascertained in the manner agreed upon by the UN Commission.[15]

In Part III the resolution, finally, called upon India and Pakistan to reaffirm their wish that the future status of the state of Jammu and Kashmir would be determined in accordance with the will of the people. It also provided that the Pakistani forces should be withdrawn first from the state. It clearly meant that the entry of Pakistani forces in the state was illegal. Indian forces were to be withdrawn subsequently after the Commission had notified that the withdrawal of the Pakistani forces had begun. Hence, in terms of the UN resolution, Pakistan has no right to even talk about Kashmir till it first vacates the Pak-occupied Kashmir (PoK) and hand it over to India, who is its rightful owner.[16]

However, at a later stage it appeared that India had committed a mistake in referring the Kashmir issue before the Security Council under Article 35 of the UN Charter. Rather India should have taken measures as provided under Article 51 of the Charter.[17] The said Article provides to the states to exercise the 'inherent right' of self-defence. This right can be exercised by a state under provisions of the Charter only when armed attack occurs on it. To defend the state of Jammu and Kashmir was a right which India had acquired immediately after the state was acceded to it. If Pakistan had attacked the state with its armed forces, India legally could have used its armed force to thwart the Pakistani aggression and should have taken back the part of territory of Kashmir occupied by Pakistan. This action, it appears, would have solved the Kashmir dispute for ever. But India did not exercise the right of self-defence, presumably, because it just did not occur to the then Indian leaders. They were also totally unaware of the political rivalry between the two blocs which prevented the Security Council on arriving any decision. The veto power of all permanent members has paralysed the whole sanctioning function of the Security Council. The system frustrates the functioning of the Security Council as an executive organ and imposes a great limitation on it.

A Larger Imperial Design

Close scrutiny of the facts indicate that the politics of plebiscite is one of the forms of imperial design. The British Government while determining the legal framework for the future political status of the princely states of India, had hoped that the larger princely states would remain independent that the subcontinental empire would consist of two dominions - India and Pakistan and that a number of large princely states would constitute the third geopolitical ingredient of the South Asian subcontinent. Their expectation was that these Princely states and Pakistan would sustain close linkages with the British Government. When the majority of Princely states acceded to India, the British plan went awry. The aspiration of Maharaja Hari Singh of Jammu and Kashmir to convert his state into an independent country was sort of a last opportunity which the British Government wished to utilize to strengthen its influence and to create strategic equation with Pakistan to meet this purpose.[18] Both Lord Mountbatten and the then British Prime Minister Clement Atlee were not happy with the accession of Jammu and Kashmir to India. It was on their advice and against his own instincts, that Jawaharlal Nehru took the issue to the UN and offered a referendum/plebiscite in that state. At the UN the imperial powers converted it into a 'territorial dispute' between India and Pakistan. It made the issue of plebiscite a complex one and laid the foundation of third party involvement in the matter.

The problem became all the more complicated because of the involvement of the Great Powers, particularly the USA. The main reason for their involvement was the high strategic significance of Kashmir. It is situated in the north of the sub-continent at the junction of five sovereign states-India, Pakistan, China, Soviet Union and Afghanistan. It has strategic significance for all of them. It also contains head waters of three important rivers of the Western part of the sub-continent–the Indus, the Jhelum and the Chenab, and has immense forest and mineral resources. Even President of the Security Council Gunnar Jarring when visited the Kashmir Valley in March - April 1957, wrote in the report he submitted to the Council that he could not fail to take note of the changing political, economic and strategic factors surrounding the whole of Kashmir question, together with the changing pattern of power relations in West and South Asia.[19]

The opening years of the fifties emboldened Pakistan mainly due to its growing understanding with the US on security - related matters. The developments which had adversely affected Indo-Pak relations include US military aid to Pakistan and its membership of Western military pacts - South East Asia Treaty Organisation (SEATO) in September 1954 and the Bagdad Pact later known as Central Treaty Organisation (CENTO) in July 1955. India was well aware of the facts and had consistently criticized Pakistan's military relationship with the US. The Indian Prime Minister Jawaharlal Nehru, in a letter to his Pakistani counterpart on 9 December 1953, complained that the US military aid to Pakistan would 'completely' change the aspects of the Kashmir problem and the question has now become 'one of militarization and not of demilitarization'[20] In the first place, the politics of aid and alliance obliged the US to support Pakistan on Kashmir and consequently drew Soviet support to India on Jammu and Kashmir making it an issue in the cold war period and secondly, it made Pakistan ambitious and, encouraged it to press India for concessions. Pakistan had now the allies willing to stand by her in case of crisis[21] which was exhibited in the coming years. Times without number and in a consistent manner some of the members of Security Council had unequivocally supported Pakistan's legitimate stand on Kashmir during discussion and deliberations. This was despite the fact that Eisenhower, the then American President, had privately assured Nehru in March 1954 that the United States considered India a pillar of the 'free world', did not intend to promote Pakistan at India's expense and cordially offered India American military aid if Nehru so wished.[22]

In response to Pakistan's membership of SEATO and CENTO, the Soviet Union effected a volte-face of its own in its Kashmir policy and called Kashmir question an internal affairs of India but decried imerialist efforts to turn the valley into a strategic bridgehead against the USSR. The uncompromising Indian stand on Kashmir received a significant boost from the Soviet leaders[23] who visited India and declared in Srinagar that Kashmir was part and parcel of India and added further that the question of Kashmir as one of the states of India, had been decided by the people of Kashmir. In February 1957 the Soviet Union used its first veto in India's favour on a Western resolution on Kashmir moved in the Security Council. It did the same in 1962 and in subsequent years. Nehru was at pains to the politics of the Anglo-American group over Kashmir in the UN. He reacted sharply by saying in the Rajya Sabha that it was India's misfortune that the two Great powers, the United States and the United Kingdom should almost invariably be against it in matter which was of great concern to it.[24] Many resolutions have since then been adopted and many recommendations have been made to India and Pakistan, but the problem remains unsettled as far as the Security Council is concerned. The Security Council has failed to find out any workable solution mainly because of the pulls and counter pulls among the two great powers and their associates.

The Real Challenge in Kashmir

Apart from the irrelevance and inappropriateness of the plebiscite demand and the doubtful political viability of an independent Jammu and Kashmir, the urge of self rule in Kashmir's popular consciousness is remarkable. Despite the coercive and manipulative of both the Indian and Pakistani authorities, mass opinion in the valley is not only confused but by and large unambiguous and unequivocal in the belief that only independent statehood would constitute genuine emancipation. The irony of fate is that the autonomist claim has been treated virtually as a form of criminal political behaviour by the Indian state since 1953, and constantly demonised as an expression of pro-Pakistan chauvinism. At the same time the popular appeal of the independence slogan is such that even overt and covert pro-Pakistan forces are usually compelled to adjust or defer to it. Neither India nor Pakistan wants to accommodate the strategic changes what would, at the very least, include Kashmiris in discussions about their future. Neither wants to revise its political philosophies, or alter the reflexive domestic opinion that supports Indian army powers on the one side and jihad on the other. Neither wants to shed the light of democratic debate on the contentious subjects of nationalism and self-determination.[25] The idea of self-determination is the transformed version of the notion of plebiscite.

The spirit of nationalism and self-determination had a long and distinguished lineage, and deep roots in Kashmir's political culture going to the popular movement against the tinpot despotism of the Dogra dynasty during the thirties and the forties.[26] Except for seven years (1975-82) of his life Sheikh Mohammad Abdullah was a crusader for Kashmir's right to self-determination, and that this faith is what won him the love and devotion of the people of Kashmir. His National Conference, despite severe repression went from strength to strength. In May 1946, on the pattern of Indian National Congress, 'Quit India' Movement of 1942, the NC launched a mass agitation called' quit Kashmir 'against the last Maharaja Hari Singh and declared that the time has come to tear up the Treaty of Amritsar–sovereignty is not the birthright of Maharaja Hari Singh. 'Quit Kashmir' is not a question of revolt. It is a matter of right.[27] Even the word 'national' in the National Conference's name refers to the territory and population of J & K. Sheikh Abdullah speaking before the Jammu and Kashmir Constituent Assembly in August 1952 referred to Jammu and Kashmir as 'our country' and made it clear that accession to India was final and complete and the issues at stake concerned the terms of membership in, and association with the Indian union.[28]

The year 1947 was a crucial one for the state of Jammu and Kashmir because the British paramountcy ceased to exist over princely states and the state was provided the option either to choose one of the dominions or remain independent. The idea of state declaring an independent one was supported by Ram Chandra Kak, the then Prime Minister of J & K and a political party named Muslim Conference. They also assured the Ruler that he would be acclaimed as the first constitutional king of a 'democratic and independent Kashmir.[29] Insistence and persuasion had led the Maharaja to cherish the dream of an independent state of Jammu and Kashmir, which at that time was looking real. But the notion was found unfeasible after Maharaja's meeting with Lord Mountbatten, who visited the state on the request of Mahatma Gandhi and Jawaharlal Nehru in the last week of June 1947.[30] This was one of the reasons, which, it appears, prevented the Maharaja of the state not to sign the Instrument of

Accession soon after the lapse of paramountcy as done by other Rulers of Indian states.

Despite several ups and downs the state of Jammu and Kashmir never abandoned the struggle for self-determination. After Sheikh Abdullah's admission of defeat in 1975, a new organisation–the People's League was at hand to keep the quest for self - determination alive. But as frustration with the Indian state's increasingly egregious authoritarianism in Kashmir mounted through the eighties,[31] more and more Kashmiris became convinced that Kashmiriyat could only be safeguarded in an independent state. As commented by Qasim Khokhar, leader of the Jammu and Kashmir Liberation Front[32] (JKLF), the eighties were an especially difficult and frustrating decade for independence activist, what with the crushing burdens of material law and Islamisation. Kashmir's democratic aspirations were callously sacrificed at the alter of the 'nation' to which Kashmiris were expected to be loyal. But the inevitable result was that when mass Kashmiri alienation from Indian 'democracy' eventually surfaced in an explosive form, as armed resistence, it was simultaneously total and violent rejections the India 'nation'. Hence the widespread appeal of the demand for azaadi or self determination.[33]

In the circumstances, the JKLF who had never enjoyed much support in the valley, emerged as the spearhead of a mass uprising, and a new generation of Kashmiri youth took up the gun in a desperate attempt to wrest the rights their father and grand fathers had been unable to obtain through peaceful means. The JKLF is still, as claimed by its leader Mohammad Yasin Malik, 'the most principled and consistent advocate of independence, that represents the wishes of the people', is not far off the mark.[34] Despite its sufferings at the hands of both - the Indian forces and pro-Pakistan gunman, organisation's ideology continues to resonate powerfully with both the middle class and the masses in Kashmir. The ultimate denial of democracy - rule through violence and coercion produced a situation by 1990-91 where the gunman came to be revered as the harbinger of freedom. For example, in April 1990, the largest political rally in Kashmir's history, surpassing even Sheikh Abdullah's funeral, took place when over 500,000 mourners turned out defying curfew orders to honour Ashfaq at his funeral, who had been killed in a shoot-out with security forces. He and countless other Shaheed[35] have become part of Kashmiri lore and Srinagar's Id Gah ground, which houses the biggest martyrs' graveyard, is practically a pilgrimage site for Kashmiris today. It was followed in early April 1991 when large anti-Pakistan demonstrations erupted in Srinagar after a JKLF area commander was killed by Hizbul Mujahideen gunman and in February 1992 after Pakistani forces shot dead at least twelve people, apart from beat and arrest of hundred more to break up a symbolic cross-border 'Unity March' from Azad Kashmir to Indian administered Kashmir by an estimated 30,000 JKLF supporters. The episode was described as a major victory for JKLF groups operating in the valley over Pakistan-sponsored factions.[36]

The regional, religious and other forms of social diversity of the state of Jammu and Kashmir prevent us applying majoritarian principle and one should remain extremely vigilant of attempts made by pro-independence factions of the state from time to time. For example, in January 1994, Raja Mohammad Muzaffar, a senior leader of the Azad Kashmir-based JKLF submitted a blueprint for a possible solution to the Kashmir question to a Conference on Kashmir,[37] organised by the United State Institute of Peace. He proposed a plebiscite throughout the territories of the former princely state with three options presented to the electorate - accession to India, to Pakistan or independent Jammu and Kashmir to be decided by a simple majority of 51 per cent of the electorate. However, the right to self determination or the plebiscite decided by simple majority, has serious flaws and risks of its own. It is not feasible in the present day circumstances due to India's implacable opposition to any notion of plebiscite, and Pakistan's manifest lack of interest in the idea except for propaganda purposes, makes the likelihood of any such exercise extraordinarily remote.

Prospects

The question of plebiscite in the state of Jammu and Kashmir as committed by Indian leaders and as provided in the Security Council's resolutions of August 13, 1948 and January 5, 1949, does not arise at the present stage. It has now become time - barred, out - dated, impractical, absolete and bear only historical importance. The resolutions of the Security Council have become invalid because the circumstances under which they were made have undergone a drastic change and as such the principle of rebus sic stantibus clearly applies. This principle is recognised not only by the classical international law but by the Vienna Convention on Treaties (1969) as well. According to it, a state is not obliged to perform its obligations under an internatinal undertaking if there occurs a fundamental change in the circumstances existing at the time the obligation was undertaken.

For India and Pakistan, Kashmir is still about their respective strengths and sovereignties and senses of security, about their titles to land and peoples, about their statures in the region and the world. Hence, they do not want independent Kashmir because each has a vital stake in Kashmir and also because they are afraid that an independent Kashmir may become an arena of world power politics. The current Indian strategy vis-a-vis the problem consists of three basic elements: first, continue the policy of sustained repression and further weaken the insurgents, second, arms and sponsor criminalised gangs that have broken away from the militant ranks, should be used to intimidate and demoralise the public as much as possible; and third try and undermine the Hurriyat Conference's standing by playing up allegations of corruption and ineptitue against some of its leading figures.

It is less than certain that any 'solution' to the struggle in and over Kashmir can be stable and final without some level of participation and acquiescence on the part of the rulers of Pakistan. But on the other, responsible political leaders and activists in Kashmir whatever their public positions and ideological commitments, know perfectly well that the gun alone cannot liberate their people. Indeed they fully realise that they themselves, and the political future of their people, are increasingly being held hostage by the environment of violence and fear. There are clear indications that some of these forces would be willing to participate in a genuine dialogue without any precondition of any kind on any side, that they feel the need of a serious, substantive talk for their people.

The likelihood of greater international involvement, particularly by the US, in the subcontinental affairs is on the cards due to the fact that the international community considers Kashmir a territorial dispute in which Pakistan has an equal status and stake. Second, despite the passage of more than fifty years, the dispute remains unresolved and it has sparked off four major conflicts between India and Pakistan. Third, the anxiety about such conflicts that qualitatively increased in the international community because of the acquisition of nuclear weapons and missile capabilities by India and Pakistan. Fourth, the phenomenon of cross border terrorism and pan-Islamic militancy has become a matter of global concern after September 11, 2001, and the assessment is that it finds fertile grounds in disputes like the one over Kashmir. Now India does not have the leverage any more of the special equation with the former Soviet Union. The insistent advice to India to remain restrained vis-a-vis Pakistan, the pressure generated to Pakistan to desist from sponsoring terrorism against India, manifest third party involvement. India has to be responsive to these realities. If we want to avoid third party involvement, we must give the highest priority to resolving the internal dilemmas in Jammu and Kashmir. At the sametime, we must convince the international community that we are willing to have a serious and substantive discussions on the issue with Pakistan.

4.2 THE FIRST EXPOSURE OF DEMOCRACY IN KASHMIR

The zigzag attitude of Kashmiri Muslims to their relations with India cannot be explained in terms of Hindu-Muslim relations in the country or in the state. It was not so much a failure of secularism in India or in the state as that of federalism and democracy at both levels due to which Kashmiri aspirations could not be fulfilled. There is no doubt that a large number of Kashmiri Muslims are alienated from India today but no pro-Pakistan sentiment is yet visible. Their alienation is more as Kashmiri than as Muslim.

The Beginning

Kashmiris thrust for equality, justice and just administration and ultimately a democratic set up went back to thirties when organised résistance commenced against the then autocratic rule of Dogra dynasty. A new generation of university educated Kashmiri Muslim youth under the leadership of Sheikh Mohammad Abdullah began to organise and the All Jammu and Kashmir Muslim Conference was formed in 1932 to coordinate the popular movement for democratic government and social justice. In 1938 a split developed in the Muslim Conference and almost its entire organisation in the Kashmir valley led by Sheikh Abdullah reconstituted as the National Conference. The Muslim Conference aimed to achieve justice only for Muslim while the new organisation (NC) realised that in a land with a multi-religious and multi-linguistic society, a communal party would not be a success, for it could never reflect the problems and dreams of the masses. Its chairman Sheikh Abdullah, in his address to the sixth session of the party, in March 1938, emphasised the need of communal harmony and mass participation in the political process of the state. Firstly, we must end communalism by ceasing to think in terms of Muslims and non-Muslims when discussing our political problems. Secondly, there must be universal suffrage on the basis of joint electorates. Without these two democracy is lifeless.[38]

On account of the unique multiple dimensions of plurality in Jammu and Kashmir it would be grave injustice to them not to recognise the fact that they are also proud Kashmiris. They are perhaps the only community of the subcontinent that has a recorded history of five thousand years.

Other ethnic identities here are Dogras, Punjabis, Paharis and Ladakhis. Gujjars are of a distinct ethnic stock-they are Muslims but have as much emotional affinity with Hindu Gujjars in the rest of the country as with non Gujjar Muslims of the state. Cultural and political differences do exist between ethnic communities belonging to the same religion but for a lasting solution, multiple identities of the people must be taken into account. The example of Bangladesh is relevant here. In 1947 the Bengali Muslims, due to pervading communal violence, became conscious of his communal identity vis-à-vis the Punjabi Muslims. But as soon as the communal threat was over, he rediscovered and asserted his basic Bengali identity.

The freedom struggle embracing all communities, thus acquired a broad political front and invited all Hindus and Sikhs who liked the party and had faith in the freedom of their country from the shackles of an irresponsible rule to participate as equals in the democratic struggle. Under the charismatic leadership of Sheikh Abdullah the National Conference in 1944 adopted a social manifesto called 'Naya Kashmir' promising radical law reform once monarchy had abolished. Despite severe repression it went from strength to strength and in May 1946, launched a mass agitation which it called' Quit Kashmir,' on the model of Indian National Congress's 'Quit India' movement of 1942. Abdullah declared to tear up the Treaty of Amritsar and challenged the sovereignty of Maharaja Hari Singh. 'Quit Kashmir' agitation, as viewed by many, was a matter of right rather than a question of revolt.[39] The political atmosphere of the state was also vitiated by Mohammad Ali Jinnah specially after the cry for Pakistan was made at Lahore in 1940. A section of the people of Kashmir began to look at political, social and economic problems through the distorting lens of religion. The distinction made earlier on the basis of Muslims and non-Muslims drew little attention as it did not affect daily relations with one another. The use of religion for political purposes threatened secularism with fanaticism which believed in freedom for one religious group. It was not prepared to look at the problem from the point of view of history and the social and economic needs of the people.

Indian Perception

The huge task of absorbing Muslim dominated Kashmir with India was not an easy one and demanded, for its accomplishment, virtues of statesmanship, generosity, farsightedness, accommodation and above all, selflessness on part of both Indian public men and Kashmir leadership.

The Article 370 of Indian Constitution which conferred a special status on Kashmir state was meant to be a temporary provision as the constitution-makers were fully confident that the close association of the people of Kashmir with free democratic India would convince them of their bright future by becoming an integral part of the Republic. The then Congress Government, while accepting the Instrument of Accession, was fully aware of the tremendous difficulties which it was sure to encounter in integrating the state. At the same time, Kashmiri leaders were expected to satisfy the people that through secularism alone they could achieve political and cultural freedom as well as economic progress within India than by forming part of Muslim Pakistan.

Owing to the lapse of paramountcy under section 7(1) (b) of the India Independence Act, 1947, the Indian states regained the position of absolute sovereignty which they had enjoyed prior to the assumption of suzerainty by the British Crown. Like other Indian states the state of Jammu and Kashmir was unquestionably competent to accede to either of the newly created dominions of India and Pakistan. Under the British regime, Jammu and Kashmir was an Indian state ruled by a hereditary Maharaja. On the 26th of October 1947 when the state was attacked by Azad Kashmir Forces with the support of Pakistan, the Maharaja was obliged to seek the help of India, after executing an Instrument of Accession, similar to that executed by the Rulers of other Indian states. By the Accession the dominion of India acquired jurisdiction over the state with respect to the subjects of Defence, External Affairs and Communication. Although like other Indian states the state of Jammu and Kashmir was included as a part 'B' State in the First schedule of the constitution of India, yet it held a peculiar position due to the fact that having regard to the circumstances in which the state was acceded to India. This dual attitude of the Government of India was incorporated in the constitution made in 1949, which, on the one hand, declared Jammu and Kashmir a part of the territory of India (Art.1) and left the application of other Articles to be finally determined by the people of the state, acting through their Constituent Assembly (Art. 370), on the other. The Indian leaders including Jawaharlal Nehru had a clear thinking that separation of Kashmir from India would pose a serious danger to Indian secularism. Its secession from India on grounds of religion would strengthen the Hindu communal forces and pose a serious threat to millions of Muslims, whose number in India is larger than even that in Pakistan.[40]

As a follow up of the provisions of the accession, work began on two fronts. To decide the future course of action the people of the state elected a sovereign Constituent Assembly to decide whether the state would remain a sovereign and independent state or become a unit of the Indian union. If it decided to remain a sovereign state, Indian leaders and people would not be a hurdle to the sentiments and aspirations of the Kashmiri people. Jawaharlal Nehru, the then Prime Minister, had a firm commitment in this regard who declared in Parliament on 7 November 1952 that we want no people in the territory of India against their will and with the help of armed forces. If the people of Jammu and Kashmir State wish to part with us, they can go their way and we shall go ours.[41] The State Constituent Assembly met for the first time on 31 October 1951 and set up several committees for the purpose. The Drafting Committee presented the Draft Constitution which after discussion, was finally adopted on 17 November 1957. This Constitution did not decide to remain as an independent and sovereign state but laid down under section 3 that 'The State of Jammu and Kashmir is and shall be an integral part of the union of India. The state of Jammu and Kashmir thus acquired the distinction of having a separate Constitution for the state. In this way the sentiments of the Kashmiris were respected and their fears of being immediately absorbed in the overwhelming Hindu majority of India allayed.[42]

Secondly, in pursuance of the one of the conditions that the Maharaja would introduce popular government in the state, immediately after the accession, as a stop gap arrangement, the Maharaja invited Sheikh Mohammad Abdullah, President of the All Jammu and Kashmir National Conference to form an interim Government and to carry on the administration of the state. The interim Government later changed into a full-fledged cabinet with Sheikh Abdullah as its head. By this proclamation the Maharaja replaced the emergency administration by a popular interim government and provided for its powers, duties and functions pending the formation of a fully democratic constitution.

It is beyond doubt that soon after accession in 1947, Indian leaders made a good start; they were quite generous in handling the Kashmir state affairs. In a short period of two years, an article was inserted to assure the Kashmiris that they would be free to shape their own destiny as they desired and nothing would be imposed on them by Indian Parliament. The constitution-makers were fully convinced that the close association of the people of Kashmir with democratic India would make them confident of their bright future by becoming an integral part of this Republic.

Turning Events

Taking advantage of the special status Kashmir registered unprecedented progress in social, economic and educational fields. After a long period of wretched poverty and semi-starvation the Kashmiris were witnessing the dawn of a new era of prosperity which was shared more or less by all classes and communities. In 1947, the people of Kashmir held Sheikh Abdullah as messiah when he claimed, with justifiable pride that he had achieved azadi for them after four centuries of slavery under Moghul, Afghan, Sikh and Dogra Kings respectively. It was their greatest hour in history to be ruled by a Kashmiri rather than foreigners.[43] As a leader of the Kashmiri people he had categorically held the view that Kashmiris interest lay with India and it was only as a part of India that Kashmir could develop as a democratic state. Between 1947 and 1951 Sheikh Abdullah in his speech to the National Conference and address to the Constituent Assembly assured the Indian leaders and public as well that Kashmir is a part and parcel of the Indian union. In May 1949 he said to Nehru, "I want you to believe that Kashmir is yours. No power in the world can separate us. Every Kashmiri feels that he is an Indian and that India is his homeland.[44]

To spell out the special provisions, as provided in Article 370 of the Indian Constitution in more and avoid subsequent difficulties, a full agreement was arrived at in July, 1952, which was called 'Delhi Agreement'. For Kashmir it was signed by Sheikh Abdullah as the leader of the Kashmir delegation. The agreement dealt with various matters, like residuary powers, citizenship, fundamental rights, the supreme court, the state flag, the president of India, the headship of the state, financial integration and emergency powers of the Union. Sheikh Abdullah was fully satisfied with the signing of the agreement and just thereafter while commencing this to the Jammu and Kashmir Constituent Assembly he said, "A satisfactory position has emerged and we are now able to assess the basic issues of our constitutional relationship with India in clearer terms. There has been a good deal of accommodation of our respective points of view. We are convinced, as ever before, that we have the full support of the Government and the people of India in the fulfilment of our democratic ideals and the realisation of our objectives".[45]

But these were too good to last. From the latter part of 1952 Sheikh Abdullah started having second thought. What prompted Abdullah to change his attitude was not the Government of India, but his own lust for political power, which, he wanted to continue under the façade of democracy. His favourable statements, speeches and utterances remain uninterrupted as long as India allowed him to rule arbitrarily and despotically over the state people. Abdullah's idea of democracy was probably that there would be an elected Parliament filled by people selected by him and with no opposition or only a nominal one, which would give sanction to whatever he desired and thus give the stamp of democracy to his dictatorial will. Towards the end of 1952 it became manifest that the public resentment against Abdullah's authoritarianism was mounting, corruption, nepotism and highhandedness were assuming intolerable proportions. He even did not care to remember the fact that Kashmir was a constituent unit of a federal republic and went to the extent of equating India with Pakistan. Abdullah and the likeminded leaders of the National Conference began to exploit the communal ambition even if these harm the interests of the people and so they tried to create and keep up tension. He kept the Kashmir pot boiling for serving self interest. However, certain ominous developments started taking shape with the Sheikh turning increasingly autocratic in his way and intolerant of any advice from the Government of India. Although his personal relation with Nehru remained as cordial as before, his utterances against India displayed a more critical tone.

The Praja Parishad agitation in Jammu and the Jana Sangh agitation at Delhi for complete integration of Jammu and Kashmir with India and the support which this agitation received from certain quarters in India made Sheikh Abdullah more suspicious and paved the way for final break between him and India.[46] In the winter of 1952-53 the Jammu Province demanded for the full integration of Jammu and Kashmir with India on the basis of one constitution, one flag and one President. The Jammu people were genuinely alarmed at Sheikh's opposition to the complete integration of the state with India. The abolition of the Maharaja and land reforms had affected Jammu more than the people of the valley. This agitation was countered very strongly by the state Government but went on growing in strength. A similar agitation was being carried on in Delhi by the Jana Sangh, a party newly formed by Shyama Prasad Mookherji, on the issue of Kashmir's complete integration with India. The agitation in Delhi was also countered strongly by the Delhi Administration. Sheikh treated the Jana Sangh agitation as symptomatic of the general Hindu mentality and categorised this as Hindu revivalism which was trying to swamp the Muslims of Kashmir and the Muslim majority areas of Jammu.[47] Pandit Nehru was greatly distressed by these harmful developments which was likely to produce a disastrous effects on the

Muslim mind in Kashmir. He said that if such an agitation based purely on emotionalism and not reason was allowed to grow, no democracy could function. The Jana Sangh agitation had given him a shock and for the first time he had started feeling doubtful about the future of Kashmir.

In all probabilities, the Government of India tried to persuade Sheikh Abdullah but was of no avail. He was adamant in his determination to strike on independent path. Other important leaders like Bakshi Ghulam Mohammad, Sadiq, Masoodi, Mir Kasim and the Hindu leaders including Saraf Dogra and D.P. Dhar felt that Sheikh was using this agitation as an excuse to get out of his previous commitments to India. Gradually, Sheikh got isolated and lost majority in all the three important bodies-the National Conference, the Constituent Assembly and the Cabinet. He conspired to assume dictatorial powers with the help of outside force. The situation became more suspicious and people expected important developments. In the evening of 8 July 1953 the Sheikh Government was dismissed and Bakshi was invited to form a ministry. Worsening situation in the state left with no option for the Government of India but to arrest Sheikh Abdullah in August 1953 with his colleagues, Afzal Beg, Choudhary Mohammad Akbar and a few others. On that very day Bakshi Ghulam Mohammad was sworn in as the Prime Minister of Jammu and Kashmir.

In Post-independence period initial years were more propitious and congenial for persuading the Kashmiris to be loyal Indians and join the mainstream of national life. The main defect of India's Kashmir policy has been that it totally ignored the state people and their human and democratic rights and laid stress on the role of individual or groups who only feathered their own nests but could not deliver the goods which were expected to do. The insistence on projecting individuals or groups and endowing them with representative character certificates through diplomatic or coercive method is fraught with negative implications.[48] Aware of the union Government's weakness in dealing with the Kashmir affairs, Abdullah consolidated his personal position and power which he was allowed to do in disregard to the pulic opinion in Jammu and Kashmir. His demands were met, his misuse of power nepotism, corruption and highhandedness were overlooked.[49] One false step led to another but with passage of time the retention of Kashmir within the union became a matter of national prestige.

4.3 PAKISTAN'S DIPLOMACY OVER KARGIL

Since independence and partition, Pakistan has been a difficult neighbour with whom our links have been many and close. As the BLP led-coalition took over the reigns of administration in New Delhi on 19 March 1998 under the premiership of Atal Bihari Vajpayee, Islamabad was apprehensive of its motives and designs The installation of a new government in India has changed the atmosphere, resulting in the successful test-firing of Ghauri, an Intermediate Range Ballistic Missile (IRBM) by Pakistan on 6 April 1998. Further, nuclear tests by both countries in May-June 1998 made Kashmir an international issue. After tests, the problem of Kashmir once again came to the fore and countries of the world in general and world's major powers in particular, demanded that India and Pakistan either denuclearise themselves, or settle the dispute They were left with no option but to choose between urging upon the two countries to change the status quo or to accept it. It would not be out of place to mention here that whenever New Delhi expressed its wish for a dialogue, Islamabad insisted for an international guarantor in respect of any bilateral accord that might be reached between the two countries. Islamabad's objectives, perhaps at the time was to involve a third party, preferably its old friend the US, as a mediator in Kashmir and the only way to accomplish this was to ensure a rapid deterioration in the situation.

In fact, the incursion into Kargil was not started in March-April 1999 as assumed by many. It began in September 1997, when Pakistan brought new long-range guns into Baluchistan and began to sell Kargil town and the surrounding villages. In 1998, its gunners continued this selling, progressively improving their accuracy till they were able to target three stretches of the road at will. But the Indian army, instead of alerting the world and warning Pakistan to stop firing, painted phosphorescent markers on the road, installed shaded night lights to pick out the markers as well as told its drivers to douse lights and speed through one at a time.[50] The Indian silence was not broken in July 1998 during the visit of Strobe Talbot to India when a journalist reported that the Leh road was closed by Pakistani artillery firing. While Pakistan's maximal goal in Kargil was to change the Line of Control (LoC) by brute force, its long-term objective was to draw a large part of the Indian Army away from the valley to facilitate the entry of militants.[51] Its Kargil adventure was simply a continuation of its decade-old policy with added means. The "brilliant" gambit of seizing the heights would balance

Siachen, expose the Leh road, revive the flagging militancy and, of course, "internationalise "Kashmir.[52] However, India had done nothing adverse to Pakistan.

Kargil occurred within weeks of Prime Minister Atal Bihari Vajpayee's bus journey to Lahore. On the issue, while India had clearly indicated that its aim was restricted to vacating the aggression and not in farther escalation, the signals from Pakistan were different. Acceptance of international community's advice and withdrawing its forces from across the Leh would amount to a defeat for Pakistan. Hence, it was seeking to save face by offering to hold peace talks. At the same time, Islamabad was signalling that it might escalate the conflict by extending it to other areas acrôss the Leh. The problem was that the Pakistani army was not in a position to withdraw without losing its credibility.[53]

The Kargil conflict had three strands˜ military, political and diplomatic. The Vajpayee government had taken a conscious decision to make the diplomatic track the prime mover over both the military as well as political. The expectation was that the external pressure would force Islamabad to withdraw the infiltrators. In order to generate such pressure, the Vajpayee government had ordered the armed forces not to cross the LoC, nor to open other fronts so as to divert and disperse the attention of the Pakistani forces.[54] More than two weeks after New Delhi went public about the intrusion from across the border, Islamabad failed in whipping up international sympathy for its action. Thus, Pakistan had lost the favour of many countries including the United States, China, Great Britain, Russia, P-5 and G-8 as well.

The first such hint of US support for India's stand over Kargil came on 30 March 1999 when its Assistant Secretary of Stale for South Asian Affairs Karl Inderfurth, in course of an interview in Washington, said that the fighting in the Kargil area of Kashmir would end only after the armed militants who had entered India-controlled Kashmir left. "They have to depart, and they will depart, either voluntarily or because the Indians take them out". Further, international support for the Indian stand on the Kargil situation gained momentum when President Bill Clinton wrote to Nawaz Sharif, the Prime Minister of Pakistan, to take steps to defuse the crisis and respect the Line of Control (LoC) in Jammu and Kashmir. At the same time, Sartaj Aziz, the Foreign Minister of Pakistan, had questioned the validity of the LoC, which was rejected by India. On the issue, New Delhi is of the view that LoC has been well defined and fully settled. The delineation of the LoC was undertaken by the military authorities of India and Pakistan in accordance with paragraph 4(11) of the Simla Agreement. The two governments approved the delineation on December 11, 1972. Adjustments of ground positions to confirm the LoC were completed subsequently. The situation in Kargil became worst, and at a later date, Clinton called on Nawaz Sharif to pull back his forces from the Indian zone of the Line of Control and warned that the deployment would hold up any effort to end the fighting between two nations.[55]

US support for India's stand over Kargil; no doubt was felt as a great relief at the time. However, many observers in their analysis held the view that it could wane if New Delhi had done anything beyond what was required to push out the intruders. Kanti Bajpai warned, "Backing us on Kargil should not be mistaken as support for our stand on Kashmir. If we cross the Line of Control unnecessarily, the sympathy will quickly shift to Pakistan". Even Stephen Cohen, the US South Asia specialist, added, "There is no real shift in the US attitude towards India. In the case of Kargil, the evidence of Pakistan collusion was pretty strong."[56] Inder Kumar Gujral, former Prime Minister had also agreed that the policy makers in Washington have understood the compulsions of India defending its own territory. This aggression has set back the US objective of the subcontinent being a region of peace and has hampered idea of a dialogue, and the real setback was to that process.[57]

Islamabad, on being frustrated and thoroughly isolated by the world community over its intrusion across the Line of Control, sent Sartaj Aziz, its Foreign Minister to Beijing for talks on the issue. Aziz discussed the Kargil issue with his Chinese counterpart and senior leaders of the country. However, the Foreign Minister of Pakistan returned from Beijing empty-handed. He failed to garner support of its close ally on the ongoing conflict with India. Describing the Kashmir issue as a "complicated affair" Li Peng, a senior Chinese leader, told Aziz that China "sincerely" hoped that Islamabad and New Delhi would exercise restraint and solve their conflict through peaceful means. "Both India and Pakistan are important countries in South Asia. China sincerely hopes they would prevent the Kashmir situation from deteriorating in order to maintain peace and stability in the region."[58] Later on, in a reiteration the Chinese Foreign Minister Tang Jixuan brushed aside Pakistan's overtures for support on Kargil and endorsed India's stand and advised Islamabad to resolve its differences with India in bilateral framework through peaceful negotiations in accordance with Lahore process. A day after his return from Beijing Aziz visited New Delhi for talks that failed because Pakistan stuck to its line.

The reasons for Beijing doing so were many. World opinion stood united against Islamabad, not only for the needless death and destruction on both sides, but even more for the possibility that Islamabad could be pushing the region ever nearer to a nuclear abyss that was too terrible to contemplate. Considering that China had supplied Pakistan with nuclear and missile technology and equipment in order to boost it as a counter-weight to India, Pakistan fully expected China to demonstrate an element of support for its old ally during Nawaz Sharif's trip to China in the last week of June 1999. Unfortunately for him, the Clinton Administration made it clear to Beijing that as a major power it expected Beijing to help defuse the looming south Asian crisis. Apart from this, Beijing has been suffering for long from the depredations of Muslim Uighurs in its Xinjiang province. The Uighurs are attempting to break away from Chinese rule and have been receiving able assistance from Pakistani fundamentalists.[59] The Kargil affair nipped in bud all that Islamabad had gained from Lahore Declaration when Indian Prime Minister Atal Bihari Vajpayee visited Lahore and leaders of both countries had displayed courageous statesmanship of the highest order.

Pakistan's diplomacy over Kargil suffered a serious setback with the outcome of the Cologne (Germany) Summit of Group-8. It seemed that the US had taken strong stand and had influenced their colleagues that it was Pakistan that was the cause of the present fighting in Kashmir. As a result, the G -8 communiqué referred to the Kargil issue and called on Pakistan to pull back the intruders. The central point of the communiqué was that hostilities had broken out because armed intruders operating from the Pakistani side on the Line of Control in Kashmir were seeking forcibly to occupy Indian territory. The G-8 countries considered India to be the aggrieved party. By reiterating the sanctity of the LoC and asking that no attempts be made to alter the status quo by force, the leaders of the G-8 had rejected Pakistan's attempts to change the situation on the ground through the use of mercenaries scavenged from Afghanistan and other parts of the world. However, the most important aspect of the G–8's communiqué was the call for India and Pakistan to settle the Kargil conflict by themselves through negotiations. Since Islamabad provoked the present crisis precisely in the hope of internationalising the Kashmir problem and inviting the intervention of the US and other foreign powers, it was bound to be bitterly disappointed at the absence of any reference to third party or UN mediation.[60] Thus, there was no reason for Islamabad to be satisfied with the outcome of the summit.

In fact, over Kargil, Pakistan faced daunting challenges on the diplomatic front to reverse the perception of much of the international community about how the latest flare-up started over Kashmir and what should be done to address this on a sustainable basis. The opposition and media in Pakistan were also angry with the Nawaz Sharif Government for "deceiving" the public on the Kargil, inviting diplomatic isolation and damaging the Kashmir cause by way it managed the conflict.[61] Benazir Bhutto, the former Prime Minister of Pakistan, while addressing a gathering in London, denounced the intrusion in Kargil as the biggest blunder in the history of Pakistan. It nearly led to the first full-scale nuclear war situation since the second world war.[62] Great Britain and Russia also, in a joint statement, expressed concern at the aggravation of situation on the Line of Control in Kashmir and appealed to Pakistan to restore status quo on the LoC by withdrawing armed groups of infiltrators.

In the circumstances, on July 4, 1999, the Prime Minister of Pakistan Nawaz Sharif met US President Bill Clinton. In their meeting, which lasted for three hours, Clinton telephoned Vajpayee to tell him what was being discussed. Ultimately, Pakistan had to agree to withdraw its forces behind the Line of Control, and go back to the Lahore accord. The Clinton-Sharif communiqué which called that "concrete steps will be taken" to restore the LoC as per the Simla Agreement, had been described by a 15-member opposition group as the "most serious setback to the country after the fall of Dhaka."[63] Earlier, Islamabad had fully expected the big powers to intervene because of the potential nuclear peril thereby effectively internationalizing the Kashmir dispute. When nothing of the sort occurred, and the entire exercise became dangerously counter-productive, Nawaz Sharif, decided it was prudent to make the best of a bad job, cut his losses and count the blessings. Despite the defiant war cries from the frustrated fundamentalists bent on continued Jehad, Sharif's retreat might have ensured his political longevity. New Delhi's restrained behaviour in not crossing either the international border or LoC and keeping the conflict confined to Kargil gave it political, diplomatic and military success.[64]

However, Bill Clinton intervened to help buy Indian restraint and prevent Pakistan's potential downfall in a full-fledged war over Kargil. For India, Pakistani withdrawal was only one issue. Pak-occupied Kashmir's hostile bases for militants are a much larger concern and, unless addressed, will continue to threaten India's stability and security in Kashmir and elsewhere. Although Clinton has set LoC's "sanctity" as a goal, the disbanding of such terrorist bases for cross border movements was not on his agenda. Despite India's growing economic charm for American business, Washington will not allow Pakistan to collapse or even come under the shadow of a militarily dominant India.[65] Thus; any US mediatory role will likely seek to safeguard Pakistani interests vis-à-vis India.

After all, Kargil has certainly served to remind the world that Kashmir is a dangerous issue that should not be left unattended. To this extent, Pakistan's claim that the Kashmir issue is now irretrievably internationalised sounds legitimate. However, by highlighting the violation of the Line of Control and by disowning its soldiers and dubbing the intruders as the Mujahideen, who later withdrew at its request, Pakistan has actually exposed its involvement in promoting cross-border terrorism. The most important lesson from Kargil is that if you are dealing with an unreliable neighbour who has lured you into war, you need to be coherent and clear in your vision.

4.4 FAULTLINES OF INDIA'S KASHMIR POLICY

Amid fear and suspicion the accession of the princely State of Jammu and Kashmir with the Union of India was completed in October 1947 after the signing of an Instrument of Accession between the then Maharaja of State and the Government of India. In initial years India got support of its main political party the National Conference and its leader Sheikh Abdullah who, at the time wanted to join India. An overriding factor in the situation is that Kashmir has over the years become a symbol as well as a test of India's secularism. If in 1947 Kashmir had acceded to Pakistan, Indians would have accepted the fact without being upset. But after the invasion of Kashmir by Pathan tribesmen and Pakistani troops and the persuasion of its leader Sheikh Abdullah, the situation became different and it all these put Abdullah in a privileged position. On the one hand he was a man of remarkable courage and integrity having mass appeal but on the other an autocrat, wayward and arbitrary.[66]

Even at that time as today the State of Jammu and Kashmir was inhabited by pro-India and pro-Pakistan elements. These communal forces had given an upper hand to Sheikh Abdullah in his dealings with the Government over the future of territory in which the secular weakness of India also remained a factor. Once Abdullah's position in state's politics became a certain he began to talk about the limited character of the accession in the Indian union and full autonomy for the state. Initially he praised India's secular democracy which is based on justice, freedom and equality for all without distinction and hoped these all to be realised while deciding the future of the state.[67] In his speeches Abdullah considered the provisions of Article 370 as secondary and laid emphasis on the identity of democratic and secular aspirations,[68] he however, also liked to add a note of caution and a thinly veiled warning, 'I would like to make it clear that any suggestion of arbitrarily altering this basis of our relationship with India would not only constitute a breach of the spirit and letter of the Constitution but might invite serious consequences for a harmonious association of our State with India.'[69]

Sheikh Abdullah not only took undue advantage from the Indian government but also tried to put the latter in perennial pressure tactics first in the name of State's autonomy and later hinted independence to be achieved with the help of the US and other foreign powers. From the start in Indian opinion the alternative to mollifying Kashmiris in the eyes of Nehru, in particular, was to hold up Abdullah as the most accredited and popular leader of the state and appease him to remain steadfast in keeping Kashmir with India. Even at the juncture Nehru pleaded with him for sanity and restraint but with little effect. His utterances before the public that Kashmir should become independent annoyed several of his colleagues and displeasure at the level of central leadership. Ultimately he was dismissed from his post in July 1953 and immediately thereafter put under arrest on charges of corruption, malpractices, disruption and dangerous foreign contacts. In his place Bakshi Ghulam Mohammad was installed as Prime Minister. Personally Nehru was not happy with the turn of events but did not interfere with the state government.

Integrating Measures

With the Sheikh Abdullah out of the way, it became easier for the central Government to work with Bakshi. The old suspicions had disappeared and the Kashmir Governments were by then convinced that the main aim of Delhi Operation was to prevent subversion, terrorisation, sabotage and conspiracy by Pakistani agents. Bakshi was a liberal-minded and large-hearted person with his feet planted strongly amongst the masses. He tried to do much for improving the material conditions of the people of Kashmir and achieved a great deal. But above all he was completely loyal to Jawaharlal Nehru and considered himself an Indian out and out. Bakshi's Government lasted till 1963 and eventually G.M. Sadiq was installed in his place.

Article 370 of the Indian Constitution stands for the special care taken and many due and undue favours shown to win the goodwill of the Kashmiris. But the arrest of Abdullah and installation of Bakshi compelled New Delhi to have a second thought on its Kashmir policy. From here and now a systematic erosion of the autonomy of Kashmir started and this was the beginning of the end of Article 370. In 1954 a constitutional order was promulgated by the President of India, which empowered the Indian Government to legislate on all matters on the Union List, not just defense, foreign affairs and communications. This order came into force on 14 May 1954 and superseded both the constitutional application order of 1950 and Delhi Agreement of 1952. The order also put a drastic curbs on fundamental liberties, freedom of speech, assembly and association in the state could now be suspended at any time on grounds of security. No judicial review was allowed as one author puts ably, "what we in India experienced for a brief period after 26 June 1975 during emergency of Indira Gandhi, Jammu and Kashmir has suffered for ...years...We cannot deny a people rights that flow out of citizenship and expect their allegiance."[70]

Other integrating measures followed further. In 1958, a constitutional amendment was effected, whereby Jammu and Kashmir was brought under the purview of central services resulting in the destruction of representative democracy, outside domination in its day-to-day administration which had no mass root. However, the peak of the process reached under Sadiq during 1964-65. Article 356 and 357 of the Indian Constitution which respectively empower central government to dismiss elected provincial governments and to assume all the legislative functions of the state, were made applicable to Jammu and Kashmir. Article 249, which empowers the central government to legislate even on subjects on the provincial list was similarly made applicable to Jammu and Kashmir. Some twenty pieces of central economic legislation were extended to Jammu and Kashmir, and the designations of head of state and premier were formally changed to governor and chief minister as in any Indian state. Further the governor was to be appointee of Delhi, rather than a nominee of the (elected) Kashmir legislature. By mid 1960s there was hardly any trace of substantive autonomy in Jammu and Kashmir.[71]

Closely related to it is the aspect of free and fair elections in Jammu and Kashmir. The people of the state had never seen genuine elections except in 1977, 1983 and now in 2002. All other elections in J&K witnessed a meaningless rituals. A democratic polity is supposed to be one in which the government and the people together create an open and civil society an integrated whole that is brought and kept together by virtue of its being open, one in which the people participate not just in things like elections and development projects, but together in creating a common future.[72]

Erosion of representative democracy continued in Jammu and

Kashmir. In the assembly elections of 1957 and 1962, the official National Conference, headed by Bakshi, won between 95 and 97 per cent of seats. The ruling party's candidates were returned unopposed in almost all seats in the valley where virtually there was no contest at all in 43 and 34 seats. The recurrent unopposed elections were earning a bad reputation. Riled by adverse reports in the international press, Nehru even wrote to Bakshi after the 1962 polls, advising him to lose a few seats in the future, so that the image of the world's largest democracy would not be unnecessarily tarnished. Further in 1967, 39 out of 75 seats were uncontested in the Valley. Congress candidates were elected unopposed in 22 out of 42 seats.

In 1977 the first reasonably democratic election was held. The Plebiscite Front, revived under the aegis of the National Conference, obtained a decisive majority in the Valley where Congress was wiped out. In post-Independence Kashmir, a new generation has arisen which is more educated, more politically conscious and self-assertive; it is in search of human and democratic rights denied to the people for three decades. The educated Muslim youth whose number multiplied several times since independence realised by 1977 that Abdullah's inconsistent behaviour had thwarted the progress of the state people in every sphere of social life. While free elections were common in all other states, Jammu and Kashmir alone suffered from gerrymandering and rigging every time elections to parliament or State Assembly. Kashmir, although disappointed with Abdullah's capitulation, obviously preferred him to the alternatives available.

Death of Sheikh Abdullah in 1982 followed a reasonably free and fair election in 1983. His party National Conference, now led by Farooq Abdullah, his eldest son, won a solid majority 47 of 76 assembly seats. This was a major achievement, since the election had been fiercely contested against the Congress (1), the party ruling Delhi. In both the above, the National Conference faced a well entrenched Congress with genuine Kashmiri support, and trounced it badly. Given a genuine contest and a Kashmiri ethno-nationalist alternative to the Congress, the Kashmiris of the valley came out to vote in droves. Seventy-four per cent cast their vote in 1977 and 73 per cent in 1983.

As a result of the assembly elections held in 2002, a new coalition government of Congress and People's Democratic party, headed by Mufti Mohammad Sayeed has taken over the reign in Jammu and Kashmir. The new dispensation had announced a Common Minimum Programme which among other things, noted that, 'the goal of the coalition government is to heal the physical, psychological and emotional wounds inflicted by fourteen years of militancy, to restore the rule of law in Jammu and Kashmir state, to complete the revival of the political process which was begun by the recently concluded elections, and to request the Government of India to initiate and held, sincerely and seriously, wide ranging consultations and dialogue, without conditions, with the members of the legislative and other segments of public opinion in all the three regions of the state, to evolve a broad-based consensus in restoration of peace with honour in the state.[73]

Negative Effects

Despite governments attempt to put democracy back on the rails in Kashmir, and thereby end the prevailing acute dissatisfaction in the state, is on the verge of failure. It has neither been able to convince the Kashmiris that the elections would be truly free and fair, nor create the conditions in which the various Kashmiri nationalist groups can agree to fight the election and thereby turn it into a genuine contest for power among the Kashmiri themselves.[74] What distinguishes democratic rulers from non-democratic ones are the norms that condition how the former came to power and the practices that hold them accountable for their actions. For democracy specific procedural norms must be followed and civil rights respected. Any polity that fails to follow the 'rule of law' with regard to its own procedures should not be considered democratic. The political history of Indian administered Jammu and Kashmir clearly does not satisfy these minimal conditions and requirements of democratic governance. Other basic indispensable component of a democratic framework, for example, a functioning political opposition, has not been permitted in the state. Democratic system rely on institutionalized oppositions and it is doubtful that any regime could long survive as minimally democratic without them.

Frustration and anger of the new generation accumulated and events began to take a new turn from mid-eighties. In late 1986 Farooq Abdullah committed a disastrous blunder and concluded a rapprochement with the centre, where upon he was reinstalled as chief minister pending fresh elections in March 1987. In exchange he agreed to contest the elections in partnership with Rajiv Gandhi's Congress (1). Although Farooq justified his decision in terms of a hard political reality he had come to accept, the arrangement met with widespread public hostility and contempt because it was an alliance with those who had disrespected and denied Kashmiriyat for forty years. The development was followed by formation of a coalition in the valley called Muslim United Front (MUF) to fight the NC-Congress alliance at the polls. In an anti-climax MUF eventually won just four seats with the NC-Congress combine taking almost all the rest with the help of rigging and strong arm tactics, booth capturing, not being allowed to vote and balantant working of administration in favour of the establishment. Mass arrests of MUF activist had immediately followed the spurious election and in fact it was in prison during 1987 that the five young men formed the Jammu and Kashmir Liberation Front (JKLF). On their release they took a collective decision to go to Pakistan-Controlled Kashmir in search of military training and weapons. Yasin Mallik currently chairman of the JKLF is one of them.

Specially after 1987 all institutional channels of protest and dissent effectively blocked and even perfectly peaceful agitations were suppressed with lethal force. The first JKLF bombing in Srinagar in late July 1988 signalled the arrival of insurgency. According to Newberg, 'Kashmiris come to insurgency when all politics seemed to fail, the politics of Kashmir's traditional politicians, politics between Srinagar and Delhi, and politics between India and Pakistan. They view themselves as victims of profound corruptions that sully the meaning of politics.[75] Indeed, most Kashmiris who developed a renewed commitment to the idea of self-determination by the late 1980 sincerely believe that they have given India's democracy more than its fair share of chances. The vast majority of Kashmiris are apparently prepared to make considerable sacrifices in order to resist this oppression. And the reason why they seem so insistent on "Freedom" which means freedom from Indian rule, is the conviction, born of their experiences, that their collective will for democratic responsible and accountable government is incompatible with their presently coerced status as 'an integral part of India.'

Two factors are mainly responsible for changing the social psychology in Kashmir. One, the growing perception and public resentment that proliferation and availability of small arms and ammunition and its use by individuals and groups with impunity is a sham democracy is a better alternative to anarchy, and a bad government is still a better option to chaos. It is a healthy development if there is an urge in initiating measures to bring an improvement in the governance of the state.[76] Good governance, as some analyst viewed it, is the way out. To some in India better governance in Kashmir means handing the state or the valley, to army rule. Others see it in terms of a clean development-oriented administration, with or without 'autonomy'. In their view, all that people in Kashmir want like people everywhere in India, is a minimum of roads, schools, dispensaries and electricity and an attentive administration. Provide these things back them up with firm security measures and the militants would be isolated.

It is true that due to over a decade of militancy, religious identities have become more pronounced and imposition of a unitary form of constitution on the state has suppressed all forms of identities except those based on religion, the distance between Kashmiri Muslims and Hindus has increased, they share a common language, culture and heritage. Militancy might have bruised Kashmiriyat, but it never succeeded in diluting it. However, it needs conducive social and political conditions to make this culture thrive again. Kashmir, apart from political problem, represents a human tragedy of epic proportions. This task of reconciliation and healing is not one that the government alone can do. Civil society as a whole in the state as well as in the rest of India, and especially organizations working in the field of inter-faith harmony would have to get involved in this process which would necessarily take many years to complete. However, a "beginning" must be made without delay.

4.5 KASHMIR NEEDS CORRECTION NOT COERCION

Cultural Composition

Kashmir has been a melting pot of ideas and cultures. It received every new creed with discrimination and enriched it with its own contribution, without throwing away its earlier acquisitions as observed by one, 'it is the cult of Buddha, the teachings of vedanta, the mysticism of Islam have one after another found a congenial home in Kashmir.' The intermingling of various ethnic groups in this part of India has provided peculiarities of the Kashmiri personality and the historical, cultural, political and geographical inputs that moulded it. The history of the people of Jammu and Kashmir is a record of constant impulses of immigration from the northwest, west, south and east directions. The alien races, ethnic groups and various religions have influenced the cultural ethos and mode of life of people of this region. Ethnic group is defined as a group of people possessing a common ancestry and cultural tradition with a long feeling of belonging and cohesiveness, living as a minority in a larger society. Each social group is the keeper of distinctive cultural traditions and the nucleus of various kinds of social interactions. It provides not only group identity but also friendship, marriage, patterns, business success and the political power base.[77]

The inside as well as outside factors have influenced the racial composition of the State of Jammu and Kashmir. Apart from the cultural heritage of the people of the state, in the process of peopling of the region, the Dards in the north-west, the Ladakhis in the east, the Gujjars and Rajputs in the south and Paharis in the south east have closely influenced the existing ethnicity of the region. The word 'Kashmiri' and 'Kashmiriyat' is a wide term which has loosely been applied for several streams of immigrants mainly from Turkey, Iran, Central Asia and Afghanistan and settled in the valley.[78] Thus, on the basis of its cultural homogeneity and geographical compactness all the people who emigrated to Kashmir from ancient times merged their individual identities into one whole. The State of Jammu and Kashmir, before its accession to the Union of India in 1947 was ruled by the Mughals, Pathans, Sikhs and Dogra Kings.

Integration in India and Alienation

With the seizure of British Paramountcy in the Indian subcontinent, princely states including the State of Jammu and Kashmir were asked to choose between India and Pakistan or remain independent. Till August 15, 1947, the day India became independent, this state failed to decide either way and increased pressure was natural from both the sides. It was in the last week of October that it had decided to accede to India keeping in view the security threats from Pakistan.

After accession the Indian leaders and public as well faced the huge task of absorbing Muslim dominated Kashmir with India. It was a difficult task and demanded, for its accomplishment, virtues of statesmanship, generosity, farsightedness, accommodation and above all selflessness on their part. As a follow up of this motivation Article 370 of the Indian Constitution which conferred a special status on Kashmir was incorporated. Initially, soon after the accession in 1947, the Indian leaders made a good start and were generous in handling the Kashmir state affairs. The inserted article assured Kashmiris that they would be free to shape their own destiny as they desired and nothing would be imposed on them by the Indian Parliament. The Constitution makers were fully convinced that the close association of the people of Kashmir with democratic India would make them confident of their bright future by becoming an integral part of this Republic. In all these affairs Seikh Abdullah, the lone leader of the Kashmiri people, remained at the heart of the scene and formed an interim Government in Jammu and Kashmir.

Subsequent political developments made it amply clear that it was too good to last. The pro-India utterances of Sheikh Abdullah took a 'U' turn in the beginning years of the fifties and the Government of India feared continuance of Jammu and Kashmir as part of the Indian Union.[79] In all probabilities, the Indian government tried to persuade Sheikh Abdullah but was of no avail. He was adamant in his determination to strike on independent path. In July 1953 the Government of Sheikh Abdullah was dismissed and he was put behind the bar in August. It was the starting point of erosion of representative democracy in the state. The assembly elections of 1957, 1962 and 1967 were a farce and registered 95 to 97 per cent of seats for the ruling clique. It disappointed the people of Jammu and Kashmir at large because they were deprived of their political right for no fault on their part.

The State of Jammu and Kashmir witnessed its first reasonably democratic election in 1977 followed by a free and fair occasion in 1983. After the death of Sheikh Abdullah in 1982, his son Farooq Abdullah made an opportunistic agreement with Congress 1, the party ruling Delhi, in 1986 to remain in power. The accord that was arrived at between Rajiv Gandhi and Farooq Abdullah led to the formation of the National Conference-Congress coalition government in November 1986, it however, simultaneously alienated the large masses of Jammu and Kashmir. The argument implied that central aid would inflow as a result of the accord, was based on narrow considerations with no match to the self-respecting people of the state.[80] In fact the party in power at the centre had no right to buy a share in the political power of a state by promising aid and the people of Jammu and Kashmir had repeatedly rebuffed attempts of earlier governments to take over their loyalty.

The accord was also full of other negative consequences. It was a denial of the basic principles of democracy and federalism. It implied that some states should be denied the right to be ruled by a government of their choice and it pushed once again Jammu and Kashmir outside the framework of federal democracy in India. It blocked all types of secular outlets of protest against governments both at the Centre and the State. It destroyed the raison d'etre of both parties and forced all types of discontent to seek fundamentalist or secessionist outlets. In no way the assembly elections of March 1987 was an improvement, blocking further secular and nationalist outlets of discontent, constitutional and democratic ones as well. Especially after 1987 all institutional channels of protest and dissent effectively blocked and even perfectly peaceful agitations were suppressed with lethal force.

In post-independence era there has been a persistent policy of denying Kashmir a right to democracy : one-party rule has been imposed on the State through manipulation of elections, opposition parties have been prevented from growing and elementary civil liberties and human rights have been denied to the people. This refusal to integrate Kashmir within the framework of Indian democracy has proved to be the single greatest obstacle to the process of Kashmir's emotional and political integration with the rest of India.[81] This is why the people of Jammu and Kashmir are so insistent on "freedom" which means freedom from Indian rule, is the conviction, born of their experiences, that their collective will for democratic responsible and accountable government is incompatible with their presently coerced status as 'an integral part of India'. It is one of the factors that has changed the social psychology of Kashmir. They began to realise that even sham democracy is a better alternative to anarchy, and a bad government is still a better option to chaos.

In the circumstances the basic human urges that we witness in Jammu and Kashmir today were translated in insurgency/violence in the beginning of the nineties. The fact that Kashmir is now reacting to decades of Congress rule and by implication, of centre's political high-handedness is by and large accepted by most scholars. It is also to note here that because of the Pakistan factor, the insurgency in Kashmir has always had to be handled with greater firmness than those elsewhere.[82] In most cases the problem is treated as merely an extension of the unresolved Hindu-Muslim conflict of the forties. There is no doubt that a large number of Kashmiri Muslims are alienated from India today. Their alienation is more as Kashmiri than as Muslim.

Expansion of Insurgency in Kashmir

Factors responsible for the birth and proliferation of insurgency in the Indian State of Jammu and Kashmir were many. Having permitted conditions within Kashmir to deteriorate to the level that they had reached in 1989, the Indian state had little option but to fight hard to break the insurgency in Jammu and Kashmir and the external support it was receiving. In fact, the democratic ideals of the freedom movement in India and its support to the struggle of the people of the princely states for a responsible government inspired and influenced the people in the valley. However, these very ideals remained elusive after the State acceded to the Indian Union. The alienation of the people of Kashmir made considerable headway due to the sequence of events that took place in coming decades. Kashmir policy of the Government of India has been marked mainly by what may be called the carrot and stick approach. But neither stick nor carrot helped win favour of the Kashmiri people. Force and aid were used as instruments to win the loyalty of the people not for the nation but for the Government and the Party in power.

Terrorism in Kashmir, or for that matter anywhere else, can not be ascribed to administrative or economic reasons alone. The main cause of it is the deprivation of political power due to which the community believes that its dignity and identity are threatened. In general a secessionist-terrorist movement often seek outlets if the political system does not have adequate provision for its expression.[83] This is what actually happened in Jammu and Kashmir after 1987. All institutional channels of protest and dissent which are essential to generating both democratic values among the citizenry and their allegiance to the established framework of authority were effectively blocked.[84] Frustration and anger of the new generation accumulated and events began to take a new turn at the close of the Eighties.

Before 1989, India and Pakistan fought over Kashmir. Since late 1989, it is Kashmiris who have done the fighting and most of the dying.[85] In early 1990 a group of young men in the Kashmir valley launched a guerilla revolt against Indian rule under the banner of a movement calling itself the Jammu and Kashmir Liberation Front (JKLF). The new organisation had received weapons and training from its part located across the border in Azad Jammu and Kashmir (AJK) as well as from Pakistani military agencies. The JKLF's stated objective was to liberate and reunite the whole of state held by India and Pakistan into a single independent state. It received mass support for freedom of Jammu and Kashmir and huge pro-independence demonstrations were organised in the valley during 1990.

Expansion of insurgency in the State has an international aspect too. The Soviet intervention that took place in December 1979 and lasted about for a decade, had several far-reaching implications. It not only made available additional armaments to the insurgents but also changed the very nature of Pak society. Social disintegration appeared to escalate in the 1980s and 1990s. As both cultivation and drug smuggling escalated, Pakistan emerged as a frontline heroin production point and transit route for the international drug trade.[86] According to a report about 5,000 Kashmiri youth were taken into Pakistan in the summer of 1988 for training and sent back in the spring of the following year. During 1988-94, over 50,000 Kashmiri youth are estimated to have been trained in Pakistan. Mujahideen, freed from the Afghan conflict, were sent to Kashmir and their numbers peaked at about 1600 in 1994.[87]

The struggle in the State of Jammu and Kashmir continued to evolve. The guerilla war rapidly intensified, to a significant degree because of an Indian response of repression and reprisal targeted not just against armed militants but frequently also against 'disloyal' civilian communities that aided and sheltered the rebels.[88] Gradually, militancy entered a new phase. It was no longer a fight between the militants and the security forces. In fact it assumed the form of a total insurgency of the entire population and was marked by demoralisation within the Political system, followed by the collapse of the administration.

Though the mid of 1990s witnessed a wane to the local support for insurgency, in the second half of the decade Pan-Islamist fighters, primarily from Pakistan, infiltrated into Indian Jammu and Kashmir in significant numbers, adding a supra-local, strongly Islamist flavour to the conflict. The protracted 'low-intensity' warfare in the interior of the State between thousands of guerillas and hundreds of thousands of Indian security forces signalled a great transformation in the military and political character of the Kashmir conflict.[89]

Thus the political history of India-administered Jammu and Kashmir clearly does not satisfy the minimal conditions and requirements of democratic governance. No Kashmir policy can succeed without taking into account the political and psychological urge of the people. The controversy over whether the policy should be tough or soft, whether it should be based on nationalist or moral appeal, on realpolitic or idealpolitik is unreal and irrelevant. What the question needs is a correct assessment, a correct diagnosis, a correct strategy. The government, despite its attempt to put democracy on the rails in Kashmir has neither been able to convince the Kashmiris that the elections would be truly free and fair, nor create the conditions in which the various Kashmiri nationalist groups can agree to fight the election and thereby turn it into a genuine contest for power among the Kashmiris themselves. What Kashmir badly needs and sadly lacks is a "healing touch" policy - a step towards a serious, sustained and multidimensional peace process.

References

1. 'Plebiscite' is a method of ascertaining the general desire of the inhabitants of a given territory or area on some specific question. This method was first used in the French Revolution to defend the wholesale annexations of territory made by the conquering French republic. It is distinguished from referendum which is a normal method or procedure of voting applied on a general system to certain

clauses of legislation. See, R.A. Edwin, Seligman, Encyclopaedia of the Social Sciences, Vol. 2, (Macmillan Newyork, 1954), pp. 163-66.

2. Sugata Bose and Ayesha Jalal, Modern South Asia-History, Culture, Political Economy (Oxford University Press, New Delhi, 2005), p. 174.
3. Balraj Puri, 'Kashmiriyat : The Valley of Kashmiri Identity', Contemporary South Asia, Vol. IV, No. 1 March, 1995, p. 57.
4. Within a week from the date the Instrument of Accession was executed, the Government of Pakistan issued a statement on Kashmir (October 30, 1947) charging India of having procured the accession by 'fraud and violence' and said that as such it could not be recognised, This view was further elaborated by Liaquat Ali Khan, the then Prime Minister of Pakistan, in a broadcast from Lahore on November 4, 1947. He declared : The accession of Kashmir is a much greater threat to the security of Pakistan. We do not recognise this accession. The accession of Kashmir to India is a fraud. See, M.M.R. Khan, The United Nations and Kashmir (1954).
5. B. Buzan and Rizvi, South Asian Insecurity and the Great Powers (Macmillan, London, 1986), p. 1.
6. Sisir Gupta, Kashmir : A Study in Indo-Pakistan Relations (Asia Publications, New Delhi, 1966).
7. Sumit Ganguly, 'India: Policies, Past and Future', in Selig S. Harrison, Paul H. Kreisberg and Deunis Kux eds., India and Pakistan–The First Fifty Year (Cambridge University Press, United Kingdom, 1999), P. 157.
8. Later on, the suggestion of the Governor–General was accepted by the leaders of India including Jawaharlal Nehru, the first Prime Minister, who issued a statement in Parliament on November 25, 1947 that, when the people of Kashmir are given the chance to decide their future this should be done under the supervision of an impartial tribunal such as the United Nations Organisation. He also wrote to the Prime Minister of Pakistan on December 12, 1947 that we are prepared to invite UN observer to come and advice us as to the proposed plebiscite. See, S.C. Poplai, ed., Select Documents on Asian Affairs, India 1947 - 50, Vol. 1 & 11 (Oxford University Press, 1959), p. 393.
9. Security Council Official Records, 1948, Document S/628 dated January 1, 1948.
10. Ibid., pp. 67-87.

11. Ibid., SCOR, S/646, dated January 15, p. 10.
12. Wayne Wilcox 'Pakistan', in Wayne Wilcox, Leo E. Rose and Gavin Boyd, eds., Asia and the International System (Winthrop Publishers, Cambridge, 1972), p. 113.
13. Verghese Koithara, Society, State and Security - The Indian Experience (Sage Publications, New Delhi, 1999), p. 111.
14. J.B. Dasgupta, Jammu and Kashmir (Martinus Nijhoff, The Hague, 1968), pp. 395-403.
15. O.H. Agarwal, Kashmir Problem Its Legal Aspects (Kitab Mahal Allahabad, 1979), pp. 76-77.
16. Vasant Sathe, 'The Pride of Kashmiriyat', The Hindustan Times, January 31, 2002.
17. B.N. Mullik, My Years With Nehru (Allied Publishers, New Delhi, 1971), p. 24.
18. Balraj Puri, op.cit., p. 90.
19. Rajkumar Singh, India's Foreign Policy - The First Study in Continuity and Change (Samiksha Prakashan, New Delhi, 2001), pp. 121-22.
20. White paper, Meetings and Correspondence Between Prime Ministers of India and Pakistan, July 1953- October 1954 (Government of India, Ministry of External Affairs, Delhi, 1954), p. 48.
21. Ahsen Mohammed Chaudhari, Pakistan and Regional Pacts (Karachi, 1958), p. 111.
22. Sumantra Bose, The Challenge in Kashmir – Democracy, Self Determination and a Just Peace (Sage Publications, New Delhi, 1997), p. 38.
23. In December 1955 N.A. Bulganin, the Prime Minister and Nikita Khruschev, the First Secretary of the Communist party of the Soviet Union, during their visit to India issued statements in Srinagar favouring India's Kashmir case. They also supported India in a report submitted to the Supreme Soviet of the USSR. See, The Hindu, December 11, 1955.
24. Jawaharlal Nehru, Rajya Sabha Debates, Vol. 39, 23 June 1962, col. 1766.
25. Paula R. Newberg, Double Betrayal : Repression and Insurgency in Kashmir (Washington, D.C., 1995), pp. 72-74.
26. M.J. Akbar, India, the Siege Within (Penguin, Harmondsworth, 1985), pp. 221-22.
27. Ibid., pp. 227-28.
28. Saifuddin Soz, ed., Why Autonomy in Kashmir (Indian Centre for

Asian Studies, New Delhi, 1995), pp. 121-39.

29. Dipankar Gupta, Political Sociology in India – Contemporary Trends (Orient Longman, New Delhi, 1996), p. 95.
30. In the month of June 1947 Mahatma Gandhi and Jawaharlal Nehru requested Lord Mountbatten, the then Governor - General of India, to visit Kashmir as both of them wanted to study the political situation of the state. They were anxious that the Maharaja of Kashmir should make no declaration of independence.
31. The Hindustan Times, January 28, 1989.
32. The Jammu and Kashmir Liberation Front (JKLF) was founded in the mid-sixties in Pakistani Kashmir. Initially it was supported by the Government of Pakistan but when it refused to abandon its pro-independence line, Islamabad terminated all aid to it and began building up Hizbul Mujahideen (HM) with a vengence. Ideologically, it is committted to an independent, democratic, secular and reunified state of Jammu and Kashmir, with the borders of the princely state in 1947 restored. It is still regarded as the most popular political movement in the Kashmir valley.
33. Dipankar Gupta, op.cit., p. 83.
34. The Times of India, November 25, 2001.
35. The term 'Shaheed' as penned by Ali Sharia' ti, the revolutionary socialist thinker of Iran, is the heart of history. The heart gives blood and life to the otherwise dead blood vessels of the body. Like the heart, a shaheed sends his own blood into the half- dead body of the dying society which has accepted submission. The greatest miracle of shahadat (martyrdom) is giving to a generation a renewed faith in itself. A shaheed is ever - present and everlasting. See, Sumantra Bose, op.cit., p. 198.
36. Rajesh Kadian, The Kashmir Tangle: Issues and Options (Vision Books, New Delhi, 1992), p. 140.
37. The proposal was presented to ' Conflict Resolution in the South Asian Region : The Kashmir Dialogue', a forum sponsored by the United States Institute of Peace in Washington, D.C. Earlier in 1991, the Pakistan - based JKLF's leader Amanullah Khan proposed a plebiscite with the same simple - majoritarian formula. See, Amanullah Khan, India Vs. India (Muzaffarabad, 1991), p. 9-10.
38. Prem Nath Bazaz, Struggle for Freedom in Kashmir (New Delhi, 1954), p. 196.
39. M.J. Akbar, op.cit., pp. 227-28.
40. Bipin Chandra Mridula Mukherjee and Aditya Mukherjee, eds. India

After Independence 1947-2000 (Penguin Books, New Delhi, 2002), p. 319.
41. The Statesman, August 8, 1952.
42. Sumantra Bose, op.cit., pp.31-32.
43. Balraj Puri, 'A Question of Semantics', The Times of India, November 25, 2002.
44. B. N. Mullik, op.cit., p. 195.
45. Ibid., p. 192.
46. Verghese Koithara, op.cit., pp.111-12.
47. Rajkumar Singh, Past, Present and Future of Kashmir (New Delhi, 2008), pp.76-78.
48. Riyaz Punjabi, 'Freeze Peace', The Hindustan Times, December 23, 2000.
49. Prem Nath Bazaz, Democracy Through Intimidation and Terror (New Delhi, 1978), pp. 159-60.
50. Prem Shankar Jha, 'Subversion in Kashmir', Hindustan Times, July 17, 1999.
51. Ibid.
52. Ibid., August 27, 1999.
53. The Times of India (editorial), June 26, 1999.
54. Ibid., June 24, 1999.
55. Hindustan Times, June 17, 1999.
56. Anita Kanungo, 'What Should We do with Pakistan', Ibid., July 12, 1999.
57. Akshaya Mukul, 'It's No Big Deal', Ibid., June 14, 1999.
58. Ibid., June 13, 1999.
59. J. Mohan Malik, 'India and China: Bound to Collide', P. R. Kumaraswamy, ed., Security Beyond Survival (Sage Publications, New Delhi, 2004), P. 135.
60. The Times of India (editorial), June 23, 1999.
61. Ibid., June 24, 1999.
62. The Hindustan Times, July 24, 1999.
63. Ibid. (editorial), July 13, 1999.
64. Vinod Anand, 'Did N-deterrence Work', Ibid., September 15, 1999.
65. Brahma Chellaney, 'The Clinton Doctrine', Ibid. July 15, 1999.
66. Bipin Chandra, op.cit., p. 320.
67. Sumantra Bose, Kashmir Roots of Conflict, Paths to Peace (New Delhi, 2003), p. 45.
68. Saifuddin Soz, Why Autonomy for Kashmir (New Delhi, 1995), pp. 121-39.

69. A.G. Noorani, The Kashmir Question (Bombay, 1964), p. 101.
70. Sumantra Bose, op.cit., p. 33.
71. Ibid., pp. 34-35.
72. Rajni Kothari, 'Interpreting Indian Politics : A personal Statement, in Upendra Baxi and Bhikhu Parekh, eds., Crisis and Change in Contemporary India (New Delhi, 1995), p. 165.
73. Karan Singh, 'Peace with Honour', The Hindustan Times, November 2, 2002.
74. Prem Shankar Jha, 'Farce Sighted', Ibid., August 19, 2002.
75. Paula R. Newberg, op.cit., p. 73.
76. Riyaz Punjabi, 'Resurrect Kashmiriyat', The Hindustan Times, July 18, 2002.
77. Majid Husnain, Geography of Jammu and Kashmir (New Delhi, 2002), p. 61.
78. Ibid., p. 62.
79. Riyaz Punjabi, 'Freeze Peace', The Hindustan Times, December 23, 2000.
80. Sumantra Bose, op.cit., pp. 44-45.
81. Balraj Puri, Kashmir Towards Insurgency (New Delhi, 1995), p.53.
82. Verghese Koithara, op.cit., p. 113.
83. Balraj Puri, op.cit., p. 84.
84. Jung Courtney and Ian Shapiro, 'South Africa's Negotiated Transition : Democracy, Opposition and the New Constitutional Order', Politics and Society, September 1995, pp. 271-73.
85. Paula R. Newberg, op.cit., p. 74.
86. Selig S. Harrison, Paul H. Kreisberg and Deunis Kux (eds.), op.cit., pp. 149-50.
87. Verghese Koithara, op.cit., p. 113.
88. Sumantra Bose, op.cit., p. 3.
89. Ibid., p. 4.

5

INDIA AND CHINA WITH BORDER DISPUTE

5.1 ESSENTIALS OF BORDER DISPUTE

The border dispute between India and China persisted due to divergence of approach on the issue. They are the only known neighbours not to be separated even by a mutually defined line of control leaving their entire 4,057 kilometer frontier in question. While China appears to fit well with the status quo as it keeps India under strategic pressure, Indian diplomacy is neither guided by the past nor by the cardinal principles of reciprocity, leverage and pragmatism. After the debacle of 1962 they resumed their border talks in 1981 but the Line of Actual Control is yet to be demarcated. The first requisite to good – neighbourly relations is a defined front line as the famous proverb goes,' good fences make good neighbours.'

Delineation of Boundary

The entire India – China border can be generally divided into three areas; the border to the east of Bhutan, the central or middle border across Uttar Pradesh, Punjab and Himachal Pradesh and the border separating Jammu and Kashmir from Chinese territories of Sinkiang and Tibet. The boundary of Kashmir with Sinkiang and Tibet is about 1,100 miles of which the frontier of Ladakh forms nearly two – thirds. Traditionally, at least from the tenth century, important points on the present alignment were recognised as the limits of Ladakh on the one hand and Tibet on the other. This whole area of the Aksai Chin plateau and the Lingsi Tang plains was administered by the Government of

Ladakh and Kashmir and utilized for grazing by the people of Ladakh. A regular sequence of official records, stretching over many years provides testimony on such matters as revenue assessment police jurisdiction, public works' projects, census returns, control of trade routes and survey and mapping operations. The boundary of middle sector lies along the major watersheds; and its delimitation secured confirmation in the treaty of 1954 between India and the People's Republic of China. The eastern sector has the trijunction of India, Burma and China and it also follows the major watersheds[1].

Before conclusion of the agreement and demarcation of McMahon line, in 1890, British rulers of India made a treaty with China that delineated the Indo -Tibetan border. The treaty was rejected by Tibetan rulers and Russia's interference appeared imminent in country's affairs. In order to check Russian influence Lord Curzon, the then Governor – General of India, sent British Indian troops in 1904 under the command of Young Husband that resulted in a treaty in 1906 with China whereby Britain accepted Chinese suzerainty over Tibet. It also provided that a British Agent would be posted in Lhasa and India would construct postal system there. By this treaty India also acquired the right to maintain troops in Tibet for the protection of trade routes. Anglo-Russian differences relating to Tibet were sorted out by an Entente signed in 1907 whereby both accepted Chinese suzerainty in Tibet. They also agreed to deal with Tibet only through China. This privileged position of China in Tibet was challenged after the Chinese revolution of 1911, led by Dr. Sun Yat-sen, when Tibet forced the Chinese troops to leave the plateau. Even subsequent attempts on the part of China failed to re-establish its authority and it warranted a situation leading to the meeting at Simla in 1914.

Thus the international alignment in this area, along the highest watershed ranges, was formalised at the initiation of the then Chinese regime. The Simla negotiations of 1913-14, and the McMahon line delineating the border of North Eastern Frontier Agency that emerged from it, had been a British response to China's attempt to assert control in Tibet.[2] The conference was held to sort out border differences between Nepal, Bhutan, Sikkim and Tibet, though it was represented by British India, Tibet and China. Arthur Henry McMahon, the then Secretary of State for India, participated in the conference as a representative of British India. In the meeting an agreement was concluded which confirmed the Chinese suzerainty, but divided Tibet into two parts- Outer Tibet and Inner Tibet. The autonomy of outer Tibet was accepted and China agreed not to interfere in its internal affairs, nor give it representation in Chinese Parliament, nor station its troops, nor appoint its civil servants, nor to turn it into a Chinese colony [3]. At the same time another boundary between outer Tibet and India was demarcated at the high mountain which divided the two countries at the watershed. Since the line dividing India and Tibet was drawn on the suggestion of McMahon, who himself drew a line by a red pen on the map, it came to be known as the McMahon Line. This demarcation passes through Tibet plateau in the north and Indian hills in the South. The map was signed by representatives of British India, Tibet and China.

From 1914 till the date of independence India's policy towards Tibet and Sinkiang was conducted by the British. The Chinese, however, refused to ratify the agreement, the then Government of India also failed to take it seriously. Because China, torn by civil wars, was not in a position to assert herself it was considered an opportunity for India to dominate. Several British officers including Olaf Caroe, one of Deputy Secretaries, had realised that the north-east frontier might one day become as live as the north-west, and pressed for the extension of the rudiments of administration, civil and military, into the areas abutting the McMahon line. In this period our relations with Tibet were conducted through a Political Officer in Sikkim, who was also in charge of our relations with Bhutan. Sir Charles Bell, a close friend of Dalai Lama, remained there for years and so long as he was incharge, it was unnecessary to keep any troops on the north-east frontier.

In Sinkiang, on the pattern of Tibet, Philip Macartney, who went to Kashgar, the remotest post of the Indian empire, was made permanent officer to look after the affairs of Sinkiang. The Government of India's policy in Sinkiang was seemingly inconsistent with their policy towards Tibet. In Tibet they did all they could to repudiate Chinese sovereignty; in Sinkiang, they did all they could to affirm it. The reason was to prevent Sinkiang from falling a prey to what then seemed a greater menace, Russia.[4] When in the middle of the thirties Chinese control over Sinkiang weakened and the Tungans had risen in revolt against the provincial Government, first, the Government of Sinkiang appealed the Chinese and having failed, turned to Russia for support. Russia was happy to intervene and Sinkiang passed on to Russian hegemony. From there onwards the Indian Government began to support Chinese sovereignty in Sinkiang. The discrepancy that we found in British India's policy towards Tibet and Sinkiang was, ultimately aimed to prevent the approach of any other strong power towards India. Throughout the nineteenth century, British foreign policy in Asia was dominated by the 'Russian bogey'. In other words, India's relations with Sinkiang and Tibet in British days were based on a mistrust of her neighbour, China and Russia and a recognition of the game of power politics.

Assertiveness of China

Earlier the British Government of India had undertaken to support the independence of Tibet, subject to the suzerainty of China. Independent India had, in a sense, inherited this commitment with a sea change in circumstances. As long as China was weak and ever since the Revolution of 1911 she had been in the throes of civil war, it was easy for Tibet to assert its independence and for India to support it[5]. When India in 1947, and China after two years in 1949, emerged into the international stage, neither of them at the time of their establishment inherited a defined space and there was considerable ambiguity about the extent of the territorial limits of the new sovereign state. In fact the alignment of these frontiers had never been properly surveyed or delimited. In the north the Himalayan hill states of Bhutan, Sikkim, Nepal, and even Tibet, had been brought within the fluid frontiers of British India through a variety of separate arrangements. For India the problem was aggravated because it was the British in Delhi or London, who had conducted surveys, negotiations and even war on border matters. In general Indians lacked experience and acquaintance with border affairs as they had never been involved with decision or policy-making.

On the other hand the People's Republic of China had come into existence on October 1, 1949, as a consequence of the Chinese civil war. After its proclamation China took hard decisions regarding its imperial heritance of far- flung frontiers and tributary states. The process for this was started even earlier and in 1939, in a seminal essay, Mao Zedong had described the territorial limits of his envisaged new China as being less extensive than those of imperial China because they excluded the tributary states of the region. Accordingly the new state recognised erstwhile frontier states like Mongolia, Nepal, Vietnam and Korea as sovereign states but at the same time laid its claim to Tibet, Hong Kong, Macao and Taiwan by virtue of legal and treaty rights, as parts of its integral space. Thus, in 1949 the frontiers or limits of PRC's sovereignty had been clearly defined and it had taken concrete steps in this regard.

From strategic and security considerations the emergence of a strong and stable PRC posed a new challenge to the Indian Policy-makers. Jawaharlal Nehru, in a letter to K.M. Panikkar, the then India's

Ambassador to China, had said that whenever China had a strong government, it had tended to expand beyond its frontiers. He viewed the happenings in China not a palace revolution, but a grass root revolution and later told the parliament while presenting the budget demand for the Ministry of External Affairs on March 17, 1950, "It was a basic revolution involving millions and millions of human beings. It is not a question of approving or disapproving; it is a question of recognising a major event in history, of appreciating it and dealing with it."[6]. While dealing with China, as most of us viewed, the only area where our interests overlapped, was in Tibet.

As expected the newly established Government of the People's Republic of China announced on January 1, 1950 that one of the basic tasks of People's Liberation Army would be to 'liberate' Tibet. When determination of the Chinese leaders found expression, K.M. Panikkar met Chinese Premier Chou En lai in which the latter had assured the Indian ambassador that though the liberation of Tibet was a sacred duty of China his government would seek this goal through negotiation and not by military action. However, despite assurance China launched a full scale invasion on Tibet in October 1950. With the use of force by China in Tibet it became apparent that the event would alter the geo-politics of the region. It made India and China immediate geographical neighbours for the first time in history and gave rise to such security concerns for India as was previously unknown[7]. More important, it raised the vital question of where the territorial limits of a partitioned and weak Indian state lay.

Regarding Tibet, India was interested in preserving its autonomy that it was maintaining for decades. On number of occasions Jawaharlal Nehru had made it clear that India had no territorial or political ambition in regard to Tibet and our relations were cultural and commercial. He also made it clear that we did not challenge or deny the suzerainty of China over Tibet[8]. In fact after the establishment of strong government in China there was a physical limit to what the Government of India could do to support the independence of Tibet. The most, India could do was to protest against the use of force and to insist that the autonomy of Tibet should be respected. In dealing with the crisis the Government of India had not only to take into account the practical possibilities of the situation, but the long-range results of any policy which they might adopt.

The occupation of Tibet by force not only brought China to India's very doors but made India anxious and its anxiety became all the more acute in view of its awareness of its own military weaknesses against China.[9]. Following Chinese action in Tibet Sardar Patel, the Deputy Prime Minister of India, in a letter drew Pandit Nehru's attention to the problems of India's security in the north and suggested measures to strengthen them. He expressed the apprehension that the Chinese and the Russians would not miss any opportunity of exploiting weak spots in the north[10]. Nehru himself was not unmindful of India's northern frontier and responding to the changed situation declared that the McMahon Line would be India's non-negotiable border in the north-east 'map or no-map',[11] but significantly made no statement regarding the frontier in Ladakh. In line, Nehru decided further to draw the Indian security perimeter along the Himalayan range, taking in Nepal, Bhutan, and Sikkim and to warn that any breach of the Himalayas would be regarded as a threat to India. Years following the occupation of Tibet India did not want to start their relations on the wrong foot and supported China on several international issues including latter's support when the United States of America intervened in Korea and advocated PRC's place in the United Nations. This led to the warming of the Sino- Indian relations, culminating in signing of a trade treaty with China in April 1954 whose preamble incorporated the much trumpeted five principles of peaceful co-existence.

Signing of Panchsheel was the last laugh for India in its relations with the PRC. In spite of the fact that Tibet had been referred as the 'Region of China' in this treaty, the PRC had accused India of being influenced by the imperialist power. After the signing of a treaty between China and Tibet on May 23, 1951, Dalai Lama left Tibet and then made unsuccessful attempts to raise the issue of its autonomy at the UN. Dalai Lama's mobilisation of world opinion in Tibet's favour was considered by China as an imperialist design and it held India responsible for it partially, if not wholly. On the other friendship with China was the cornerstone of the entire edifice of Nehru's worldview and structure of policy, and he placed his trust on the 'Chineseness' of communist China, on its national pride and its 'Asianness'[12]. Despite strong domestic pressures and fears following the extension of Chinese sovereignty to Tibet and the harsh Soviet and Chinese criticism of him, non-alignment and India, Nehru took deliberate measures to avoid confrontation. However, in years to come the question of frontiers and borders became alive and immediate issue for both which it had not been in 1950.

In post- Panchsheel phase, though in a mild tone, India and China began to warm up the issue of territorial delimitation. Basing himself on the view that India's northern frontier was a traditional one and that there was no doubt as to where it lay, Nehru had decided in September 1954 that the whole boundary should be shown on maps as a continuous line and no reference need to be made to undermarcated areas. But unfortunately, no map on a larger scale could be issued. In the meantime, China had been issuing maps of varying scale showing boundary alignments which were never the same but included Aksai Chin, NEFA and various little pockets of Indian territory within China. When India objected to this they simply said that they were merely following Kuomintang maps and it did not satisfy India. Later on, nature of the border dispute enlarged and the Government of China stated that they had not as yet undertaken a survey of their boundary nor consulted with the countries concerned and they would not make changed on their own[13]. Thus, for the first time they virtually repudiated the traditional alignment shown on Indian maps and implied that the boundary was an open issue which should be the subject of discussion. In response Nehru wrote a letter directly to Zhou expressing his surprise at Chinese attitude which was contrary to what he had been since 1949 and what he had repeatedly said in parliament.

Realistically speaking, the reassurances of China and the apparent relaxation in tension between the two did not, in substance, mean more than a mere temporary postponement of more vital issues whose seriousness came to be realised only afterwards. Minor border incidents and incursions took place before 1955 that might be considered as insignificant, they however, began to take a large amount of Indian territories in following years. In 1955 and 1956 the incident of border crossing happened and on several occasions Chinese troops were found on the Indian side of Shipki La. At about the same time major incursions began with full knowledge of the Chinese authorities where India delineated the limits of her territories, started levelling a caravan route across the inhibited plateau of Aksai Chin. From Sinkiang to Tibet, this road was meant to open Western Tibet to Chinese immigrants and to divert its trade from its traditional southward direction into Western China and the Soviet Union. It was completed in about two years and simultaneously Chinese patrols were also regularly visiting southern Demchok, a village in Kashmir near the Tibetan boundary; and a party of Chinese soldiers was seen in 1956 in the Nilang area in Uttar Pradesh. The Chinese Government also asserted their claims to Bara Hoti, two miles south of Tun Jun La.

In the circumstances Chou En- lai, the Chinese premier, visited India in December 1956 and assured that although China had never recognised the McMahon Line, his country felt, they should recognise it because it was an accomplished fact and because of their friendly relations with India. When Nehru suggested that the two sides should agree on some principles which bases the minor boundary disputes, the visiting guest only said that the question could be solved or should be settled early. This oral commitment and word strengthened Nehru's faith in premier's friendship. The period of patch up of differences appeared to have gone some way in consolidating their friendship which contained seeds of future trouble[14]. Further China alleged that "The American Chiang Kai-shek clique with fugitive reactionaries from Tibet" had for sometime been active in the Indian town of Kalimpong.

Divergence of Approach Deepened

From the start Indian and Chinese approaches to the territorial issue remained poles apart. While for Nehru the question of the territorial definition of India continued to be as an ex-colonial modern state and he failed to make it a priority goal of foreign policy, Mao regarded the territorial formation of the PRC with utmost seriousness and took hard decisions in this regard. Now the basic policy defects of India began to impart dividends and from 1958 divergence of approach to the territorial issue surfaced. Incidents occurred at Bara Hoti inspite of the renewal of the understanding as well as agreement not to send armed personnel to the area. In July 1958 the Government of India received information about the intrusion by Chinese troops into the Ladakh region of Kashmir and occupation by them of India's Khurnak Fort. About at the same time the news of Chinese troops crossing into the Lohit Division of NEFA and establishment of outposts at Lapthal and Sangch Malla along the Indo-Tibetan border came to which India dispatched protest notes. Height of the event was on 14 December 1958 when Nehru personally wrote to Chou En-lai rebutting the Chinese claims. India was shocked when in his reply the Chinese premier said that "the Sino-Indian boundary has never been formally delimited" and that the so-called "McMahon Line was a product of British policy of aggression against the Tibet region of China." Obviously by that time China's borders with its neighouring states in the Himalayan region except India, had been finally settled and its troops had been posted all along the Sino- Indian border. Complaints and counter-complaints were pushed in the background as Sino-Indian border conflict took a serious turn causing great anxiety.

However, fluctuating Chinese instance could easily be attached to the developments in Tibet. In general Nehru sought to work out a policy which would harmonise our seemingly conflicting objectives : to help the Tibetans while maintaining friendship with China and to ensure the security of India in a new context without casting off the anchor of non-alignment[15]. The background of Tibetan revolt of March 1959 was prepared by the Khampa who raised a voice against China in 1956. Initially its centre was east of Tibet province and this unrest now spread to Tibet itself. In this phase of downward slide in Sino-Indian relations even the decision of the Government of India to prevent armed Khampas from crossing the border and, in case of those who managed to cross over, to disarm them and send them back to Tibet did not help to stem the steady decline. Further the Chinese authorities charged that this revolt was engineered by the privileged class of the old social order. These elements were encouraged by foreign vested interest and imperialist.

The last event that destroyed Sino-Indian border understanding was the revolt of Tibet in the middle of March 1959. This sudden uprising in Lhasa, the capital of Tibet, led to the outbreak of hostilities between the Tibetans and the Chinese forces. A proclamation declaring independence of Tibet was issued by the Tibetan cabinet and the Seventeen Point Agreement, made between Tibet and China in 1951, was also declared null and void. As the situation worsened the Preparatory Committee for the Tibetan Autonomous Region set up by the Chinese was recognised with Pancham Lama as chairman. The revolt was put down by the people's Liberation Army of China with a heavy hand and it entrenched itself well across the borders of India. At the end of March 1959, the Indian Government granted asylum to Dalai Lama and admitted several thousand Tibetan refugees who accompanied them. The flight of Dalai Lama and his arrival in India placed the already brittle relations a heavy strain from which they never recovered.

Before and even after the outbreak of the Tibetan revolt India adopted cautious and correct approach, deliberately framed to please the Chinese. From January this year India was faced with the problem of numbers of Tibetan refugees is thing to cross over. Nehru, maintaining a correct position, ordered that no Tibetan should be permitted into India. Again when he received reports of fighting in Lhasa, refused to give any general commitment that refugees would be let in. He was quite clear about the future of Tibet and India's policy thereof. Nehru's meeting with Dalai Lama on 24 April 1959, made the latter known 'Let us face the facts. The whole world can not bring freedom to Tibet unless the whole fabric of the Chinese state is destroyed. Only a world war, an atomic war, could perhaps make that possible. In the same vein he was clear in regard to India's Tibet policy and said 'There was no question of India intervening in Tibet; the most that India could do in helping the Tibetans to have a square deal, was to assist a situation gradually to develop which would induce the Chinese Government to moderate their policy in Tibet. India's policy side approach was appreciated by the Chinese Government.

What vitiated the atmosphere was the other side of the coin. Particularly in case of political asylum to Dalai Lama India was guided by reasons more than one. Nehru's decision to grant asylum to Dalai Lama had the near-unanimous support of public opinion in India. This humanitarian act suited the guest as he was respected in India as a high priest of Buddhism [16]. There was also wide-spread sympathy for Tibet because of the 'cultural kinship'. Despite being affirmative in 1954 when Panikkar said about the asylum of the Government of India if Dalai Lama had ever sought, this time in 1959 China regarded the grant of asylum as an unfriendly act. It condemned India's attitudes and actions as inconsistent with the Panch Sheela and charged India 'expansionist' with holding the Dalai Lama 'under duress'. Later it was also charged India with encouraging the rebels and interfering in China's internal affairs [17]. In the meantime the Prime Ministers of the two countries met in April 1960 but failed to cut much ice. In fact the summit was the last real opportunity for arriving at a common approach to the border problem – weakened the prospect of a negotiated settlement. Even three meetings of the officials of the two countries held in Peking, New Delhi and Rangoon respectively in 1960 failed to find any solution rather they made perceptions even more obvious. Simultaneously relations between the two went on deteriorating and border incursions becoming more frequent they assumed more menancing dimension.

Earlier at the close of the year 1959 pressed by Chinese advances and strong public sentiment Nehru decided to pursue the 'Forward Policy' with a view to exercise effective control upto its borders. The sole purpose of this decision was to establish checkposts and despatch patrols, wherever possible, up to the boundary and to constitute a special board to complete the building of roads in the border areas within two years to make clear that any further Chinese advance was obvious aggression. This step of the Indian government was necessitated as the Chinese had been steadily moving southward into Ladakh and a parallel Indian position became essential. This might halt the flow of Chinese encroachment and help to create a climate where good sense would prevail and negotiations could begin [18]. By the end of 1961, about 50 posts were established by Indian forces all along the border. Meanwhile, the PRC improved its relations with Nepal, Ceylon and Pakistan.

The early months of 1962 saw a continued exchange of diplomatic notes with China protesting at the patrolling and the establishment of border posts by India. In March and April 1962 some posts were established by India on the Depsang plains and on post twelve miles north-east of Daulat Beg Oldi. These posts were intended to affirm Indian sovereignty over these border areas rather than to withstand Chinese attack but it was misinterpreted by China and the latter had resorted to aggressive tactics. Intense Chinese activity was reported in the western sector, especially in the Chip Chap, Chang Chenmo and Pangong regions, but many protests were lodged by India when there was confrontation or firing. Expressing readiness for talks, disappointed Nehru remarked on 3 October 1962 when B.M. Kaul, India's Chief of the General Staff, met him, 'India had tolerated Chinese incursions into her territory for far too long and a stage has come when she should take-or appear to take-a strong stand irrespective of consequences'.[19]

The climax of India- China border dispute came on September 8, 1962, when Chinese troops crossed the McMahon Line in NEFA in the eastern sector and occupied a good part of Indian territory. Pressed by political compulsions Nehru told the media on October 13, 1962 that his Government had asked the army to throw the Chinese out of our territory. Many people in the country including B.M.Kaul were surprised and acknowledged that this might have provoked the Chinese to launch a massive attack on October 20, 1962.[20] By October 25, Chinese were inside India about 16 miles south of McMahon Line. Further the Chinese began attack on a very large scale on November 15 in both NEFA and Ladakh sectors. The victorious Chinese reached a spot in Assam overlooking river Brahmaputra, plains of Assam and the Bay of Bengal in the eastern sector. Suddenly on November 21, 1962, the Chinese announced unilateral cease-fire. Timely help by Britain and the US perhaps compelled China to cease-fire and withdraw to the point chosen by them[21]. The Indian armies abided by the cease-fire and did not impede the Chinese withdrawal in the eastern sector, although this meant that the Chinese would remain in possession of about 2,500 square miles recently occupied in the western sector. While the Chinese asserted that they would withdraw to the 'line of actual control' as on 7 November 1959, they also let slip that, in fact, to do so would mean withdrawal from about 6,000 square miles of territory which they had occupied.

1962 enabled China to establish an international identity

ideologically and political distinct from that of the Soviet Union. Its military victory and its unilateral withdrawal enhanced its image and standing in the third world. It paved the way for China to play an independent role in world affairs. By contrast, for India, the year proved a trauma. The collapse of India-China amity effectively destroyed the structure of Nehru's foreign policy. It did more : it shook the foundation of his worldview. After 1962 the two concerns became most pressing for it. The one was territorial definition and consolidation which became the core problem in its relationship with all neighbours, especially China and Pakistan. The other was an active search for security vis-à-vis China. In the aftermath of the war Nehru, perhaps as his last brave act, attempted to moderate the mood of the Parliament and advised it not to shut the door to the possibility of future talks with China, and not to cast China as an 'enemy'. It, however, was a definite end to a more expectant past and a new beginning for India and China in almost every aspect of state life.

Today the map-marked McMahon line is the on- the-ground divide in the east except for China's occupation of the Thagla ridge and some area in the vicinity of Longju. The Sino-Indian boundary is still undemarcated and China has not foreclosed its claim that include nearly the whole of Arunachal Pradesh and some areas on the Indian side of Karakoram range in the north-west. China signalled its ascension to great power status in post-1962 period by becoming a ballistic missile-armed, thermo-nuclear power the border, however, remained peaceful with India effectively accepting China's occupation of Aksai Chin and China not contesting India's return to the NEFA following the war.

5.2 PERCEPTIONS BEHIND THE BORDER NEGOTIATIONS

Departure of the British from the subcontinent in 1947 deprived India of the necessary military strength that England had represented for so many years- a strength that was clearly indispensable for the implementation of viable defence system. In the post-Independence situation in India the new political leaders who were at the helm of affairs were unable to continue to follow a forward policy in the north. Poverty-stricken and problem-ridden India had, in their view, other priorities to judiciously use her unexploited resources. Furthermore, they had a different political goal, which was to contribute to the promotion of peace and welfare of mankind. In the meantime the regional security environment had also changed considerably from the time of the British. The new India had now to face an unfriendly and suspicious Pakistan. On her northern frontier soon after the termination of the Chinese civil war India had to reckon with the Chinese occupation of Tibet. It made border with China alive and unstable. The Indian political leaders had generally come to the conclusion that the border threat stemmed more from Pakistan than from China.

Thus, in Indian calculation Pakistan, not China, became the focal point of country's defence strategy. Though the possibility of attack on the subcontinent was only from the northwestern frontier region, they did not feel any need to extend their military strategy or expertise. At the juncture, Nehru's conviction that China would not take any strong action against India played a decisive role. On the basis of different intelligence and diplomatic reports, he allowed himself to be convinced that China's growing adverse relations with the two superpowers and her serious domestic economic situation would restrain her from taking any military action. He, however, did not lack political understanding of the potential problems and, in a communication to K.M. Panikkar, the Indian Ambassador in China, noted that whenever China had a strong central government, it had intended to expand across its frontiers. This historical tendency had now been reinforced by a vigorously pulsating and dynamic new China, both radical and militantly nationalistic.

Indian Perceptions

The defeat and humiliation of India on the battlefield in 1962 generated a new mood in the country- a mood of re-evaluating country's concept of national security. For the first time India's foreign policy was no longer allowed to remain the domain reserve of the political leaders and accusing fingers were pointed at those who were guilty of having neglected India's defence. China, since the establishment of Communist rule on October 1, 1949, was viewed by India as a threat to its security. Despite his faith in peace, friendship and cooperation in dealing with the nations of the world Jawaharlal Nehru was alert to the danger from China and in 1952 he instructed the Director of Indian Intelligence to regard China as an intelligence target along with Pakistan.[22] India and China- the two giants of Asia were also assigned to play a role in the region and viewed in this context India always thought of China as a potential foreign policy partner who shared a concern to moderate the effects of super power imperialism in world affairs.[23]

Despite apprehensions, Nehru could not believe that relations with China could or would deteriorate as they did in the late 1950s and the early 1960s. When it happened, his China policy failed to know the full extent of the change in Chinese motives and designs. Not after the outbreak of the war but even before in December 1958 it had become known in Delhi that the Chinese had established a number of posts in the Aksai Chin area of Ladakh, true to the intuitive approach to foreign affairs, Nehru said in the Indian Parliament, "The normal idea is that security is protected by armies. That is only partly true; it is equally true that security is protected by policies. A deliberate policy of friendship with other countries goes further in gaining security than almost anything else."[24] He called this attack a strange twist of history that had brought us face to face with something that we had not experienced in this way for over a hundred years or more. The Chinese aggression on our border during the last five years, bad as it was and indicative of an expansionist tendency, though it troubled us greatly, hardly led us to the conclusion that China would indulge in a massive invasion on India. Charging cynicism and duplicity on the Chinese side he drew the conclusion that Chinese interpretation of various lines changes with circumstances and that they accept the line which is more advantageous to them. Sometimes they accept part of a line and not the rest of it which is disadvantageous to them.

India, to Nehru's satisfaction, faced this challenge with 'new anger, new determination and new gratitude'- anger at Chinese perfidy, determination to accept no dishonorable settlement and gratitude to those countries which had rallied to her aid.[25] The reaction to Chinese behaviours was far from defeatist and led Nehru to speak of the war repeatedly as a blessing in disguise.[26] After independence, foreign policy became a responsibility of the national government under Jawaharlal Nehru. A variety of factors enabled him to play a unique role in this realm. His personal position was so dominant that, as one of his biographers remarks, he was "the philosopher, the architect, the engineer and the voice of his country's policy towards the outside world."[27] And lastly, his personal strength, acquired during the freedom movement, and greatly augmented after independence, established him as a world statesman par excellence, so that his opinion and authority could not be successfully challenged and undermined even by the events of 1962. But the conflict left a strong mark on it for a number of years in all the three spheres, domestic, regional and international. Nehru himself said that India had been living in an unreal world, and that "We are growing too soft and taking things granted," but he added "We are not going to give up basic principles because of our present difficulty."[28]

The conflict with China suddenly subjected foreign policy to what appeared at the time intolerable pressure. In the new situation there was not much scope for the stock in trade of Indian diplomacy- mediation, peace-keeping amelioration of tension with which she played in the past a dramatic role on the international scene. In preparing for a long phase of Chinese hostility, the domestic situation and the military requirements had to be placed in world context. India, experiencing a crisis of the spirit, had found herself, and this new mood should be utilised to achieve both industrial advance and military readiness.[29] Defence and developments were parts of the same process; and planning, socialism and non-alignment were all ways of preparing the nation to face renewed Chinese aggression. Real strength, as Nehru said on January 18, 1963, came not from the purchase of arms but from the building of an industrial base which could be converted, when the need arose, into a war machine, the development of power and transport, increased productivity in agriculture, improvement in public health and spread of technical education. Thus, in domestic dealings the war crisis reinforced the importance of the kind of socialism suited to India.[30] On the other exercise in favour of the search for a way to honorable negotiations with China remained in active consideration.

Nehru's successors- Lal Bahadur Shastri, Indira Gandhi and others who succeeded to the throne had not only reaffirmed their resolve to cling to old lines of policy, but had moved in measure albeit still tentatively towards negotiations with China. On assuming office Shastri had made it clear that if the intention of China was really to arrive at a settlement and if Peking would not put forward at the negotiating table claims to large areas of territory with threats to take them by force, then there could be negotiations between the two countries. He clearly viewed Chinese motives behind the attack and said in Parliament on 20 September 1965, "The basic objective of China is to claim for itself a position of dominance in Asia, which no self-respecting nation in Asia is prepared to recognise.[31] The annual report of the Ministry of External Affairs for the year 1964-65 also spelt out India's perception of Chinese motivations. It said, "India was the key to the "vast intermediate zone' of Asia, Africa and Latin America, China would like to see India reduced to the status of a secondary power in Asia and to destroy the policy of non-alignment which has earned for India so much respect and prestige in the Asian-African world."[32] After Shastri, Indira Gandhi became the Prime Minister of India who, in a statement, on February 16, 1966, reiterated that India was prepared to talk with China "should proper conditions arise."

However, apart from keeping the door opened for talks with China, post-Nehruvian strategy was also faced with a dangerous situation and

India finally resulted in the adoption of a dual method of upgrading the armed forces, and of seeking a military alliance with the Soviet Union. It gave a new direction and a broader definition to the concept of national security. Gradually successors of the throne gave the concept of national security a wider dimension and created a triple defence strategy–a strategy of upgrading India's armed forces, a strategy of seeking a military alliance and, finally, a strategy of greater institutionalization of the Indian system for the identification of national security objectives.[33] In her quest for national security, India has indeed come a long way since her independence. She has, through the years, acquired a military clout that no one in the region can challenge – probably not even China in the conventional sector.

Perceptions of China

In contrast of India, the people's Republic of China had a long history of a tacit but clear strategic military doctrine. Since the third century B.C. till 1911, the 'barbarians' from across the land frontiers remained the main threat to the Chinese empire. Whenever they threatened any part of the regime, armies were raised to repel them or to extend the empire in the process of subduing them.[34] For a brief period in pre-revolution phase China became weak and unstable because of warlordism and internal warfare between Nationalist and Communist forces. It was followed by the establishment of a strong central government in China which adopted a doctrine, combined with Soviet strategic thinking and the Communist party's experience in fighting Japan and the Guomindang armies for several decades. By 1949, the geopolitical situation had changed and the Soviet Union had become China's ally, while the United States of America which had been China's ally all along, had now become an enemy. Thus, the Chinese strategic military doctrine, in early fifties, identified US imperialism as the grand strategy to encircle China prior to invading it. Even India's forward policy in the border area was interpreted as part of US imperialist encirclement of China.

In formulating Chinese attitude towards India and the world at large Mao Zedong played a significant and decisive role. Mao's theoretical analyses of formidable power, especially those written in his early years, and his old leadership of the peasants in China have earned for him a unique place in world history. But basically he was an outstanding Chinese figure, rooted in indigenous tradition. A hard-headed nationalist, he was determined to regain for his country not only equality among the nations but a prime position in Asia. He combined throughout his life the roles of both a revolutionary and a nationalist and at the start, each strengthened the other. Under his leadership and inspiration China became an ambitious nation and a skilled practitioner of realpolitik[35] By the time India and China had awakened modern communication, broke down the physical barriers and brought them face to face in a period when they were going through an acute phase of nationalist stirrings and hyper-sensitive responses to foreign countries, because of their experience with imperialism and rather late emergence as nation-states, abrasive responses that rubbed off against each other too.

In the years following China's attack on India people felt a need to reassess the motives behind the aggression. It was a failure of diplomacy which is, in fact, meant management of international relations by means of negotiations; the method by which these relations are adjusted and managed by ambassadors and envoys; the business or art of the diplomat. Possible motives are important to be mentioned here not only because they are related to China's general policy in foreign affairs but because they will reveal the extent to which those motives have determined the nature of Sino-Indian relations. Motives behind the attack were closely related to the Chinese anxiety to keep the Sino-Indian border issue alive. It also explained the causes of the series of Chinese intrusions into the Indian territories during the 1960s. Even hardening of the Chinese attitude towards India in late fifties and early sixties was based on country's calculation of gain and loss. It is said to be a mixture of Chinese imperialism militant nationalism, and revolutionary zeal of militant communism[36]

Desire for attainment of great power status, as considered by many, was the prime motive behind the Chinese attack. For several years in the beginning India introduced Communist China to the world, especially to Asia. After some years they knew that China is able to make more rapid and greater progress than India, former's dependence on the latter for status became intolerable. As a first step China insisted on India accepting a subordinate status, renouncing non-alignment and generally moulding her foreign and domestic policies to suit China's view of herself and of the world. Viewed in this perspective if the creation and non-recognition of India's northern frontier was the expression of independence in world politics, the aggression of 1962 was intended to show that China had not only the desire but also the capacity to be a great power.[37] However, a scholar, Neville Maxwell, considering the effects of India's forward policy and its unilateral declaration of ceasefire argued that military action by China was decided on to bring India to the negotiating table and to show her that any attempt to achieve a settlement on her own terms, by moving into Chinese-held territory, was futile.[38] On the other the Chinese showed their reasonableness in having border settlements with Nepal, Pakistan and Burma.

While dealing with the People's Republic of China we can hardly overlook the strategic aspect of the issue. In fact, one other purpose of the Chinese military action was to hold on to the Aksaichin and the strategic highway which is so vital for controlling the difficult provinces of Tibet and Sinkiang. As the war was an expression of the politico-military strategy of China, Nehru, keeping it in view, said in November 1962, 'I don't see any real compromise. What they have in mind is different from our thinking. There is no bridge between us." But later on he also added 'India was not going to be one of the small fish which this huge crocodile in the pond of Asia was seeking to devour.[39] In the face of China's attitude that either one is for them or against' a self-respecting nation like India could hope for no lasting friendship with her.[40]

Ideological differences between China and the Soviet Union had also motivated the former to launch a massive attack on India. The Sino-Soviet rivalry at the time was centered in Asia and China regarded India as an ideological obstacle and sought a dominating position in Asia. In addition to this the Soviet influence of Asia has been much more than the Chinese influence. Obviously Chinese aggression was launched in the hope that the attack on India would compel the communist parties of Asian countries to come to the Chinese fold. It, however, realised a deeper objective, that was to find out what attitude would the Soviet Union take towards China after the aggression and it became clear that the Soviet Union could not be relied upon even in a conflict with a non-communist country. In international arena the behaviours of China was criticised widely and was based on the fact that it had forgotten the futility of war as a traditional means of the achievement of great power status. The Chinese behaviours in post-aggression period also testified that the attempt made on the part of China had been to build up her power and not bother about the settlement of the border question.

Perceptions Experienced and Analysed

In post-1962 period relations between India and China were put on rails with the establishment of ambassadorial level contact in April 1976. It could not be done earlier because Peking was engaged in a full-scale campaign against India whose chief purpose was to carry the conviction that India was no longer non-aligned but was firmly in the imperialist camp. In the meantime China shifted its position on Kashmir, moved closer to Pakistan and gradually became a major source of military and economic aid to Islamabad. Particularly in case of Nepal and Sri Lanka China adopted the policy of creating or encouraging dissensions between them and India. The border question was, in addition, made complicated with Pakistan giving China a direct access to the disputed territory of Kashmir. It was reported at the close of the sixties that Pakistan was building a road from Mor- Khun in Northern Kashmir to Khunjareb Pass on the Kashmir-Sinkiang territory. The entire alignment of the road ran in Indian territory under Pakistani occupation. The road was strategic one and would help extend the Chinese road network in the Tibet-Sinkiang area into Northern Kashmir. The Government of India viewed that 'it will give easier access to Chinese troops from areas under the illegal occupation of China in North-east Kashmir and from Tibet into the Gilgit area in Pakistan-occupied Kashmir which lies to the North of ceasefire line.[41]

China's strategic relations with Pakistan and construction of Karakoram highway on a disputed land with the help of the former had marred the prospect of border talks between the two. But in spite of these negative developments India, on her part, did not shift its policy towards China either on Tibet or on Taiwan. It also backed fully China's efforts for representation in the United Nations. By the time Indira Gandhi took the reign of administration in January 1980 a lot of change had been made in China's internal and external policies. Considering the proper perspective, she opted for a policy of establishing contact with the Chinese. As a major breakthrough she met Huo Guofeng, her Chinese counterpart, on the occasion of Tito's funeral in May 1980 and an agreement was announced when Huang Hua, the Foreign Minister of China, visited New Delhi in June 1981. With no major gain on the border side it could be counted as slow serpantine movement of adjustment and accommodation. They agreed that the officials of the two countries should take up the problems and seek settlement through periodic and on going discussions. Huang Hua mentioned that the three principles: historical background, existing realities and national sentiments of the two countries should constitute the framework for addressing the border problem. Among the positive developments, the most important was Indian Prime Minister's visit to Beijing in December 1988.

For India the central issue was border problem but with the visit of Rajiv Gandhi in December 1988 India changed the track and decided to push relations with Beijing ahead without waiting for a border settlement. Indian view received further impetus in May 1992 when R.Venkataraman, the President of India, visited China and emphasised the creation of conditions of tranquility on the border. During the visit they acknowledged in their statements that the border problem was a serious road block and needed redress through serious negotiations. Side by side several meetings of Joint Working Group (JWG) were concluded to strengthen the process of peace and tranquility on the border and both sides agreed to facilitate greater mutual confidence in their relations.[42]

The two countries moved in direction of getting peace and tranquility on the border and as a mark of success they agreed to keep the border dispute apart and develop friendly relations when P.V. Narasimha Rao, the Indian Prime Minister paid a visit to Beijing in 1993. Until the border dispute is resolved, Rao and Li peng agreed to maintain peace on Line of Actual Control (LAC). They also greed to undertake specific confidence building measures like informing each other on their military exercises, but unfortunately no consensus was arrived at the reduction of troops on the border. It seems that the original impetus given and policy orientations initiated by Deng Xiaoping, Rajiv Gandhi, Li Peng and Narasimha Rao has lost momentum.

As a result of the understanding reached between the two during Narasimha Rao's visit to Beijing "to skirt border dispute" and develop friendship Jiang Zemin, President of China and Head of the Chinese Communist Party paid an official visit to India in November 1996 and among others, signed an Agreement on Confidence Building Measures. The signed agreement provided that the two countries would reduce their military strength along the Line of Actual Control and that no military activities would be undertaken by either country that affected the other country. The preamble of the agreement laid stress on the relevance of Panchsheel and stated that it was aimed at a fair, reasonable and mutually acceptable settlement of the complicated border issue. However, Atal Bihari Vajpayye, who was the leader of opposition at the time, called for cautious approach towards China. He wondered why President Jiang Zemin was maintaining a mysterious silence on the border issue.[43]

Differences between India and China on many other issues have been narrowed down but by no means eliminated. Some of the operational confidence building measures have been put in place since 1993, but the CBM's agreed upon in this time and later in 1996 can be fully implemented only after the problems affecting the Line of Actual Control are settled. The fact of the matter is that the Chinese seemed reluctant to take even the interim step necessary to move towards a solution of the boundary question, namely, to delineate the Line of Actual Control in the seven segments where there is a difference of opinion between China and India.[44] China has no intention to resolve the boundary question. It remains opposed to India's nuclear weaponisation and missile programme. On the other Chinese defence cooperation, particularly with Pakistan, remains a major security concerns of India to which there has been no satisfactory Chinese response.

Even today, China remains concerned about India's policies on Tibet. This concern is heightened by the incremental support that the Dalai Lama is getting from the international community. The China visit of Atal Bihari Vajpayee, the Indian Prime Minister, in July 2003 was a classic exempler of Indian diplomacy in practice. Despite elusive statements and concessions from the Indian side, the Chinese spoke in measured terms on Sino-Indian relations and gave no ground. In the period since the negotiations began, China has emerged as a global economic and political force and strengthened its leverage vis-à-vis India, both directly and through its mass transfers of weapons of mass destruction to Pakistan.[45]

As viewed by the Indian establishment China desires a normal relationship with India, they seem insistent about having this on their own terms. Another Indian view is that Chinese relations with Pakistan and Myanmar could be an exercise for creating a Chinese cordon sanitaire around India. In an atmosphere of mistrust, net result would not be easy to come by. Prolonged and hard-nosed discussions would follow. But as they are neighbours, big countries, vast landmasses, ancient civilizations, modern, independent, nationalist countries they have to live together and learn to make adjustments and accommodations.

5.3 INDIA AND CHINA WITH PANCHSHEEL IN ASIA

The famous five principles of Panchsheel or peaceful co-existence-mutual respect for each other's territorial integrity and sovereignty, non-aggression, non intervention in other's domestic affairs, mutual benefit and equality and peaceful co-existence were first incorporated in the Sino-Indian Agreement on Tibet in April 1954. In succeeding years it occupied the form of a norm in the world community. It became a general principle of right conduct to which a community expects all its members to conform which shape the very structure of international relations. Alongside the five principles various other codes of a similar nature can be found in the constituent charters of such bodies as the United Nations, the Non-aligned Movement, the Organization of African Unity and so on.[46] But for India and China these principles remained more than a declaration. China elevated the five principles as the cornerstone of its foreign relations with all states. It continues to stress peaceful co-existence in current pronouncements of foreign policy. India too has made strenuous and successful attempts to have these principles accepted by the non-aligned movement and incorporated as 'basic principles of international law' through the Declaration on Friendly Relations passed by the UN General Assembly.

When the principles of Panchsheel were recognised by India and China it was the honeymoon phase of Sino- Indian relations. At this point they espoused common principles on international security and international relations. Coming out of their own anti-colonial struggles, both countries adopted different systems of statehood, but they shared a common antipathy to western global hegemony. The change in the geopolitical situation today has been accompanied by the rapid rise of India, and especially China, as the economic powerhouse of the future. In the circumstances China's biggest worry is American unilateralism and the avowal of George Bush to convert the world into an American dream of democracy. Similarly, India, with its adherence to Nehruvian non-alignment also opposes American unilateralism.[47] Prevailing situation needs friendly ties with India and China. It is this common goal that allows both countries once again to espouse common security principles, based on the old ideals mooted in Panchsheel.

The origin of the essence of this peace ideology can be traced back to the fourth- fifth century AD's work of Buddhaghosha, Visuddhimaggo which mentions the five principles that a Buddhist follower has to follow. Before its enshrinment in the India-China Treaty on Tibet, these five principles were first proposed by Dr. Surkarno as Pantja Sila in Indonesia, a Buddhist country, on 1st June 1945. In Indonesian context these were nationalism, humanism, freedom, social justice and faith in God.[48] There is no doubt in the fact that this ancient principle belongs to the Indian tradition, it was considered by the signatory of the treaty differently. While Chinese emphasised the Asianness of the doctrine of Panchsheel by using it in their dealings with Afro-Asian states and rarely in their dealings with the managers of the world system, that is western states, India laid stress on its global and modern relevance by relating it to the UN Charter.[49] However they did not hesitate in calling Panchsheel an Asian value. The Chinese, in particular, gave the concept a cultural dimension.

Super power Rivalry in Asia

In the post-World War II period the world was divided into military and ideological blocs, each trying to bring within its orbit as many countries as it could. The United States of America abandoned her traditional policy of isolationism and established firm partnership with the peoples of Europe, Asia, Africa and Middle East. Soon it established bilateral and multi-lateral security arrangements with more than forty countries. On the other was the Soviet Union, its arch rival, whose leaders openly affirmed their faith in the doctrines of Marx and Lenin and exhorted the people to make preparation for the inevitable conflict with the capitalist countries. It pushed Bulgaria, Hungary, Rumania, Yugoslavia, Albania, Czechoslovakia, Poland and East Germany into the Communist orbit. Going a step further the USSR also took the first major step in consolidating the solidarity of the communist states by setting up the Communist Information Bureau (Cominform) of the major European communist parties.[50] The relations between the two superpowers were marked by an under current of mutual distrust and jealousy. Perkins and Duesen called these differences as inevitable because "their objectives were widely different, on one side was the idea of free society, on the other an iron despotism; on one side was an economic system which put the major emphasis on the ingenuity and enterprise of the individual, on the other an economic system the state controlled virtually the whole economy; on one side was the hope of tranquality and orderly development, on the other the hope of revolution and of the coming of a new order, on one side was a reluctance to use force, on the other a disposition to invoke force whenever and wherever it could be done without undue risk. In such a situation neither side could do justice to the motives of the other"[51]

In one way or the other hegemony was considered to be the maximum goal of superpowers in Asia. The perception of the two powers and their interests in Asia, in the developing countries, and in the world in general, has for most of the time been fairly divergent. At the minimum, the basic national interest of the United States, as in case of any nation, has been its national security- the protection of territorial integrity and political independence. In case of the US, the changing milieu of international environment have pushed the security principle from the national boundaries to the whole Western Hemisphere and transcending finally to the preservation of power equilibrium in Europe and Asia. Later the concept has widened to the effect of equating any communist advance in world politics- territorial, political, economic, cultural or military, with threat to American security. This led the United States to speak and act in the name of thc so-called free world or free nations not excluding feudal-monarchial, unpopular, authoritarian and corrupt regimes of the time. Western leaders and Americans, in particular, consistently argued that their actions were in support of nationalism, the freedom of choice of new governments, and orderly processes of political change.[52] The United States' government also made it clear that it would not permit changes to take place which compromised its security or that of its allies.

In the background of US relations with the countries of Asia, the Soviets embarked on the course of competitive co-existence in the hope that it would lead to the ultimate triumph of proletarian internationalism. In general the main objectives of the foreign policy were- strengthening and developing the world socialist system, the unity and cohesion of the socialist countries and their friendship and fraternity; giving an all -out support to the national liberation movements and fostering solidarity and with the independent Asian, African and Latin American countries, and promoting peaceful co-existence.[53] The range of goals of Soviet policy in Asia was meant to have maximum and minimum objectives. At the high end of the scale must inevitably be the desire to exert hegemony over Asia- either as an expression of Russian power or of communist ideology. Hegemony can be thought of in various ways; a total communisation of Asia along the Soviet model is the extreme case and is unlikely to achieve. But attainable would be a situation in which the other Asian states have no strong and reliable external support and none of them would be strong enough to resist Soviet domination.

The USSR under Stalin was concerned with Asia- it had to adjust to the existence of a Communist regime in China and had to take a position vis-à-vis the rash of Communist revolts in the South East Asia at the end of the 1940's. But the efforts applied in Asia was extremely small. The Soviets had only limited resources and these were overwhelmingly committed to Europe where the Soviets perceived the greater danger and more hopeful prospects. By the beginning of the Khrushchev era the basis of a change in Soviet Policy towards Asia was evident because the situation in Europe had stabilised and China refused to become another Soviet satellite like Mongolia. In fact Moscow approached Asia not as a target for Communist revolutionary activity but as a collection of nations with whom it was possible and often profitable to deal on a state-to-state basis. Since many Asian countries were glad to reciprocate the relationship, the USSR became an acceptable player in the Asian balance-of-power game. However, the importance of both the nations was never undermined and even in that period there was much talk in Washington as well as in Moscow that the future of Asia would be determined by the competition between India and China.

Position of India and China in Asia

So far as the position of Asia in world politics is concerned in post-1945 phase it has been swept by political and social revolutions. It has released the forces which have subsequently changed the face of Asia and fundamentally altered its role in world affairs. The colonial and traditional regimes that existed earlier have been replaced by a wide variety of new states. Powerful new forces of the time-nationalism, Communism, the drive for self-determination and demands for social change have shaped the development of the region. New elite groups and political leaders had emerged in every Asian state, and they all were dedicated to political, economic, and social change. Apart from the leaders in Communist China and its small Communist neighbours, a majority of the new leaders in Asia professed belief in some form of parliamentary democracy comparable to that in the West.[54] In the early 1950's despite conflicting interests of many sorts to divide the states in the region, a powerful slogan of "Asian Solidarity" came which found its expression in Sino-Indian Treaty on Tibet in 1954. Later on several developments had marred its prospect in this part of the world.

The signatory nations of the principles of Panchsheel- India and China are the two giants of Asia. In population, human resources, and potential they far outstrip any other country of Asia or even many of them combined. In spite of their differing social and political systems, both had been exploited by western imperialism and colonialism. Both had ancient cultures that had survived many internal upheavals and external onslaughts. And lastly they both had just emerged from foreign domination as proud, nationalist entities. Additionally China also enjoyed a certain natural advantage in geopolitics. It virtually looked down upon the hills and plains of India from its higher mountain tops in Tibet and Sinkiang.[55] Even before the establishment of Communist rule in China, Jawaharlal Nehru strongly advocated friendship with the country whose culture he admired. He sincerely believed that if India and China stood together they would be a pillar of strength and add a voice of reason and maturity to international affairs.

In consolidating Asia and preserving its unity India was far a head of China. Nehru looked at the Indian situation in the wider perspective of western domination over the whole of Asia. The latent feeling of "Asianism" in Nehru found expression in a new form, in a sort of pride in Asia, in the need for finding Asian solutions to Asian problems in Asia and not in the courts and chancelleries of Europe.[56] India took initiative in organizing two conferences at New Delhi in 1947 and 1949 respectively. Inaugurating the Asian Relations Conference in New Delhi on 23 March 1947 Nehru said "In this crisis in the world history, Asia will necessarily play a vital role. The countries of Asia can no longer be used as pawns by others, they are bound to have their own politics in world affairs. In this atomic age, Asia will have to function effectively in the maintenance of peace. Indeed, there can be no peace unless Asia plays her part. Emergence of Asia in the world affairs will be a powerful influence on world peace.'[57] As a true well wisher of Asia Nehru convened a Conference on Indonesia in January 1949 when the Dutch launched a second invasion on that country.[58] India had been taking special interest in the liberation struggle of the Indonesian people and it was one of those countries which raised the issue of Dutch aggression against Indonesia in the United Nations. India regarded herself as the moral conscience keeper of Asia. India's voice echoed the feelings of the other parts of Asia, Africa and the world. As more and more countries became independent, India tried to widen this area of "Peace and Protest" in Asia.

The year 1949 witnessed the end of Chinese civil war and establishment of a Communist rule. In the affairs of China India kept herself non-partisan and Nehru, in his note to the then Ambassador of China suggested 'The situation is difficult because of the civil war that is going on. While maintaining close and friendly relations with Chiang Kai-shek's Government, should not allow himself to become a partisan in the civil conflict.[59] However, turning China red and the dramatic events were hardly a favourable sign for India because they had not only skewed the Asian balance of power in favour of the apparently monolithic Communist world, but had, with the Chinese occupation of Tibet, brought a dynamic and an unfriendly Communist state to the very doors of India. The situation became more delicate as a formal alliance with the West was excluded in view of the forthright decision of the government to make non-alignment its article of faith. An alliance with the Communist world was equally impossible due to the profound ideological and political gap that separated those who were in power in India from those who were the decision-makers in Communist countries.[60] In response to the need there arose a broad consensus among the Indian decision-makers to deploy different efforts to face the new situation.

To meet the new threat India adopted a two-pronged policy -on the one hand it decided to bring about a modest improvement in country's defences and advocated a way of befriending the Chinese, on the other. In pursuance of its first strategy new treaties were negotiated with the Himalayan states of Bhutan (1949), Sikkim (1950) and Nepal (1951). Discreet steps were taken to improve communications throughout the mountainous tribal areas, to increase the number of check-posts in the middle sector, and to extend the rudiments of effective administration in the North-East Frontier Agency right up to the McMahon line.[61] Most of these steps were primarily diplomatic, administrative and police and aimed to bring about an improvement in India's defence system.

The above defence- related steps proved unable in satisfying the minds of Indian people at large and there appeared a general consensus among the decision-makers that political rapprochement with the Communist world was really the only rational substitute for any military confrontation. It was in this background that a diplomatic offensive was launched to seek some normalisation with the Communist countries. China, being geographically and spiritually nearer to India became the first objective of Indian diplomacy. Nehru cherished hopes of making friendship with China. His faith in a resurgent Asia, free from the domination of Europe and America was strong. He demanded the admission of Peking into the United Nations, insisted on the return of Formosa to the People's Republic, and declined to accept the invitation of the United States to go to San Francisco to sign the Japanese Peace treaty only because the China had refused to accept the American draft treaty. Very soon the single minded policy began to pay off and it became increasingly evident that Peking was slowly abandoning its belligerent line. But India's refusal to sign the Japanese peace treaty was welcomed by the Chinese press editorially which expressed the view that such an action proved 'that the age was past when imperialist governments can do whatever they please.'[62] Peking also appreciated India's determination to adopt an independent line on many controversial issues concerning China in international affairs.

Modern people's Republic of China emerged as a result of the civil war between Ideologist as well as the nationalist forces of the country. In the period of internal clash to rule over China the nationalist forces were supported by the United States of America, a group which stood opposite to the Communist party. Several fact-finding missions and experts were sent to China by the US, who, despite admitted corrupt practices in the Chinese National Government of Kuomintang pleaded in favour of supporting them politically, morally and financially. They suggested.'it is highly preferable that the United States have a free, though immoral Government in China than to have a hostile Government- no matter how pure and moral- dominated by Communist influences.' The Nationalists gained a good deal of military successes practically till the end of the first half of 1948, but by spring 1949 the Communists strengthened their rural mass base and were in full control of North China. Mao Tse-tung, the supreme leader of the Communist party of China appeared confident, of establishing the people's Republic. He declared after the Communists convened the people's political Consultative Conference in September 1949, 'our nation will never again be an insulted nation. We have stood up.'[63] On 1, October 1949, 'People's Government started its affairs and Chiang Kai-shek took his Government to the island of Formosa (Taiwan) to survive as the so- called legitimate government of China under the American patronage and protection.

To the surprise of none the new regime of China was aimed to spread Maoist radicalism in the non-communist countries and it necessitated apposition to the West and the US in particular. As the new dispensation owed some differences on several issues with the USSR, it required co-existence with numerous middle powers on the basis of expediency. Chinese aid was given principally to Peking - oriented parties which were expected to remain faithful to Maoist principles of strategy and accept Peking's guidance.[64] According to the steps already decided the advanced capitalist states, especially the US, were alleged to express their class character by pursuing aggressive policies against China and the Asian Communist movements. Peking was happy to counter US and its interventionist activities and by increasing China's own armed strength to make it a more significant deterrent. On the other with a view to cultivate intimate relations with the neutral countries of Asia, Africa and Latin America Peking signed treaties of mutual non-aggression or friendship with Burma, Nepal, Afghanistan, Guinea, Combodia, Indonesia etc. and settled outstanding differences with them through diplomatic channels. As a supplement China also strengthened its cultural relations with a large number of foreign countries and used economic weapon to further its interests.

Basically Chinese leaders believed in Marxian –Leninist ideology and stood for proletarian internationalism. For the attainment of this objective they thought it desirable to establish intimate relations with other Communist powers, especially the Soviet Union. In this period China tried to maintain her revolutionary fervour in internal and external affairs and propounded the new doctrines of 'the inevitability of war' and 'permanent revolution'. The importance of the Sino–Soviet cooperation was acknowledged by different Chinese leaders who asserted that the unity of the two could play an extremely important role in the unity of peoples of the world.[65] Thus, when the Chinese Communist leaders began to build up a Socialist system in early years, they were evidently agreed that the Soviet Union should be accepted as a model.

Death of Stalin in 1953 witnessed some ideological dilution in Soviet policy which included "revisionism" and "peaceful Co-existence". Chinese viewed these concepts as basic change in Soviet policy. They considered it grave and fundamental danger and total hostility towards the USSR was viewed as the only correct response. As a result in sphere of ideology Peking decided to work as effectively as possible against the Soviet diplomacy in the developing areas which allegedly seek to advance Moscow's great power aims at the expense of the national Communist movements. Chinese associated the struggle against revisionism as their duty in order to establish friendship and cooperation with other Socialist states that evidenced the intensity of Chinese hostility towards the USSR.

"Peaceful Co-existence" as Chinese consider, is a line of diplomacy that facilitates expedient compromises and settlements with the imperialists and their allies. The diplomacy itself carries formal commitment to certain principles which concern the regime's dealings with other governments and there is no justification of another peaceful co-existence if the theme of diplomacy is taken into account. Thus in the post-1953 period Chinese leaders were evidently unwilling to recognise that Stalin's ideological authority had passed to the USSR's unstable collective leadership.They disapproved Khrushchev's liberalisation in the USSR and his new foreign policy which stressed co-existence with the West and the promotion of Communism in the Third World by peaceful methods. In spite of public respect for Moscow's leadership China's government accelerated extraordinary new programme of Socialist economic development, apparently in the hope of demonstrating that the regime had a superior dynamism with a view to give great inspiration to Communist movements in Asia and elsewhere.

Wide Reactions

India's thrust for Asia, its refusal to be a part of any post- war alliance and China's stiff attitude towards the USA along with ideological differences with USSR culminated in the signing of a treaty between the two on Tibet in April 1954. It was the high time for Asian solidarity that symbolised in the five principles of Panchsheel. These principles were included in the preamble of the treaty under which Tibet was referred as the Tibetan Region of China and India was permitted certain reciprocal facilities of trade and pilgrimage in relation to Tibet. Further China tried to befriend the nonaligned and the developing countries and signed the Bandung Declaration of the Afro-Asian Heads of Government held in April 1955. The Conference provided a real golden diplomatic opportunity to the People's Republic of China to carve out a major diplomatic entry for itself in the region along with several other regions of Asia.

Signing of the treaty by the two Asian giants-India and China on the basis of five principles was not liked by the USA while the USSR was less than happy. In reference to country's hostility with PRC and mistrust of nonaligned India, the US had stiffened her opposition to Communist China's entry into the UN and created difficulties for India by arming Pakistan. The USSR welcomed it hoping that it would hasten the entry of India into the socialist camp but at the same time also wondered why India was getting closer to China than to them. Most Asian countries including the nations of South East –Vietnam, Cambodia, Laos and Indonesia heartily welcomed it except Pakistan who was jealous of India and closely aligned with the USA and the West. The Non-aligned world, in general, became ease that the two Asian nations were trying to solve their mutual problems peacefully and bilaterally without third-party intervention.[66]

India was overwhelmed with joy and Nehru tried his best to develop a modus Vivendi through this treaty with China. He believed that peace in Asia could not be maintained or would not endure without India and China having an understanding about each other's policies and cooperation. Hope in India was natural that the treaty would create and enlarge the area of peace in Asia as a whole and especially in South and South-East Asia. Beyond doubt the treaty was not an arrangement to divide Asia into segments of spheres of influence, but it was an instrument to solve the problems of Asia in Asia through Asians. However, interpretation of the treaty was different from China's points of view. For Peking, it was an undoubted gain in as much as it gave her greater respect and credibility in Asia, Africa and the Third World. It did not consider that the treaty solved all the problems pending between her and India. In fact Nehru and his advisor had overlooked small but important proviso in the Tibet Trade discussions, that it did not cover "pending, unresolved issues between the two countries," and the Sino- Indian border was one such issue. One error led to another followed by a disaster in 1962.

Most of us consider today after 50 years of Panchsheel that these principles need some rethinking in context of developments and globalisation. Politically too, the world at large revolves round the United States. A close look at recent foreign policy pronouncements emanating from both countries highlight three issues which China and India share a common interest. These are opposing US unilateralism, support for multilateral organizations and diversification of trade. Things can change for the better if countries of the region stand together and do not allow the powers of the world to dominate them. Strength lies in unity and cooperation and not in becoming pawns on the chess board of big powers.

References

1. Sarvepalli Gopal, Jawaharlal Nehru : A Biography 1956-1964, Vol. III (Oxford University Press, Delhi, 1984), pp. 303-4.
2. Verghese Koithara, Society, State and Security – The Indian Experience (Sage Publications, New Delhi, 1999), p. 68
3. V.N. Khanna, Foreign Policy of India (Vikas Publishing House, New Delhi, 2004), p. 113.
4. K.P.S. Menon, Many Worlds Revisited – An Autobiography (Bharatiya Vidya Bhavan, Bombay,1981), pp. 139-42.
5. IBID., p. 270.
6. Jawaharlal Nehru's Speeches 1949-1953, Vol. II (Publication Division, New Delhi, 1954), p. 226.
7. Mira Sinha Bhattacharjea, '1962 Revisited', in G.P. Deshpanda and Alka Acharya, eds., 50 Years of India China -Crossing a Bridge of Dreams (Tulika, New Delhi, 2001), pp. 430-32.
8. Jawaharlal Nehru's Speeches, 1949-1953, pp. 254-55.
9. Rajkumar Singh, India's Foreign Policy: The First Study in Continuity and Change (Samiksha Prakashan, New Delhi, 2001), p. 103.
10. For the text of the letter see Indian Constitutional Documents: Munshi Papers, Vol. 1 (Bombay, 1967), p.178.
11. Nancy Jetley, India- China Relations, 1947-1979 : A Study of Parliament's Role in the Making of Foreign Policy (Radiant, New Delhi, 1979), p.19.
12. Mira Sinha Bhattacharjea, op.cit., p.435.
13. Memorandum of the Foreign Office of China, November 3, 1959 as quoted in Sarvepalli Gopal, p.83.

14. Mahendra Kumar, Theoretical Aspects of International Politics (Educational, Agra, 1976), pp. 294-95.
15. The Economist (London), April 4, 1959.
16. M. Brecher, India and World Politics (London, 1968), p. 145.
17. People's Daily (Peking), April 24, 1959.
18. A.S. Whiting, The Chinese Calculus of Deterrence (Ann Arbor, 1975), pp.10-11.
19. B.M. Kaul, The Untold Story (Delhi, 1967), p. 368.
20. Ibid., p. 387.
21. V.P. Dutt, India's Foreign Policy (Vikas, New Delhi, 1987), p. 279.
22. B.N. Mullik, The Chinese Betrayal (Allied, New Delhi, 1971), p.84.
23. Jawaharlal Nehru, Indian Foreign Policy : Select Speeches, September 1946-April 1961 (Government of India, New Delhi, 1961), p.395.
24. Ibid., p.79.
25. Sarvepalli Gopal, op.cit., p. 239.
26. The Hindu (Madras), April 27, 1963.
27. Michael Brecher, Nehru : A Political Biography (London,1959), p.564.
28. Jawaharlal Nehru's speeches, 1957-1963, Vol.IV (Publication Division, New Delhi, 1964), p.230.
29. Loksabha Debates, February 27, 1963, Third Series, Vol.13, cols. 1307-42.
30. The Hindu, January 20, 1963.
31. Asian Recorder, October 1965 (New Delhi, 1965), p. 6715.
32. Annual Report, 1964-65, Ministry of External Affairs (New Delhi,1965), p.28.
33. Harish Kapur, India's Foreign Policy, 1947-92 Shadows and Substance (Sage Publications, New Delhi,1994), pp. 27-34.
34. Giri Deshingkar, 'Strategic Doctrines', in G.P. Deshpanda and Alka Acharya, eds., op.cit., pp. 333-34.
35. Sarvepalli Gopal, op.cit., pp. 238-39.
36. Mahendra Kumar, op.cit., pp. 301-2.
37. Ibid., p. 303.
38. Maxwell, N., India's China War (Cape, London, 1970), p. 348.
39. The Hindu, January 4, 1963.
40. The National Herald (Lucknow), January 18 and 31, 1963.
41. Foreign Affairs Record, July 1969 (Government of India, New Delhi, 1969), p.142.

42. The Indian Express (New Delhi), February 2, 1992.
43. The Times of India (New Delhi), December 3, 1996.
44. J.N. Dixit, 'Beijing on Our Mind', The Hindustan Times (New Delhi), August 3, 2000.
45. Brahma Chellaney, 'Forever Shanghaied', Ibid., July 29, 2004.
46. Raymond Cohen, International politics, the Rules of the Game (Longman, Newyork, 1981), p.93.
47. The Hindustan Times (Patna), January 28, 2005.
48. G.H. Jansen, Afro-Asia and Non-Alignment, (Faber and Faber, London, 1966), p.127.
49. G.P. Deshpande, 'Verbalities and Realities of Foreign Policy' in G.P. Deshpande, Alka Acharya, op.cit., p.387.
50. Deva Narayan Mallik, Postwar International Politics- A Ouadripartite Survey (Veena Mandir, Muzaffarpur, 1973), p.183.
51. Dexter Perkins and Glyndon G.Van Deusen, The United States of America – A History, Vol.II, pp.666-67, as cited in H.K.Chhabra, Foreign Policies of Major Countries, Vol.III (Surjeet, Delhi, 1980), p.256.
52. Wayne Wilcox, Leo E.Rose and Gavin Boyd eds; Asia and the International System (Cambridge, Massachusetts, 1972), p.256.
53. V.M. Khostov and L.N. Kutakov, 'The Foreign policy of the Union of Soviet Socialist Republic' in Black and Thompson eds., Foreign policies in a World of Change (Newyork, 1963), pp. 256-77.
54. Johna, Garraty and Peter Gay eds., The Columbia History of the World (Harper and Row, Newyork, 1972), pp.1117-34.
55. V.P. Dutt, India's Foreign policy (Vani Educational, New Delhi, 1984), p.277.
56. T.N. Kaul, India, China and Indo China (Allied, New Delhi, 1980), p.8.
57. Jawaharlal Nehru, op.cit., p. 251.
58. Ibid., p.253.
59. K.P.S. Menon, op.cit., p.230.
60. Harish Kapur, 'India and the Soviet Union', in K.P. Misra ed., Foreign Policy of India- A Book of Readings (Thomson press, New Delhi, 1977), pp. 245-46.
61. Lorne J. Kavic, India's Quest for Security : Defence Policies; 1947-65 (Berkeley,1967), pp.46-61.
62. People's Daily (Peking), September 16, 1951.
63. Clande A. Buss, Asia in the Modern World (Macmillan, Newyork, 1964), pp. 538-45.

64. Lin Piao, Long Live the Victory of People's War (Foreign Languages Press, Peking, 1967), p. 37.
65. H.K. Chhabra, op.cit., pp. 100-3.
66. T.N. Kaul, op.cit., pp.12-14.

6

INDIA, SRI LANKA AND THE LTTE

6.1 GENESIS OF POWER DEVOLUTION IN SRI LANKA

In post-Prabhakaran phase, once again, it is absolutely essential to re-commence the peace process through devolution of political powers in Sri Lanka. Till date the government's actions have divided the people and not united them. From the first Bandaranaike-Chelvanayakam Pact of 1957 to the present proposal of Mahinda Rajapaksa the yester governments have denied the basic characteristics. The internal ethnic war does not develop in vacuum or automatically, but stems from deep rooted socio-economic and political grievances that cannot be redressed by normal political means. Even in Sri Lankan context all the people whether they be Sinhala, Tamil, Muslim or Burgher - all accept that the territorial integrity of the country must be safeguarded. Let us commit ourselves to a negotiated political solution acceptable to all communities based on democracy.

Social Composition

Most of the countries in South Asia are multicultural and multi-national. These countries are composed of plural societies, communities or cultures. They have their independent cultural traits and world views and they need careful management, especially because that leads to inevitable competition and often conflict among these disparate groups. As Sri Lanka is a mosaic of cultural, religious, ethnic and linguistic diversities, the heterogeneous nature of the island is responsible for generating a plethora of internal and external threats to the nation. It is suffering from the problem of ethnicity and struggling to establish peace and social stability since independence. The communal and ethnic conflicts, the separatist tendencies, inter-state terrorism and the practice of militarization are the prolong challenges to the island.[1] If Sri Lanka had been provided with the federal constitution at the time of independence the Sinhalese and the Tamil leaders might have been able politically to bargain with each other from their political power bases at the centre and the region and the prolonged ethnic conflicts could have been prevented.[2] In addition, Sri Lanka's ethnic conflict has attracted inter-state concern partly because of the socio-cultural interaction between the Tamils of Sri Lanka and Tamils across the Palk Strait while the cross-state links of the immigrant Indian Tamils have figured even more positively in Indian concerns. This had enhanced creating the singularly complex situation of a majority community, the Sinhalese, developing a minority psyche which aggravated the Sri Lankan ethnic strife.[3] However, the roots of the conflict in Sri Lanka has its roots in colonial period and earlier as well.

Despite the small size, the island of Sri Lanka is marked by a relatively wide diversity with pluralism, which accommodates diversity and regards diversity as inevitable. The Sri Lankan society is composed of the mutually exclusive Sinhalese, Ceylon Tamils, Moors, Malays, Burgher and Eurasians, Europeans, Afghans and Baluchis and Veddas. Among them the principal ethnic community in Sri Lanka is the Sinhalese who constitute about 74 per cent of the population. The second largest ethnic group, the Tamils, constitute about 18 per cent. Another important ethnic group is that of Moors or Muslims who make up some 7.4 per cent of the total population while other small minorities like Malays and Burghers constitute some 0.4 per cent. The caste system of Sri Lanka has also developed its own characteristics and shares an occupational role with its Indian prototype but it is based on hereditary roles and functions rather than on principles of purity and impurity. Its political life has been closely bound up with these communal and other traditional social differentiations. These traditional groupings formed the basis of politically most significant loyalties, interests and demands.[4] Hence today Sri Lanka has to recognise that its patriotic identity of Sri Lankan must be built upon a confederative principle that recognises the existence of several communities as well as three nations within the entity Lanka (Ceylon). The three nations are the Sinhalese, Tamils and Muslims. The communities are the Malays, Burghers, indigenous Vaddas, Colombo Chetties, Borahs, Sindhis, Parsees and Memons.[5] In other words in many individuals their Sri Lankanness has been generated through their ethnic identity as Burgher, Malay, Sinhalese, Tamil, and so on.

In the social set-up of Sri Lanka it is commonly held that the Sinhalese originally came from north India and settled in the island about 500 years before the Christian era.[6] They used a Sanskrit - derived language and most of them are Theravada Buddhists, but with the influence of the Hindu caste system also readily apparent.[7] Most of the Sinhalese practice a variant of Buddhism which had received continuous support from the rulers since it was introduced on the island in the 3rd century BC. Caste in Sinhalese society is the result of the impact of Brahminical Hinduism on a Buddhistic social structure wedded more to egalitarian concepts of birth and status. Politically too, the relevance of caste is significant and even at the time of making the first constitution of independent Sri Lanka several commissions and draft schemes advocated provisions on caste-basis.[8] From a geographical standpoint, the Sinhalese are categorised as Low-country and Up-country or Kandyan Sinhalese. The Low-country Sinhalese are mostly concentrated in the west and the south of the island and have a experience of 400 years of European rule. Unlike them the Kandyan kingdom maintained its independence for long time and was late in coming under the European influence. They have largely preserved their social pattern which was feudal, hierarchical and conservative in nature. As an effect of European while the Sinhalese of Low-country took to Christianity and English education, the Kandyan Sinhalese have emphasised traditional Buddhist education rather than English education.

The Tamils of Sri Lanka in racial and cultural terms, possessed distinct identity as a minority group and traced their ancestry to the same period as that of the Sinhalese arrival and challenge the Sinhalese versions of the historical origins of Sri Lanka. They are, however, divided into Sri Lankan Tamils and Indian Tamils depending on their descent. The Ceylon Tamils, also called the indigenous Tamils, are the descendants of those Tamils who reached Sri Lanka in the wake of the Chola invasions beginning with the rule of the Chola Prince, Elara. The Ceylon Tamils ultimately settled in Northern and Eastern provinces which constitute the dry zone of Sri Lanka as opposed to the wet zone inhabited by the Sinhalese. The largest concentration of the Ceylon Tamils is to be found at Jaffna in the extreme north.[9] The Ceylon Tamils are mostly Hindus, the rest of them being Christians. In a sense, the Ceylon Tamils are both Ceylonese and Tamils - Ceylonese because they enjoy Ceylonese citizenship, and Tamils because they have cultural affinity to the Tamils of South India. The Ceylon Tamils make up about 12.6 per cent of the total population.

The Indian Tamils, on the other, are the people who had been brought from the Indian mainland by the British to work on the coffee, tea and rubber plantations in the island. They began to immigrate into Sri Lanka from the first half of the 19th century in the wake of the introduction of the plantation economy into the island were composed of two categories of persons-estate labourers and non-estate immigrants. The estate-labourers were mostly Tamils, hailing from the Tamil-speaking districts of South India.[10] The non-estate immigrants, also called free immigrants, were commuters between India and Sri Lanka holding temporary residence permits, and were composed of miscellaneous passengers from the north, south and west India and of the South Indian labourers who were employed otherwise than as estate labourers.[11] The Indian Tamils constitute 5.7 per cent of the total population and are mostly concentrated in the plantation areas situated in the central highlands. Although Indian Tamils are not indigenous to the island they had the same legal status as the Sinhalese and the Sri Lankan Tamils during the British rule.

The Ceylon Muslims comprise two groups-the Ceylon Moors mostly of Arab and Indian extraction who came as traders to the island during the seventh to the fifteenth centuries and inter-married with the natives, and the Malays of more recent origin, descendants of Javanese mercenaries brought by the Dutch. A large proportion of the Muslims on the east coast are herdsmen and cultivators, but generally there are Muslims engaged in minor commercial pursuits and these activities take them to the interior and remote parts of the island.[12] Most of the Muslims are Tamil-speaking and they live adjacent to the Ceylon Tamil community residing in the northern and eastern parts of the island. However, on the issue of language there is a divergence of opinion between the Muslims of Sinhalese areas and the Muslims residing in the Tamil-speaking areas.

The Burghers, a very small, are the descendants of those Portuguese and Dutch settlers who married in local families. Hence they are of mixed ancestry and include the offspring preferring to call themselves Eurasians or, more recently, Euro-Ceylonese. They speak English and are Christian in religious faith. The Burghers, during British rule wielded an influence in the public life of the island quite disproportionate to its number but with independence and the switch to nationalistic goals with the decision in 1956 to adopt Sinhalese as the official language, large number of them migrated to Australia while others have settled in Britain and Canada. Another group of minority, the Veddas are generally looked upon as one of the earliest known inhabitants of Sri Lanka and are believed to have migrated to the country originally from south India.

Thus, in a plural society such as that of contemporary Sri Lanka with solidarity patterns based upon shared religion, language, ethnic identity, caste and region commanding a loyalty rivalling at least in some situations that which the nation state itself is able to generate, a national consensus on basic social and political goals is hard to establish. With a view to keep the social and political fabrics intact in the early Post-Independence phase some attempts were made by the political parties in power to forge a measure of unity.

Initiatives for Devolution

The present day political leadership in Sri Lanka has realised the earlier mistakes and blunders made by the early governments after independence in 1948 and began pondering on the new pattern of political system which would be based on the federal style without using the term federation. In fact the privileges enjoyed by minorities including the Tamils in the island took a U turn in Post-Independence era and internal scene changed particularly against the Tamils. The Presidential system which was adopted soon found to be unsuitable to the heterogeneous nature of Sri Lankan society pushing the country into ethnic mess. Prior to independence the Tamil interests were looked after by the Tamil Congress who broke away from the Ceylon National Congress formed in 1919. In 1951 a split took place in the Tamil Congress itself and as a result the Federal Party (F.P.) came into existence under the leadership of S.J.V. Chelvanayakam, who pleaded for a federal set up in order to safeguard the rights of the minority Tamils. In the same year the Federal Party in its resolution also stated the formation of a separate state for the Tamil community in Sri Lanka.

Both the communities-the Sinhalese and the Tamils alongwith other groups awakened to safeguard their individual identity in Post-Independence era. In this context the Sinhala-Buddhist majoritarian became forerunner. The two main groups-the Buddhist Committee of Enquiry and the Eksath Buddhist Peramuna began to enquire into the state of Buddhism in Sri Lanka. It resulted in the publication of a report in 1956 called 'Betrayal of Buddhism' which demanded several things for the protection of Buddhism in the country. It gave air to the language controversy and made the Sinhalese and the Tamils intensely hostile to each other. The enactment of the language policy the 'Sinhala only' by the coalition government under the leadership of S.W.R.D. Bandaranaike helped to bring about an intense feeling of togetherness among all the Tamil political parties of all complexions-the Federal Party, the Tamil

Congress including those who resigned from the UNP Party and the UNP government.[13] The Post-Independence political developments in the island only exacerbated communal disharmony that further strengthened the roots of alienation among Tamil groups. In a sense the unitary system of Sri Lanka has completely failed on account of the parochial and inhuman attitudes of the Sinhalese political society in satisfying the preserved aspirations of the multi-ethnic people and therefore, the demand of decentralization of democratic processes has been raised from time to time.

The general sense of alienation among the Tamils and the government language policy passed in 1956 compelled the Federal Party to adopt a four-point demand at its annual convention held at Trincomalee in August 1956 with the threatening to take direct action by non-violent means if they were not met within a year. It included among other things (a) Enactment of a democratic constitution based on the federal principles and the establishment of one or more Tamil linguistic state or states, (b) Restoration of the Tamil language to its rightful place enjoying absolute parity of status with Sinhalese as an official language of the country, (c) Enactment of laws recognizing the right to full citizenship on the basis of a simple residential test of all persons who have made this country their home, and (d) Immediate cessation of colonisation of traditional Tamil-speaking areas by the Sinhalese people. In the circumstances to accommodate the Tamil grievances and contain the communal killing, the then Prime Minister of Sri Lanka, SWRD Bandaranaike signed an agreement with Chelvanayagam in 1957 which is known as B-C Pact. It recognised the Tamil as the language of administration in the north and the east, and also provided some measure of autonomy for these regions.[14] This pact was supposed to permit reasonable use of Tamil in the Northern and Eastern Provinces and also for regional councils with powers in agriculture, education and selection of candidates for colonisation scheme.[15] But on account of the Sinhalese pressure and United National Party's opposition, the demand of the regional council for Tamils could not be contended by the government on the plea that any attempt towards federalism will be vicious for the unity and integrity of Sri Lanka. Likewise the subsequent Dudley Senanayake-Chelvanayagam (D-C) Pact of 1965, though well-intentioned, and which dealt with, inter alia, regional autonomy also collapsed by 1968.

From the beginning the Tamil parliamentarians along others reaffirmed and reiterated their dedication in preserving the unity and integrity of the country, as they said "We are not asking for the division of Sri Lanka on the racial basis. We stand for division of the powers and thereby achieving unity in diversity. "They described the federal system as the "Panchsheel," which means cooperation and the co-existence, As part of its policy and to meet the Tamil demand of federalism the Sri Lankan Freedom Party government headed by Mrs. Bandaranaike introduced a District Political Authority (DPA) system as a measure of the administrative decentralization in 1973. The main duty of the district political authority was to control, direct and coordinate all matters pertaining to the district. However the system failed on account of incapacity and the parochial approaches of the heads of DPA.[16] On the other hand, it created a psychological setback to the Tamils which led to the transformation of their demand from federal to the secession with the start of Tamil Eelam Movement.

Further realising the potentiality of the Tamil Eelam Movement, the United National Party government of J.R. Jayewardene formulated the new scheme for the devolution of powers in 1978 which was known as the District Development Council (DDC). It was consisted of the elected members of the parliamentary group and the executive committee headed by the district ministers who were under the control of and responsible to the President of Sri Lanka. As a result of its composition the DDC had become an exercise in deception and had been puppets in the hands of President.[17] Consequently, the Tamils obsessed with the frustration and resentment. The new situation compelled the Tamil Federal Party change its name and manifesto, becoming the Tamil United Liberation Front (TULF) committed to independent Tamil state.[18]

The large scale devastating communal riots of 1983 made the issue of devolution of power a burning topic in the country and the July 1987 proposal of J.R. Jayewardene resulted in the signing of Indo-Sri Lanka Accord at the end of the month (29 July). The signed Accord had two aspects in which the first dealt with India's commitment to uphold Sri Lanka's sovereignty and territorial integrity on the condition that the latter agreed to grant a reasonable amount of autonomy to the Tamils to their satisfaction. The second aspect of the Accord dealt with Sri Lanka's commitment to disallow any extra-regional power to dabble in its affairs which had either a known or a potential intention to harm India's security interests in the region. In the Accord India expressed itself openly and unequivocally as being opposed to the Eelamist demand for a separate Tamil state in Sri Lanka, but at the same time brought pressure to bear on the Sri Lankan government to carry out its own pledges to effect a political solution of the ethnic crisis by implementing the principle of devolution of power from the centre to the provinces in Sri Lanka.[19] In general the devolution of power from the centre to the provinces involved three basic issues: first, the extent of powers to be devolved; second, the relations between the centre and provinces; and third, the unit of devolution.

In one of its most controversial parts, the Accord had virtually acknowledged the Tamil 'homeland' demand by providing for a temporary merger of the northern and eastern provinces but at the same time recognised the justifiable reservations of Muslims and Sinhalese communities in the eastern province by providing for breaking up the merger to allow the reversion of this province to its separate existence if a referendum so determined before the prescribed date.[20] As a follow up of the Accord the Sri Lankan Parliament had passed the 13th Amendments to the constitution and the Provincial Council Act no. 42 to devolve power for the participation of the Tamil people into the democratic process. However, the Tamils considered all these provisions as biased and prejudicial as they had not real powers and almost all the powers were rested with the Sinhalese. The said Amendment and the Provincial Council Act refused the constitutional recognition to the North-Eastern Province as areas of historical habitation of the Tamils. The devolution of power remained a controversial issue right up to the sign of the agreement in July 1987.

Recent Developments and Prospects

As promised during the Parliamentary election campaign of 1994, President Chandrika Kumaratunga came out with a detailed devolution package within the framework of a proposed new federal constitution. It proposed to give federating units much more powers than any time in the past. It also talked about the permanent merger of the Northern and Eastern provinces in which the Tamils would have their say. However it soon proved a fiasco when the government of People's Alliance (PA) came under pressure from the United National Party and the Sinhala forces in general. President Kumaratunga also retracted from its original stand on federalism and went in favour of more safeguards for the central authority. Further the idea of the so-called Tamil homeland was also diluted beyond recognition through providing various possibilities in respect of the territorial reorganisation of the Eastern Province. On the other hand for the majority of Tamils in Sri Lanka an independent homeland is no longer a point. All that they want is a measure of self-rule in the Tamil majority area within Sri Lanka.[21] Under the proposed peace package, as felt by the Indian origin Tamils of Sri Lanka that they are being sidelined and ignored by the People's Alliance Government of Mrs. Chandrika Kumaratunga. The matter was raised by S. Thondaman, Chief of the Ceylon Workers Congress (CWC) who wrote a letter to the secretary of the ruling People's Alliance in which he complained that the government's devolution packages carry no meaning for the community.[22] It charged that neither the government nor the devolution scheme had addressed the basic and pressing problems of the community. President Chandrika Kumaratunga also failed to get the support of opposition parties on the proposed framework for devolution of power.

In line after assuming power President Mahinda Rajapaksa worked hard to end the prolonged civil war by employing sundry mechanisms. First of his initiatives was APRC (All Party Representative Committee) in 2006 to find political consensus on power sharing between the conflicting communities, but the genuine efforts of the President could not confer affirmative result due to the traditional rivalry of major political parties and lack of participation of Tamil parties. Subsequently continuing his efforts, the President had appointed a group of multi-ethnic experts to evolve a political package acceptable to all sections. It was a seventeen-member multi-ethnic panel in which six Sinhalese, four Tamils and one Muslim was included. For devolution to be meaningful it is recommended that the majority of the subjects and functions be categorized as belonging to the national sphere or the provincial sphere with a provision for a concurrent list consisting of a minimum of subjects and functions.[23] But President's move at the juncture was not liked by the UNP and the SLFP including the extremists organizations like JVP (Janatha Vimukti Peramuna), Mahajan Eksath Peramuna and others.

In the circumstances Mahinda Rajapaksa, the President of the island and his government adopted two track policies. The Political solution for the Tamil masses and the military solution for the Tamil Tigers and very recently in May 2009 the President became victorious when the leader of LTTE Velupillai Prabhakaran was killed by the security forces of the country. Many of us feel that in Post-Prabhakaran phase the Sri Lankan identity must now be built upon a confederative principle that recognises the existence of several communities as well as the three nations within the entity Lanka- the Sinhalese, the Tamils and the Muslims. Self-generating initiatives and mechanisms by the civil society can be the best solutions.[24] Tamils must exhibit their sense of nationalism for Sri Lanka. Moreover, all the Peoples living in Sri Lanka must develop the sense of humanism that motivates the people to come together for the common objective of fraternity. Almost all the mechanisms should be pondered over and a system like the federal should be chosen on the basis of other successful federal systems. The significance of federal system must be explained to the protesters of the system as it does not pose threat to unity and integrity of the nation but is useful for ethnically heterogeneous societies.

6.2 ETHNICITY AND CHEERLESS VICTORY IN SRI LANKA

Globally, the region South Asia is considered as a disturbed and troubled part of the world on account of ethnicity and ethnic wars continuing in the area. It is a potential challenge to internal stability and occurs more in the underdeveloped regions of the world than elsewhere. In case of Sri Lanka the ethnic divide between the Tamils and the Sinhalese has widened after independence of the country in 1948 and after decades of violent confrontations, LTTE, an extremist outfit of Tamils, demanding a separate home land for Sri Lankan Tamil (Eelam State) has been miserably crushed and defeated by the Sri Lankan armed forces in May 2009. With this a new phase of uncertainties has commenced in the island which at best be hoped to end in near future.

Ethnicity in Sri Lankan Context

The ethnicity-related war in the South Asian region is a common phenomena particularly in Bangladesh, India, Pakistan and recently more violent in Sri Lanka. It is a large scale violent incident entailing an organised and prolonged military engagement and confrontation between regular government forces and highly mobilised insurgent or militant groups. There is continuity in fighting: military attacks/operations are extended over a considerable part of the country's territory. Importantly, the warring parties and their grievances and goals are solely defined in ethnic terms. Whereas the government represents the dominant majority ethnic group, civilians belonging to the minority ethnic community invariably constitute the insurgent or militant forces.[25] In the situation winning the war is the fundamental objective of the combatants and compromise is hard to negotiate so long as the asymmetry of power between the ethnic parties is not altered. In general ethnicity has gained prominence in today's politics for two additional reasons. First, the growth of sectarian political parties throughout the region has amplified and redirected ethnic issues to the political limelight. These parties have risen or have been resurrected by parochial interests, because of government's inadequacy or inability to remove ethnic grievances. These parties differ from national parties in that they have a narrow political base; represent the interests of only particular ethnic groups or segments thereof; and are dedicated to achieving political ends through violence. Second, the ethnic factor in South Asian politics is sustained also by the international role of the regional countries.[26] For instance, the Pakhtoonistan movement in the NWFP has been inspired and sustained by successive Afghan governments and the Sri Lanka's Tamil secessionist movement received full support from the neighbouring Indian state Tamil Nadu.

In general the separate cultural identities of regions, far from losing social significance and becoming blurred have in fact reasserted their cultural and regional identities by politically mobilising themselves in order to confront the state system which has failed to recognise or protect their interests. The Sri Lankan Tamils have rejected the continued validity of national symbols and values and have redirected their allegiance to ethnic symbols and values in order to fight for greater influence within their societies.[27] The present position of Sri Lanka have been interpreted by some as a clash between two subnationalism, that of the dominant Sinhalese Buddhist elite and of the minority Tamil elite of the northern peninsula.[28] But more often it has been seen in political terms in which the Sinhalese have consistently sought to diminish the cultural and political salience of the Tamils in post-Independence Sri Lanka. Despite the fact that there was an apparent communal harmony during the British period in Ceylon, the seeds of the cleavage between the Sinhalese and the Tamils were laid in the colonial Sri Lanka. The first wave of discontent was felt by the minorities during the independence movement when the practice of communal representation, prevalent during the colonial administration, was abandoned and fearing the dominance of Sinhalese in the new system, the Tamils began to agitate for the equal sharing of legislative and executive powers.[29] The volume of grievance-formation increased in the Post-Independence era of the island country.

Unlike India from the early years of administration the Government of Sri Lanka, following the majoritarian principle decided to build the nation on the basis of religion (Buddhism) and language namely Sinhala. At large the decision of Bandaranaike's government pertaining to language, education and settlement schemes affected the Tamil community both politically and economically. By making Sinhalese the sole official language in 1956, by abolishing the denominational system in 1960 and by introducing the weightage system for technical and higher education the interests of Tamils were affected materially. In addition the fear of marginalisation and suppression was intensified by the scheme of land colonisation under which the north and the east of the island-the traditional homeland of Tamils, were began to be inhibited by the Sinhalese population and the Tamils became concerned of being reduced into a minority even in their homeland areas. In reaction to the policies of the successive Sri Lankan governments sections of the two dominant Tamil parties, the Federal Party and the Tamil Congress united to form the Tamil United Liberation Front (TULF) in 1975 and on May 14, 1976, it adopted the Vaddukoddai resolution which called for the creation of a separate Tamil state of Eelam. In 1977 the founders of above two political parties had passed away and in their absence the militant groups which were already in the field were unleashed. Among these the Liberation Tigers of Tamil Eelam (LTTE), founded on May 5, 1976, vowed to achieve a separate state or Eelam through bloody and violent confrontation with the Sri Lankan state.

Forms and Manifestations of LTTE

The Liberation Tigers of Tamil Eelam commonly known as the LTTE or the Tamil Tigers was founded in 1976 as a successor to the Tamil New Tigers, a militant group, is a separatist organization formally based in northern Sri Lanka. Since its inception this organization has waged a violent secessionist campaign that sought to create an independent Tamil state in the north and east of Sri Lanka. Further this campaign evolved into the Sri Lankan civil war which was one of the longest running armed conflicts in Asia. Barring scattered violent actions here and there the LTTE carried out their first major attacks on July 23, 1983, when they ambushed a Sri Lanka Army troops transport and killed 13 soldiers leading to the Black July riots against the Tamils of Sri Lanka. The subsequent anger amongst the Tamil community resulted in numerous Tamil youths joining Tamil militant groups to fight the Sri Lankan government and it was considered start of the insurgency in Sri Lanka. In the violence of July and August 1983, at least several hundred people almost all of whom were Tamils were killed. A large number of killings were performed in particularly gruesome, sadistic fashion and corpses were often mutilated or burned. It was for the first time that Tamils of the commercial and professional classes of Colombo were attacked.[30] In effect the incident had dashed any hope that ways can be found to sustain a minimally workable plural society in Sri Lanka. It made them a weaker community. Their intensified isolation resulted in future antagonism, since any group that is perceived to be exclusive became a potential target.[31] They remained deeply uncertain and confused about the future.

Unlike the earlier communal disturbances between the Tamils and the Sinhalese the communal riots of July 1983 had left a clear message for the then government of Sri Lanka and Jayewardene was under tremendous pressure from the Tamils of Sri Lanka who wanted a solution to the problem. Jayewardene realised that time was running out and something must be done to ease the prevailing tension. It followed a series of inter-ethnic dialogue that included the Thimpu Talks (1985), the Indo-Sri Lanka Accord (1987), the Mangala Moonesinghe Select Committee (1991), the devolution proposal announced by President Chandrika Kumaratunga (1995-97) and the latest ongoing peace negotiations between the Government of Sri Lanka and the LTTE. Of the attempts the signing of Indo-Sri Lanka Accord (1987) was most significant from the view point of power devolution as well as easing prevailing tension in the country. The Accord had two parts-the first dealt with India's commitment to uphold Sri Lanka's sovereignty and territorial integrity while the second part dealt with Sri Lanka's commitment to disallow any extra -regional power to dabble in its affairs which had any intention of harming India's security interests in the region.

However, for the LTTE the Accord had no meaning as it did not address any of the Tamil demands, namely, an end of the illegal Sinhala colonisation, recognition of the Tamils as a nation, the permanent merger of the northern and eastern provinces, and the withdrawal of Sri Lankan troops from the province. As a follow up of the accord India sent a Peace-keeping Force (IPKF) to ensure that peace returned to the strife-torn Tamil areas. In operational terms this meant the disarming of the LTTE cadres. But the political power of the LTTE emanated from its guns and, understandably it refused to surrender them without any credible guarantee that political power would be handed over to it. In post - 1983 riots period violence on both sides increased alarmingly, as the Tamil militants have trained abroad with the PLO and in South India.[32] The Tamil extremists reject the notion of a Sinhalese Buddhist theocratic state, and are convinced that until the Sinhalese are driven out of the Tamil-majority areas there can be no lasting peace.

The Tamil Tigers, who during the height of their power possessed a well-developed militia cadre, are notorious for recruiting child soldiers, for carrying out civilian massacres, suicide bombings and various other high profile attacks, including the assassinations of several high-ranking Sri Lankan and Indian politicians like Rajiv Gandhi, the Indian Prime Minister, who signed Indo-Sri Lanka Accord (1987). They invented the suicide belt and pioneered the use of suicide bombing as a tactic. They also pioneered the use of women in suicide attacks, and used light aircraft in some of their attacks. At present they are proscribed as a terrorist organization by 32 countries, but have extensive support amongst the Tamil diaspora in Europe and North America, and among Tamils in India. Over the course of the conflict, the Tamil Tigers frequently exchanged control of territory in north-east Sri Lanka with the Sri Lankan military engaging in fierce confrontations in the process. Despite heavy fighting continuing between the Tamil Tigers and the Sri Lankan forces, the concept of an independent Tamil Eelam propounded with fanfare at Vaddukoddai in 1976 remained a faint and receding dream. The days of large scale and senseless violence against civilians, whether unleashed in the name of liberation or fighting terrorism seem to be over.[33] The conflict between them is manifested in a variety of ways ranging from political protest to ethnic violence and terrorist insurgencies to guerilla warfare.

Earlier to the present Rajapaksa regime of Sri Lanka, President Chandrika Kumaratunga under the auspices of Norway as a peace-negotiators, had signed Ceasefire Agreement with LTTE to resolve ethnic war and safeguard territorial integrity of the country. As a result both the parties maintained peace to greater extent. But the LTTE used the opportunity of prolonged peace to build its warfare strategies including air force. It procured advanced arms to fight against government reviving civil war in a more powerful way and even started air attacks.[34] In the circumstances a change of guard took place in Sri Lanka in which Rajapaksa became the new President of the country in November 2005.

The Last Debacle

The entire milieu of ethnic crisis and extremism of LTTE in the island changed abruptly in November 2005 when Mahinda Rajapaksa took over as the new President of Sri Lanka. Earlier Sri Lankan governments, in an effort to appease the majority Sinhalese population, have consistently failed to address Tamil grievances and this has helped the Tigers to build support among the Sri Lankan Tamil diaspora. But the present dispensation after assuming power had worked hard to end the prolonged civil war by employing sundry mechanisms. First of his initiatives was All Party Representative Committee (APRC) in 2006 to find political consensus on power sharing between the conflicting communities. The committee, in its interim steps, recommended to move forward the process of earnestly implementing the devolution and official language provisions of the Sri Lankan Constitution. It also stated that the final political package will require a constitutional amendment, that some of its provisions will also need to be approved in a referendum and that all this will take time once a favourable climate is established.[35] However, genuine efforts of the new government could not confer affirmative result due to the traditional rivalry of major political parties and lack of participation of Tamil parties. Further Mahinda Rajapaksa appointed a group of multi-ethnic experts to evolve a political package acceptable to all sections. But even this could not work.

On the other the overall defence situations in Sri Lanka deteriorated further in March 2007 when the LTTE, for the first time had carried out an air attack. The Hindu, a daily newspaper, described the event editorially as a dangerous development for the strife-torn country. It not only worsened the prevailing volatile security environment but also posed a new challenge in the fight against terrorism. The ongoing undeclared war between the Sri Lanka military and the LTTE seems to have entered a perilous phase.[36] In other words the LTTE's air raid had raised fundamental questions about the strategy employed by the government. It made nonsense of the government's claim of defending the integrating of our country and protecting its people-the primary duty of any government of Sri Lanka.[37] In line both the UNP and SLFP signed a memorandum of understanding (MoU) in October 2006 to cooperate in all the spheres of national interest. This pact was first of its kind in the Sri Lankan political history, but the parochial and narrow interests of both parties killed it. Subsequently, on account of frustration, lack of cooperation from fellow parties and failures in all initiatives, the President was left with no option but to wage a powerful military attack on LTTE. Faced with increasing attacks from LTTE, the President pulled out Norwegian brokered Ceasefire Agreement reached in 2002 for the period of six years. The Government of Mahinda Rajapaksa hoped that its military campaign would finally mark an end of the LTTE. Since 2006, when both sides resumed major military operations, the conflicts has killed and wounded thousand of civilians and displaced hundreds of thousands, leaving many suffering from disease and hunger.

In relation to the decades-old ethnic issue the Government of Mahinda Rajapaksa used two - track policies-the political solution for the Tamil masses and the military solution for the Tamil Tigers. It ensured the basic needs and safety of the internally displaced Tamils amidst targeting LTTE in the remaining strongholds and areas. In May 2008, for the first time after many decades, in north-eastern province, elections were conducted very successfully and a Tamil Chief Minister Pillayan, a TMVP worker and former LTTE leader, was appointed changing the entire political misconceptions towards democratic process. Now the Tamil community has genuinely realised that the agenda, tactics and uncompromising attitude of Prabhakaran could not establish congenial milieu for the comprehensive development of Tamils, and therefore, they made their own plan and strategy.[38] Such positive developments were taking place due to very rational political leaders of all communities.

But Rajapaksa continued his avowed military steps against Tamil Tigers. He held the firm belief that army solution should be based on what can be implemented and added further that unlike his government, the previous governments have not been bold enough to implement their promises. He also assured the nation while commenting on the feasibility of military solution that in an era of globalisation he would not retard the economic growth. The new President with his core group had made a political resolve in August 2006 to launch a fight-to-finish campaign against the Tigers. On the political front, they adopted a shrewd strategy, borrowing some of the LTTE's own tactics, such as continuing to make politically correct statements on matters of peace development and steps towards conflict resolution while meticulously planning operations for an all-out war. To impress upon the international community that it was keen on keeping the door open for negotiations, the government did not ban the LTTE as a terrorist group. On the propaganda front too, like the LTTE, it created the Media Centre for National Security (MCNS) in June 2006 with the sole aim of countering the pro-LTTE portal Tamil Net.[39] The motto, in the battlefield, as described by the army chief, was: 'Go for the kill, maximum casualties and destruction of infrastructure of the enemy with minimum possible damage to the troops"[40] The government had made it amply clear that the ongoing war is not against the innocent Tamil people, but against the LTTE. It is not against humanity, but against militancy.

The success story of Sri Lankan security forces started from the year 2007 when it recaptured almost all of Sri Lanka's Eastern Province including large areas of rebel dominated territory south of the strategic eastern port city of Trincomallee. This area served as the lifeline for some 40,000 government troops deployed in the northern Jaffna Peninsula. The government adopted severe military attacks as a final weapon against the beleaguered and obstinate LTTE. It had gained at its optimum level of success in eliminating LTTE completely in the national interest of Sri Lanka. The war of Sri Lankan security forces intensified from December 2008 and the end came soon in May 2009 when the military capabilities of LTTE was decimated and it resulted in acceptance of its defeat and death of LTTE's supremo Prabhakaran, revered by some as the 'Sun God'. With this a new chapter has been opened in Sri Lanka's multi-ethnic society and politics. Now the government has found an opportune moment to exhibit the world that their island country is an appropriate example of an inclusive democracy acting on people's wish and mandate in the larger interest of the nation.

6.3 LTTE IN SRI LANKA : FADED NOT FINISHED

The ethnic divide between the Tamil and the dominant Sinhalese communities deepened further in post – Independence period causing a serious setback to the growth of harmonious relations between the two neighbouring countries- India and Sri Lanka. They both from the beginning maintained their cultural rivalry and were conscious enough to preserve them at any cost. After the independence of Sri Lanka, the successive governments of the country deliberately made their divide wide particularly to take political advantage and communal segregation at the level of Sri Lankan government along with social divide that made Tamil community of Indian origin a neglected segment of Sri Lankan society and politics.

Dissatisfaction among the Tamils gave birth to several extremist groups who held faith only in violent activities. They considered formation of a separate state (Eelam) as solution of their problem and started fighting violently for their avowed purpose. The 1970s saw emergence of more than thirty militant groups owing to the unemployment, lack of opportunities for higher education and the imposition of an alien language. Among the militant groups who owed their allegiance to violence, LTTE, formed in May 1976, was solidly nationalistic. This organisation continued its violent activities and defied all governmental proposals and suggestions. It started a well planned strategic, declared war against the Sri Lankan Government and its armed forces in and outside the country for the last four decades.

Of late in the year 2008-09 the LTTE fought a decisive war with Sri Lankan armed forces which proved a debacle for it and all its bases in the island were destroyed by the government and its brutal armies, however, the root cause of militancy is yet to be resolved completely. Until or unless alienation of Tamils of Indian origin in country's society and politics is stopped, dissatisfaction and its networking at national and international levels are bound to re-emerge sooner or later and any discrimination or fault on the part of Sri Lankan government and its dominant majority community may prove disastrous for the nation as a whole which might endanger even its sovereignty and integrity. The challenge now is to address the cause of war.

Formative Backgrounds

Sri Lanka is suffering from the problem of ethnicity and struggling to establish peace and stability in the island for decades. The traditional rivalry between the Sinhalese and Tamils is fostered by the British plantation economy but even before the coming of colonial masters they both maintained separate kingdoms- the Tamil kingdom in the North and the lowland Sinhalese kingdom in the south. In due course as it generally happens mutual suspicion between the Sinhalese and the Tamils laid the seeds of the cleavage. The large majority of the Ceylonese are Sinhalese, claiming descent from Indo-Aryan migrants and speaking a Sanskrit-derived language. Most of them are Theravada Buddhists and occupy the central hill areas providing the labour force in the southern coastal metropolitan region. A large Tamil minority from south India is divided about equally into two distinct groups (a) Ceylon Tamils who have resided in the island for several centuries, are Ceylon citizens and are well represented in commerce, the professions, academia and government service; and (b) The Indian Tamils, mostly descendants of migrants brought to Ceylon as plantation workers during the British period who do not hold Ceylonese citizenship. Unlike the former group who is important both politically and economically, the latter lacks the political prerogatives of citizenship but is organised into labour unions.[41] However both speak Tamil, a non Indo-Aryan Indian language as their mother tongue and are Hindus, which distinguishes them from their Sinhala neighbours.

The British, at first, after taking the entire administration under a unified control in 1833 tried to create a homogeneous society in the island. Improvement in means of transportation and communication across the country broke down the regional isolation of the social groups. In addition the spread of a market economy, growing urbanisation, and economic relationships tended to bring the diverse groups into a single network of trade and commerce. In the circumstances it was natural that some aspects of colonial policy tend to affect the majority interests more than the minority interests for the simple reason that the minorities being already conscious of their numerically inferior status do not react so sharply to those aspects of the policy as does the majority, but when the majority reacts to those policies it indirectly harms the interests of the minority. In other words the British failed to do so as they could not overcome certain forces which acted as obstacles against integration. Advancing social mobilisation generated new aspirations and demands and widened concern with educational opportunities, urban employment and governmental services, heightening the potential for communal conflict.[42]

Thus in course of time Sri Lanka became a mosaic of cultural, religious, ethnic and logistic diversities. Sinhalese and Tamils are the most dominating communities. The heterogeneous nature of Sri Lanka is instrumental in generating a plethora of internal and external threats to the nation. Since 1833 the first legislative assemblies were entirely communal in composition. This gave opportunity to the communal leaders to take different postures in politics. In the 1920s while the Sinhalese favoured territorial principle in representation in the legislature, the Tamil preferred communal principle. Further the introduction of territorial representation and universal adult franchise by the Donoughmore constitution in 1931 completely changed the carefully adjusted ratio of representation of the Sinhalese and the Tamils from 2:1 to 5:1. The Tamils reacted forcefully by boycotting the general election under the Donoughmore constitution and as a result four Tamil constituencies in the Northern province did not return members to the first State Council. As the independence of the island approached, the Tamils became communally conscious and fervent by the time Soulbury Commission arrived in 1944 to prepare a new constitution. Although the commission did not agree with the fifty- fifty scheme of representation put forward by the newly formed Ceylon Tamil Congress, it provided for certain safeguards under which seats were distributed in the nine provinces on the basis of area as well as population. The new provision also prohibited the enactment of any law on matters affecting particular communities or religious groups.[43] In fact, the most important factor in antagonism between Tamils and Sinhalese was British English education that was adopted by Tamils more widely than Sinhalese and as a result, the former grabbed most of the opportunities generated and provided by the British. This consequently resulted in resentment and jealousy among the Sinhalese. They felt that they had been discriminated in their own country.[44]

After independence in 1948, the internal scene changed against the Tamils. It witnessed the resurgence of Sinhalese and Tamils on the one hand and successive Sri Lankan government's anti-Tamil enactments on the other. Even during the movement for independence the minority Tamils sought constitutional means to safeguard their privileged position in the professions and the government, which was much more than what thc Sinhalese were willing to concede subsequently. The Sinhalese on the other hand, wished to consolidate their political power over the island because they saw the Tamils as constituting a direct threat to the survival of Sinhala Buddhism and the Sinhalese language. But the moderate Sinhalese are willing to share the country with the Lankan Tamils, provided the latter learn Sinhalese and accept the fact that Sri Lanka is and will always be, a Sinhalese Buddhist country. The extremist Sinhalese believe that devolution of any kind will only hasten secession.[45] If Sri Lanka had adopted a federal system and natural and unbiased policies, stability and peace would have been maintained and the present day agony of people would have been avoided.

The independence of Sri Lanka was followed by the rising tide of Sinhalese nationalism and the process saw the revival of Buddhism and traditional culture that had already been started by a second layer of elite-the Ayurvedic physicians, the Sinhalese school teachers and the bhikkus of the Sangh who formed a link between the modern Sri Lankan polity and pre-colonial Sinhalese kingdoms. They were sore that their language, religion and culture were relegated to a secondary place. In the mid-1950s a Sinhalese revivalist movement which had developed over several decades emerged forcefully on to the political stage. Initially it had begun as a protest against Westernisation and the use in public institutions of the English language which was spoken by only a small elite minority of Sinhalese, and many of these anti-Western pro-vernacular sentiments were shared by the predominantly Hindu Tamil minority. But during 1955 and 1956, the Sinhalese movement grew increasingly chauvinistic and required feature ever since.[46] Further Sinhalese chauvinism has intermittently proved a major threat to social cohesion and national integrity sparking major outbursts of anti Tamil violence in 1958,1977,1981 and most savagely, in 1983.[47] The chauvinistic view of the Sinhalese majority as a nation, indeed as the nation, means in clear contradiction to the concept of Sri Lankan as a modern, pluralistic nation-state. The Sinhalese are equally proud of their culture, religion and language. They consider themselves to be the first settlers and Sinhalese Buddhism as the native religion of the island since the third century B.C.[48] They are acutely aware that as a distinct linguistic and ethnic group Sri Lanka is the only place for them. But on the other they are psychologically disposed to seeing themselves in the minority because of the presence of Tamil in South India with whom the Lankan Tamils have a strong sense of ethnic affiliation.

The Sinhalese paradigm of one country, one nation, one language and one people compelled Tamil youths to rise against Sinhalese chauvinism. Though the Sinhalese and the Tamils were self-conscious about their differences and were mutually suspicious, they were not intensely hostile prior to the language agitation of 1955-1956. Language was central to the self identification of both Sinhalese and the Tamils, and was deeply embedded in the sub nationalist sentiments of both communities. Like the Sinhalese, the Tamils of Sri Lanka take pride in their ancient culture and language[49] and the more zealous among them point to their distinct Tamil dialects as opposed to the Indian state of Tamil Nadu. They considered themselves the authentic bearers of the pure Tamil tradition, and constitute a Dravidian race. Tamil extremists reject the notion of a Sinhalese Buddhist theocratic state, and are convinced that until the Sinhalese are driven out of the Tamil-majority areas there can be no peace. Laying equal claim to the island as their homeland, they refuse to concede to Sinhalese majority tyranny.[50] Soon both the communities became rivals in establishing their cultural superiority and the administrative hegemony over each other.

The present tragedy is the result of political and cultural rivalry between the two communities and the ineptitude of the national leadership in reconciling their differences. In the early post-independence phase, some attempts were made by the premier conservative politician among the Sinhalese, D.S.Senanayake to forge a measure of unity among the middle and upper classes of the various groups in Sri Lanka's multi-communal society. But a rift developed between the two groups with the enactment of the citizenship laws of 1948 and 1949 and it was the immediate pretext for the formation of the strongly Tamil nationalist Federal Party (FP) in 1949.[51] The Ceylon Citizenship Act No.18 which came into operation on 15 November 1948 laid down that a person would be entitled to the status of a citizen of Sri Lanka either by the right of descent or by virtue of registration. Likewise the next enactment, Indian and Pakistani Residents (Citizenship) Act No. 3 of 1949 an Indian or Pakistani Residents of Sri Lanka was to be granted the Citizenship status of the country through registration.[52] The Federal Party which was formed in 1949 to look after the interests of Sri Lankan Tamils, concentrated on three objectives; (a) an autonomous region for the indigenous Tamil-speaking peoples comprising the northern and eastern provinces linked to the rest of the island under a federal set up, (b) parity of status for the Tamil language with the Sinhalese language and (c) citizenship rights for all Indian Tamils who wish to make the island their permanent home.

The alienation of Sri Lankan Tamils not only initiated but also matured in 1955-56 when island's government took a number of decisions to spark their sentiments and requirements as well. The two main political parties of the country- Sri Lanka Freedom Party (SLFP) and United National Party (UNP) had changed their language policy to Sinhala only as the official language of the island from the two languages policy for which they had stood since the State Council resolution passed in 1944. It led directly to a reaction from the Ceylon Tamils who saw the legislation as a threat not only to their culture and their identity but also to their means of livelihood. However, to contain the communal killings that followed the Bandaranaike-Chelvanayagam pact was signed in 1957 but soon thereafter the former had abrogated the pact. This resulted in the swing of Tamil opinion more firmly behind the Federalists. The Tamil demonstrations led to counter-riots and ultimately to the island wide holocaust in the 1958 and the declaration of emergency.[53] The voice of Sri Lankan Tamils, the Federal party allied itself briefly with the ruling party's National Government formed after 1965 general elections till 1968 to maximize gains for the Tamil, but it was never done by the government due to the pressure of SLFP and the Federal party resigned from the cabinet in 1968.

These events had a number of grave consequences. Since the Sinhalese leadership reneged on its commitments each time, the Tamils lost confidence and began to view the negotiated settlements with Sinhalese as futile exercise. The failure of these negotiated settlements which would have partially ameliorated the cultural, economic and political grievance of the Tamils, led to a strong resurgence of Tamil nationalism by the end of the sixties and to significant shifts from moderate to militant sentiments within Tamil ranks since then. Even under the new constitution the government of Mrs. Bandaranaike in 1973 introduced standardization in education that facilitated Sinhalese admission to universities but prevented many qualified Tamil students from seeking university admission.[54] It was done at a time when massive unemployment was already an issue. There was also widespread discrimination against Tamils in government appointments. The issues of discrimination responsible for bringing tussle and bickering were language, administration, education, employment, colonisation of land and the power devolution. With Tamil political leaders failure in political bargaining and power politics, Tamil youths raised arms against the government. The armed uprising gave birth to political violence as the only means. The Tamil youths sought the means of armed struggle for the establishment of Tamil Eelam- a separate Tamil state. During this period, Tamil militancy emerged in Tamil areas with plenty of Tamil militant organisations to fight for their rights against the oppressive rule of Sinhalese. The ethnic conflict has become a central problem in Sri Lankan politics, which led to the emergence of political terrorism of LTTE.

LTTE : Aims and Objects

The Liberation Tigers of Tamil Eelam (LTTE) was formed on May 5, 1976, under the leadership of Velupillai Prabhakaran with the demand of a sovereign Tamil state in the northern and the eastern parts of the island.[55] It was a self-proclaimed representative of Tamils and has been demanding the separate state of Tamil Eelam dividing Sri Lanka. Formative backgrounds of the LTTE showed that it was due to the lack of consensus on basic socio-economic and political issues in society. This undermines security and stability of the nation. In the context of traditional homeland of Tamils which gave foundation for the demand of separate Tamil State, the Federal Party (based on two – nation theory) of Tamil community in Sri Lanka stated in the party's resolution of 1951; "The Tamil speaking people in Sri Lanka constitute a nation distinct from that of Sinhalese by every fundamental test of nationhood; firstly that of a separate historical past, in this island at least as ancient and glorious as that of Sinhalese; secondly by the fact of their being a linguistic entity, entirely different from that of Sinhalese, with as unsurpassed classical heritage and a modern development of language which makes Tamil fully adequate for all present day needs and finally by reason of their territorial habitation of definite areas, which constitute over one-third of the island".[56] The concept of Tamil-Nation was basically to bring together Tamils and the Muslims living in Sri Lanka. Infact the political failure of democratic system and chief political parties in resolving Tamil grievances led to the demand of separate Tamil state. The tragedy of Sri Lanka's history is that so many Tamil patriots of yesteryear were led to discard their Lankanness and adopt a separatist Eelam identity or to discard their island roots altogether.[57] In other words their Sri Lankanness has been generated through their ethnic identity as Burgher, Malay, Sinhalese, Tamil, and so on.

Terrorism in Sri Lanka began in 1970 with the formation of a militant student body called the Tamil Students Movement to protest government plans to limit access of Tamil students to universities. Very soon this movement went underground and turned to avert terrorist activities.

Violence escalated in Jaffna from 1972 onwards, beginning with the publication of a new constitution seen by the Tamil United Liberation Front (TULF) as anti-Tamil. The year 1972 witnessed the formation of two Tamil terrorist groups such as, the Tamil New Tigers (TNT) and Tamil Eelam Liberation Organisation (TELO), while other active Tamil guerilla groups included the People's Liberation Organisation of Tamil Eelam (PLOTE), the Tamil Eelam Liberation Army (TELA), the Eelam Peoples Revolutionary Liberation Front (EPRLF), and the Eelam Revolutionary Organisation of Students (EROS). They all were averse to political bargaining and sought an armed solution to the Tamil problem. At political level too the Federal Party and Tamil Congress joined hands in a Tamil United Front (TUF) and rejected the republican constitution of 1972. The TUF, in its national convention in May 1976 endorsed to change its designation as TULE and resolved that the restoration and reconstitution of the free, sovereign, secular and socialist state of Tamil Eelam......... has become inevitable.[58]

In context of evolution of the Tamil extremist movement the years 1977-78 were of crucial importance. Decades after independence, Tamils supported a more federal system and the concept of a separate state was proposed by the Tamil United Liberation Front (TULF) who went on to campaign in the 1977 election for an independent state for Tamils in Sri Lanka. They won and went to parliament to represent the northern and eastern provinces but was later banned from the parliament by the Sri Lankan government for advocating an independent state for Tamils. On the other among the militant groups, the LTTE avowed to achieve a separate state or Eelam through bloody and violent confrontation with the Sri Lankan state. Its arrival on the centre-stage of Tamil politics was signalled by the murder of four policemen in Velvettithurai in April 1978. The incident triggered off a confrontation with the government that injected a new and most complex dimension to Sri Lanka's ethnic problem and eventually plunged the country into a virtual civil war. As a response to the happening the government first banned the LTTE and other similar groups in May 1978 and then imposed emergency in Jaffna in January 1979 that continued for a year. However the government's action had radicalised the extremists and boosted their popularity among the Tamils.

Since its inception, the LTTE has grown out to be a massive army with the whole hearted support of the Tamil people and some years later it maintained thousand of brave soldiers, with a naval wing that had become a formidable on in the subcontinent. And as the racist policies of the successive Sinhala governments continued it made the Tamil civilians to more and more hardships. In that kind of situation the LTTE had become the army that the Tamil people could look up to in order to put an end to all the troubles and win back the Tamil's homeland, Tamil Eelam. The LTTE in previous years possessed a well-developed militia cadre and were notorious for recruiting child soldiers for carrying out civilian massacre, suicide bombings and various other high profile attacks, including the assassination of several high-ranking Sri Lankan and even Indian politicians. They invented the suicide belt and pioneered the use of suicide bombing as a tactic. They also pioneered the use of women in suicide attacks and used light aircraft in some of their attacks. They were proscribed as a terrorist organisation by 32 countries, but have extensive support among the Tamil diasporas in Europe and North America, and among Tamils in India. In course of the conflict, the Tamil Tigers frequently exchanged control of territory in north east Sri Lanka with the Sri Lankan military, engaging in fierce confrontations in the process.

The LTTE carried out their first major attack on July 23, 1983, when they ambushed a Sri Lanka Army troop transport outside Jaffna. Riots had taken place earlier also but the 1983 riots were unprecedented in the sense that in this case even the elite members of the Tamil community were targeted. The deadly attack on police sparked riots in Colombo and elsewhere in which thousand ofTamils died. It was taken as the beginning of the ethnic conflict which followed attacks and counter attacks and support on both sides for violence grew since 1983 there had been on-and-off civil war, mostly between the government and the LTTE. As a result hundreds of thousands of refugees were displaced internally or had fled to Tamil Nadu and around the world. From here onwards the LTTE had begun its armed conflict with Sri Lankan government and relied on guerilla strategy that included the use of terrorist tactics. The Tigers had integrated a battlefield insurgent strategy with a terrorist programme that targeted not only key personnel in the countryside but also senior Sri Lankan political and military leaders in Colombo and other urban centres.

In post-riot periods, the LTTE made its organisational structure wide and placed immense emphasis on the cult of martyrdom. Its leadership was organised along a two-tier structure; a military wing and a subordinate political wing. Overseeing both was a central governing committee headed by the LTTE chief , Velupillai Prabhakaran. The central committee had also an International Secretariat, which was in charge of the outfits, global network. Gradually the LTTE had gained power and began to operate in cooperation with other Tamil militant groups which shared their objectives, and in April 1984, it had formally joined a common militant front, the Eelam National Liberation Front (ENLF). By the same time a especial drive was started to recruit women and children as cadres of the LTTE. Earlier in 1983 the Women's Front of the Liberation Tigers was formed which began combat training in 1985. In October 1987, Prabhakaran set up the first training camp exclusively for women in Jaffna for the second and successive batches. Like men the women cadres underwent the same tough training and were divided into fighting, intelligence gathering, political and administrative units. Children have featured prominently in the LTTE's protracted guerilla and terrorist campaigns and according to an estimate conducted by the Sri Lankan Directorate of Military Intelligence, there was as much as 60 per cent of LTTE's fighters were below the age of eighteen. Until 1986 the LTTE had sufficient adult units in operation. In 1987 a deliberate policy of recruiting women and children into LTTE cadres was initiated after the signing of the Indian Peace–keeping Force (IPKF) Accord.

The much-publicised India-Sri Lanka Accord of July 1987 was not approved by the LTTE and its supremo Prabhakaran had explained that the accord did not address any of the Tamil demands, namely, an end of the illegal Sinhala colonisation, recognition of the Tamils as a nation, the permanent merger of the northern and eastern provinces, and the withdrawal of Sri Lankan troops from the province and as such, refused to surrender without any credible guarantee that political power would be handed over to it. After much hue and cry and opposition on the part of Sri Lankan government the IPKF withdrew to its land in March 1990. It was followed by the new wave of violence which erupted between the LTTE and Sri Lankan security forces. One of the consequences of the Indian troop withdrawal for the politics of the north-east region was the ascendancy of LTTE in the areas which were vacated by the IPKF. Withdrawal of the Indian forces proved fatal to India and Sri Lanka and on May 21, 1991, Indian Prime Minister was killed by an LTTE suicide bomber and prominent Sri Lankan leader premadasa by its suicide cadre during a May Day rally in Colombo in 1993. As a result in January 1995 the Government of Sri Lanka and the LTTE agreed to hold talks but without lasting success and attacks as well as counter attacks on both sides continued for years to come or until February 2002 when the two enter into a ceasefire agreement. However it too failed to bring lasting peace in Sri Lanka. The continuing violence and confrontations took several precious lives of diverse fields and paved the way for a near end point as the year 2006-07 approached.

Recent Debacle and Prospect

The year 2006 was important for the decade–old ethnic problem of Sri Lanka . At the juncture the domestic regional and international community and almost all the confidence building measures faded, the only mechanism left with the state was to fight the complex network of terrorism and use the full-fledged command of the military might of the nation without responding to pressures around. Earlier political solution was held as the supreme mechanism to resolve ethnic crises in Sri Lanka and in this direction plenty of measures and efforts were put in so far but in vain. The recent conflict in Sri Lanka unlike earlier was between the LTTE and the government as well as between stubborn Sinhalese and Tamils. This is not the problem particularly of Sinhalese or Tamil or Muslims, but it has encircled the entire population in Sri Lanka which has tired of violence and is dreaming of peaceful habitation.[59] With this objective in view the Sri Lankan army began to target the LTTE's hideouts and having destroyed its bases increased the inevitability of peace. According to a study conducted by a Mumbai think-tank Strategic Foresight Group (SFG) Sri Lanka has emerged as the most militarised society in South Asia and concluded that it could get worse unless urgent action is initiated towards ending the decades–old conflict.[60] It also said, 'For the LTTE, which is essentially a military outfit, expenditure on weapons and the maintenance of a war economy gets top priority. It does precious little for the economic well being of the people under its control, despite running a few social and economic organisations.[61]

In that kind of situation and under a calculated strategy the Rajapaksa government managed to finish the tigers militarily. He made a political resolve in August 2006 to launch a "fight – to- finish campaign against the Tigers. The LTTE provided the much – needed excuse for the assault when its cadre closed down the Mavil Aru sluice gates in the east denying water to more than 30,000 civilians. The presidential core team in the campaign included the defense secretary, his younger brother and the army chief Lt. General Sarath Fonseka which proved a lethal combination for the LTTE. When fighting again erupted in mid 2006, the Tigers were now compelled to fight the Sri Lankan forces on their own terms. By the summer of 2007, the government had recaptured all of the LTTE's eastern territory, forcing them back into their Vanni heartland.[62] At the moment the government seemed using two track policies. The political solution for the Tamil masses and the military solution for the Tamil Tigers.

In addition when in action the government pursued a well thought policy in regard to political and other issues attached and at the sametime borrowed some of the LTTE's own tactics, such as continuing to make politically correct statements on matters of peace, development and steps towards conflict resolution while meticulously planning operations for an all – out war in course of the fighting perhaps to impress upon the international community that it was keen on keeping the door open for negotiations, the Rajapaksa government did not ban the LTTE as a terrorist outfit. On the battle front, the motto was, "Go for the kill, maximum casualties and destruction of infrastructure of the enemy with minimum possible damage to the troops."[63] The current phase of hostilities witnessed the maximum use of air power but despite large scale aerial missions, it was only in the last phase of the war from December 2008 that the curtain came down on Eelam War IV in the early hours of May 18, 2009, with the decimation of LTTE's military capabilities and the acknowledgement of the death of LTTE's supremo Velupillai Prabhakaran by organization's international representative.

Velupillai Prabhakaran's death has left a big void in the LTTE's leadership. If Prabhakaran is no more, it will not be an immediate end of the LTTE. It will however be the beginning of the end and the decline and fall would be quite rapid. But it would be a fatal mistake to see the military death of the LTTE as a demise of the cause that gave birth to the Tigers. The cause, the legitimate grievances and aspirations of the Tamils and other minorities in the island nation is not only alive but kicking. A durable solution to the Tamil question can be found only on the basis of justice and equality. The grievances of the Tamils have to be redressed and their legitimate aspirations addressed within a united Sri Lanka. It has provided the island country the real prospect of converting its political structure into a federal one offering genuine space for cultural and political out on only in which ethnic identities can be preserved much more effectively.[64] It is a sure recipe for further rupture in the already strained relations among various communities in the multi ethnic and multi linguistic island nation but at the sametime its failure would cause a return of militant politics.

References

1. Vinod F, Khobragade, 'Ethnic Politics in Sri Lanka-Political

Solution to Tamil Cause and Military Solution to LTTE,' Subhash C. Kashyap, ed., South Asia Politics, Vol. 7, No. 11, March 2009 (New Delhi, 2009), p.24.

2. Ibid., 'Re-Thinking Power Devolution in Sri Lanka,' Vol.6, No.1, May 2007 (New Delhi, 2007), p. 23.
3. Bertram ESJ Bastiampillai, 'Ethnic Conflicts in South Asia and Inter-State Relations Especially in Relation to Sri Lanka', in Shelton U. Kodikara, ed., South Asian Strategic Issues-Sri Lankan Perspectives (Sage Publications, New Delhi, 1990), p. 84.
4. Lucy M. Jacob, 'Regionalism in Sri Lanka', in Ramakant, ed., Regionalism in South Asia (Aalekh Publishers, Jaipur, 1983), p. 175.
5. Michael Roberts, 'Some Pillars for Lanka's Future', N. Ram, ed., Frontline, Vol. 26, No. 12, June 6-19, 2009 (Chennai, 2009), p.29.
6. P.C. Roy Chaudhury, Lands and Peoples of the World Sri Lanka (Sterling Publishers, New Delhi, 1985), p.38.
7. Leo E. Rose, 'Nepal, Burma and Ceylon', in Wayne Wilcox, Leo E. Rose and Gavin Boyd, eds., Asia and the International System (Winthrop Publishers, Cambridge, Massachusetts, 1972), p. 231.
8. Bryce Ryan, Caste in Modern Ceylon:The Sinhalese System in Transition (New Brunswick, 1953); Also see Soulbury Report, Paragraph 273.
9. H.P. Chattopadhyaya, Indians in Sri Lanka (O.P.S. Publishers, Calcutta, 1979), p.100.
10. Ceylon Census of Population, 1871 to 1921, Vol. 1, Part II, 1921, pp. 37-38.
11. H.P. Chattopadhyaya, op.cit., p. 103.
12. A. Jeyaratnam Wilson, Politics in Sri Lanka 1947-1979 (The Macmillan Press, London, 1979), pp. 47-48.
13. Lucy M. Jacob, op. cit., pp. 178-79.
14. Shaukat Hassan, 'Problems of Internal Stability in South Asia', in Shelton U. Kodikara, ed., External Compulsions of South Asian Politics (Sage Publications, New Delhi, 1993), pp. 267-68.
15. Lucy M. Jacob, op. cit., p. 180.
16. Vinod F. Khobragade, op.cit., p. 24.
17. Ibid., p. 25.
18. Gananath Obeyesekere, 'The Origins and Institutionalisation of Political Violence', in James Manor, ed., Sri Lanka in Change and Crisis (Croom Helm, London, 1984), p. 156.
19. Shelton U. Kodikara, ed., op. cit., pp. 165-66.

20. Ibid., p. 166.
21. Seema Guha, 'The Lankan Tug-of War', The Times of India, July 28, 1997.
22. The Hindustan Times, August 21, 1997.
23. Vinod F. Khobragade, op.cit., p. 23.
24. Michael Roberts, op.cit., p. 24.
25. P. Sahadevan, 'Negotiating Peace in Ethnic Wars', Bansidhar Pradhan, ed., International Studies, Vol. 43, No. 3, July-September 2006 (Sage Publications, New Delhi, 2006), pp. 239-40.
26. Shaukat Hassan, 'Problems of Internal Stability in South Asia', Shelton U. Kodikara, ed., op.cit., pp. 272-74.
27. Ibid., p. 276.
28. A. Jeyaratnam Wilson, 'Race, Religion, Language and Caste in the Subnationalism of Sri Lanka', in Michael Roberts, ed., Collective Identities, Nationalism and Protest in Modern Sri Lanka (Marga Institute, Colombo, 1979), pp. 462-73.
29. Tilak Gooneratne, 'The Present Situation in Sri Lanka', Asian Affairs, London, XVII, Part I, February 1986, p. 35.
30. James Manor ed., op.cit., p. 22.
31. Ibid., R.P. Slater, 'Hill Country Tamils in the Aftermath of the Violence', pp. 217-18.
32. Bruce Matthews, 'The Situation in Jaffna', The Round Table, No. 290, April 1984, p. 28.
33. P.K. Balachanddran, 'Eelam : A Receding Dream', The Hindustan Times, January 19, 1998.
34. Vinod F. Khobragade, op.cit., p. 26.
35. The Hindu (editorial), January 28, 2008.
36. Ranil Wicremesinghe, 'The Way to Resolve Sri Lanka's Political Crisis', Ibid., April 6, 2007.
37. Ibid.
38. Vinod F. Khobragade, op.cit., p. 27.
39. B. Muralidhar Reddy, 'The War is Over', N. Ram, ed., op.cit., pp. 7-8.
40. Ibid., p. 8.
41. Wayne Wilcox, Leo E. Rose and Gavin Boyd eds. op.cit., p. 229.
42. Vijaya Samaraweera, 'The Evolution of a Plural Society', in De silve, K.M ed., Sri Lanka: A Survey (London, 1977), pp. 88-89.
43. Lucy M. Jacob, op.cit., pp. 176-77.
44. Vinod F. khobragade, op.cit., p. 24.
45. Marshall R. Singer, 'Report on the Pressures and Opportunities for

a Peaceful Solution to the Ethnic Conflict in Sri Lanka', Journal of Developing Societies, April 11, 1986, p.15.

46. James Manor, ed., op.cit., pp. 2-3.
47. Ibid.
48. Shaukat Hassan, op.cit., pp. 268-69.
49. Bryan Phaffenberger, 'The Cultural Dimension of Tamil Separatism in Sri Lanka', Asian Survey XX1-11, November 1981, p. 1146.
50. Marshall R. Singer, op.cit., pp. 13-16.
51. A. Jeyaratnam Wilson, op. cit., p.41.
52. H.P. Chattopadhyaya op.cit., pp. 225-28.
53. Lucy M. Jacob, op.cit., pp. 179-80.
54. Frontline (Madras), April 5, 1985, p. 42.
55. Sugata Bose and Ayesha Jalal, Modern South Asia- History, Culture, Political Economy (Oxford University Press, New Delhi, 2004), p. 187.
56. Vinod F. Khobragade, op.cit., pp. 24-25.
57. B. Muralidhar Reddy, 'Democracy Deficit & two Movements' Frontline, N. Ram, ed. op.cit., p.27.
58. The Ceylon Daily News, October 5, 1977.
59. Vinod F. Khobragade, 'Re- Thinking power Devolution in Sri Lanka', op.cit., p.26.
60. The Hindu (Madras), September 27, 2006.
61. Ibid.
62. Tom Farrell, 'For Him no Sacrifice was too Great for the Objective of Eelam', Ibid., May 20, 2009.
63. B. Muralidhar Reddy, op.cit., pp. 5-8.
64. Malini parthasarathy 'The Mirage of Eelam'. The Hindu, April 24, 2009.

7

INDIA, NEPAL AND THE MAOISTS

7.1 DEMOCRATIC EXPERIMENTS IN NEPAL

Nepal is a small country with big problems. Since the multi-party rule was ushered into Nepal in 1990, it has tried all kinds of political experiments in government formation. Needless to say, all these experiments have failed to provide political stability. Again in the situation of chaos and confusion King Gyanendra sacked Nepal's coalition government of Sher Bahadur Deuba on 1 February 2005 and declared emergency in the Himalayan Kingdom. However, the agitation in favour of popular sovereignty began after a year of King's takeover. It was launched in unison by the Maoists and the seven-party alliance (SPA) of parliamentary parties with the call of "mass mobilisation programme" on 6 April 2006. In decades it was for the first time that the two principal players - Maoists and the SPA were struggling together for the restoration of democracy in Nepal. Ultimately a decisive moment came in the history of Nepal when King Gyanendra administered the oath of the office of Prime Minister to Girija Prasad Koirala, leader of the Nepali Congress, apart from restoring the Parliament of Nepal which was dissolved in 2002. The choices each makes will help to determine the fate of Nepalese society and politics.

Historical Sketch

The modern state of Nepal was founded by Prithvi Narayan Shah in 1769 who defeated more than seventy-five small hill principalities, either voluntarily or after unsuccessful resistence to the Gurkha armies. It was the Gurkha conquest under his leadership that gave the country a single name and a strong central government in modern times. His emergence as a strong monarch out of the prevailing chaos and uncertainty, made the Kingdom state-centric and not society centric. The state-centric approach is described as the perception that operators of the state system play the most decisive roles in the determination of public policies. In the system even state is defined as all those individuals who occupy political offices that authorise them and them alone to make and apply decisions.[1] The system so established, checked the development of political consciousness and a clear sense of identity with the symbol of nationalism. For hundreds of years, the central government in Nepal was run by a number of interrelated families, with the most influential and powerful of them keeping the Prime Ministership or to chief executive position to themselves.[2] Centrally appointed governors provided the link between Kathmandu and the rest of the country.

Prithvi Narayan Shah died in 1774 but till 1846 the King ruled and reigned. During this period the Kings of Nepal undertook to rule directly with authority. Under the circumstances a political system was evolved which relied for its effectiveness on plots and rumour-mongering, bluster and bullying, and primarily on manoeuvres and counter manoeuvres. It was the primary obligation of the common people or the masses to support the elite in the government and in the landed aristocracy. The government existed for the elite rather than for the people. The organs of the government were used largely for the personal gain and the masses were exploited rather than benefited.[3] Considerations of the common people seldom figured in the calculations of the rulers.

In between the period the Gurkha Kingdom of Nepal had a conflict of interests with British India since the British ascendancy in India. One of the British expansions was directed to North India, towards which Nepal was also trying to expand. In 1814-15, there was a war between the British and the Gurkhas which resulted in the defeat of the latter. After that the Gurkhas developed cordial relationship with the British in India, who guaranteed the survival of Nepal as a state[4]. The famous treaty of Sugauli (1815) was ratified in March 1816 by which the Nepalese relinquished much of their newly acquired territory and agreed to allow a British residency to be established at Kathmandu. The Gurkhas also provided the British with soldiers who fought in the defence of British imperial interest. In those years, Bhimsen Thapa (1806-37) was the Prime Minister of Nepal who greatly increased the power of his office at the expense of monarch and paved the way for the establishment of the Rana line of hereditary Prime Ministers. Later on, Jung Bahadur, a member of Bhimsen family became prominent in the government and after a Kotmassacre, assumed power on 17 September 1846.

Jung Bahadur, the first ruler of Rana family, adopted a friendly and cooperative attitude towards British India and during India's first struggle for freedom (1857-58) he stood firm as a friend of the British. Although he died in 1877, his policy towards the British survived. Almost all Rana Prime Ministers followed his suit and noted among them was Chandra Shamsher, who ruled Nepal with much ability. However, the contradictions between the King and the Rana Prime Ministers and within the Rana family, were internal to their system of family oligarchy. Externally, the Rana regime was hostile to and incompatible with the modern concepts of power, authority and legitimacy which, in nutshell, required the broadening of the regime's base by making it people-oriented.[5]

But the winds of change began blowing in thirties when anti-Rana organisations were formed and the Prachanda Gurkha in 1931, and the Praja Parishad in 1935. Several Nepalese leaders of the time including B.P. Koirala and D.R. Regmi took a very active role in Indian Nationalist movement and even jailed by the British. In the changed circumstances they began to think of founding an organisation to carry on the struggle for democracy in Nepal. They founded the 'All India Nepali National Congress' at Varanasi on 31 October 1946 with the guidance and support of Indian socialists like Jayaprakash Narayan and Ram Manohar Lohia, in particular. The then Rana regime received a great jolt in August 1947 when the British withdrew from the Indian subcontinent and the new Indian dispensation refused to cooperate with the Nepalese autocracy as earlier. Further, for a number of years Kathmandu witnessed political instability which resulted in 'Delhi Settlement' with the help and interference of the then Indian government. Ultimately, King Mahendra who assumed power in March 1955 promised for holding the first ever Parliamentary elections in 1959.

Dawn of Democracy

In that kind of situation Nepal needed first a constitution which provided for Parliamentary system and acting on the idea King appointed a Constitution Commission with Bhagwati Prasad Singh as Chairman and four other members. On 12 February 1959, the King gave Nepal a 77–Article Constitution which ensured a Parliamentary form of Government based on universal franchise. It was presented to the nation just a week before the Parliamentary elections were to be held. The constitution was modelled on the British pattern and incorporated all the characteristics of a parliamentary democracy. The Parliament was to be made of two Houses – the House of Representatives (Pratinidhi Sabha) and the Senate (Maha Sabha), including the King. Pratinidhi Sabha was an elected House having 109 seats.

The election process for the House of Representatives started on 18 February and ended on April 13, 1959. The Nepali Congress, the largest of all political parties, who commanded a mass base, won 74 seats out of 109. The Nepali Congress polled the highest number of votes, however, the percentage of its polled votes was less than 15 per cent of the total electorates and about 37 per cent of the total votes polled. Next to it was Gurkha Parishad who got 19 seats.[6] In total nine political parties participated in this first general election of Nepal's history.

Further developments followed as per the schedule. On 4 May 1959 B.P. Koirala was elected leader of the Congress Legislative Party and the next day, the Constitution had accepted the principle that the leader of the majority Party in the House of Representatives would be the Prime Minister.[7] After a gap of ten days King Mahendra invited B.P. Koirala to form his government and consequently, on 27 May 1959, a 19 – member Council of Ministers was constituted with[8] Cabinet Ministers and 11 Deputy Ministers. Contrary was the fact that formation of the Council of Ministers took place prior to the commencement of the Constitution which came into force on 30th June 1959 and the Parliament was inaugurated by the King on 4th July 1959.

Under the new Constitution which provided for the Parliamentary System, several arrangements were simultaneously made that undermined the Parliamentary sovereignty. In it, the King was empowered to reject the recommendation of the Prime Minister to summon or dissolve Parliament. Another infringement was relating to the post of the Prime Minister in which the King was given a discretion to appoint even an outsider to the office of the Prime Minister if he found no person commanding the confidence of the majority in the House. The King was given power to dismiss the Prime Minister after consulting the Rastra Parishad (Council of States). But above all, the constitution itself was the result of the King's promulgation. The first elected government of Nepal, under the premiership of B.P. Koirala was allowed to function having sandwiched between people's aspirations and King's uncontrolled powers.

As a result months after the formation of the new dispensation signs of clash between the King and the Prime Minister began to take shape towards the end of 1959. Provocation was provided by Koirala's assertion at a public meeting in Nepalganj that he derived his authority from a mandate of the electorate, which implied that he could not be thrown out at the pleasure of the King. The growing power and prestige of Koirala both inside and outside Nepal pained King Mahendra and he feared the end of royal power in Nepal.

Post-dismissal Effects

The fear of His Majesty was translated into action on December 15, 1960, when King Mahendra took over the government by a Royal Proclamation, dissolved parliament, deposed all ministers including B.P. Koirala. The reasons for abrogating the system were explained in the royal proclamation which stated that stability and progress expected to be brought about by the elected government had remained unfulfilled; administration was paralysed and lawlessness had become rampant; selfish and group interests had gained momentum. Thus for ending this sorry state of affairs and for furthering the cause of democracy suspension of parliamentary system had become necessary in the national interest.

The official version of the causes was inadequate. Politically, two charges were levelled against the Parliamentary system that brought its end. In the first place there was no adequate background for the smooth functioning of the Parliamentary system and the people were not prepared for the system. Secondly, the political parties, instead of enlightening the public were misleading and confusing the people. However, at the heart of the matter remained the fact that King Mahendra was opposed to political parties because he viewed every kind of organised popular force as a threat to his absolute power.[9] The King suspected that the Nepali Congress leaders were indulging in a plot for the eventual abolition of monarchy.

Externally too, it was considered as a serious setback to the democratic efforts in the country. Since the coming of King Mahendra in 1955 he adopted the policy of diversifying Nepal's political and economic relations with regional and world powers at large. They all helped Nepal in the hope that the country, having self-reliant economically would be able to stand on its own feet politically broadening the base for democratic norms. Cooperation between the two elements of the time – the King and the Nepali Congress was the need of the hour. By taking over the government, the King had virtually imposed a dictatorial rule in Nepal. The event reminded the prophetic words of King Tribhuvan who told Koirala nine years ago" you don't know my son (Mahendra). He is a thorough reactionary .... a diehard Rana supporter .... He will make

Nepal, and he will make all of you, weep.[10]

The changeover from democracy to dictatorship continued in Nepal for decades. King Mahendra ruled and reigned till his death in January 1972. His death was followed by the coronation of his son King Birendra, during whose dispensation, the agitation for restoration of democracy was fastened. The age-old system of absolute monarchy in Nepal was replaced by constitutional monarchy on April 8, 1990. King Birendra agreed to the demands of the people for putting an end to partyless Panchayat system. He agreed to a new constitutional arrangement in which he would continue to be head of the state but the governance would be the responsibility of a cabinet answerable to Parliament.[11] An Interim Government was formed on 19 April 1990 with Krishna Prasad Bhattarai as the Prime Minister of the country. Elections on a multi-party basis were held in May 1991, resulting in a clear, though thin majority for the Nepali Congress.[12] Next to it was the Communist Party of Nepal, who registered a strong presence in Nepalese legislature.

Democracy Restored

With the coming of Democracy in Nepal in the early nineties social and political power of Maoism was felt in Kathmandu. For centuries and with the advent of King Mahendra, despite diversification of foreign economic relations of Nepal with major regional and world superpowers, the country remained backward in spheres of agriculture, industry, trade and commerce, health facilities, road and transport, education etc. On the otherhand Nepal not only established its diplomatic relations with various countries but made them strong from politico-strategic points of view, especially at the cost of its age-old intimacy with New Delhi. Though Nepal's diplomatic relations with China was established in August 1955, the latter had left far behind India and other powers in influencing the Palace and the people of the country. The main reasons for forceful entry of Maoism in Nepalese society and politics were the economic backwardness of Nepal and Kathmandu's strong political relations with the Peking. However, no less important role was played by the internal dissensions of the Nepali Congress which not only made Maoism a strong force in Nepal but The Communist Party of Nepal - United Marxist- Leninist emerged as the single largest Party in the general elections, held in November 1994 and formed government under the premiership of Manmohan Adhikari.[13] The Nepali Congress was only a few seats behind the Communists, it was a moral defeat, accepted so by Koirala.

Despite the establishment of constitutional monarchy Nepal lacked political stability on account of dissensions among the leaders of Nepali Congress and rising power of Maoism. Economic and social backwardness of Nepal added fuel to the fire and a large section of the people began to lean towards the Marxist ideology. Gradually Nepal was moving towards a phase of lawlessness. It gave birth to Maoist insurgency which disliked the King and the Political system, equally.

In fact, the deteriorating condition of Nepal was a failure of the political system itself. The Parliamentary system has been failed miserably in managing popular aspirations of economic well-being and social justice. Political leaders and elected representatives of the people gave priority to their preoccupations with power and pelf rather than to the concerns of their wider social constituencies. However, the king himself played a significant role in deserting the political system and did not hesitate to quietly patronise the unfolding Maoist rebellion during 1996-2001. In an abrupt and dramatic development the bloody night of June 1, 2001, came and the Crown Prince Dipendra murdered his parents along with other relatives. Gyanendra, the younger brother of King Birendra, became the new King of Nepal. The year not only witnessed a complete transformation of the monarchy following the palace massacre but it also lent greater stridency to the Maoist rebellion that had already gained a considerable social support and self confidence to challenge the kingdom's armed forces.[14]

In 1996 the Maoist had established themselves in three remote mountain districts in the west of the Himalayan Kingdom. The coming years provided them wide public sympathy for their proposed socio-economic programme. Today, they control 69 of the 75 districts of Nepal. The primary target of the Maoist is the monarchy, but to tap nationalist sentiment, they also inveigh against Indian 'hegemonists' who allegedly prop up the oppressive system.[15]

Recent Developments

Later in a dramatic development the history of dismissing an elected government was repeated on 1 February 2005 when King Gyanendra sacked Nepal's coalition government of Sher Bahadur Deuba and declared emergency in the Himalayan Kingdom. The King said in an address on nationwide television. "I have exercised the rights given to the Crown under the present constitution and dissolved the Government in the larger interest of the people. For the larger interest of the Nepalese general public, the nation and democracy and people's fundamental rights, we have decided to form a new Government under my own chairmanship."

After the takeover, the country was in turmoil. What Nepal badly needs and sadly lacks is a peace process that aims to provide the Maoist with face-saver which, in turn, integrates them into the mainstream of Kingdom's politics. It may yield the immediate peace that the King has promised Nepali people in his takeover address. On the otherhand, the Maoist do not appear to be inclined towards a genuine peace process. They know that such a process will eventually call for their laying down of arms and adjusting their revolutionary notion of new democracy with a multi-party Parliamentary order.

The new change has brought the king face to face with all the popular political forces of Nepal, the armed Maoists and political parties. The event has also isolated him from his erstwhile supporters in the international community, particularly India, the US, the European Union and Britain. His only hope of restoring his authority lies in conciliation and negotiation, whose possibility is not only limited but difficult too.

Since the takeover the democratic and Maoists forces of Nepal began to come closer to each other to fight against the autocratic rule of King Gyanendra. The first such effort was made in November 2005 when they signed the 12-point agreement which was denounced by the palace and the United States of America. As there seemed no way out the SPA and the Maoists undertook the second understanding on 19 March 2006. On the day of agreement they both released identical statements separately and unequivocally declared that people's movement is the only means of ending the conflict, establish loktantra and restore people's sovereignty in Nepal.[16]

The People's movement took a decisive turn at the end of April 2006 and leader of the Nepali Congress Girija Prasad Koirala was administered the oath of Prime Minister of Nepal on the last day of the month. The Parliament, which was dissolved in 2002, was also restored and it unanimously approved a proposal to hold elections for a special Constituent Assembly to draw up a new constitution that would decide the future of monarchy in the country.[17] The struggle for democracy in Nepal has perhaps entered its most difficult phase only now.

7.2 EMERGENCE AND SPREAD OF MAOISTS IN NEPAL

The success of the Chinese revolution had a profound impact on the world, creating a wave of joy amongst the oppressed countries in South

Asia on the one hand and sending shivers down the spine of the developed capitalist countries of Europe and especially America on the other. Personalities like Mao Zedong and Zhou Ea Lai started to be worshiped as cult figures, not only in China, but in many other countries as well.[18] Chinese revolution served as the required fuel to ignite the hidden passions of freedom for many a third world countries and the kingdom of Nepal is one of them. But the success of the Maoists in Nepal should not be overemphasised as a stupendous achievement of Maoism. In fact it is a product of more than 50, if not 200, years of political distortions. Monarchy in Nepal has reigned supreme for 40 years, governing through a corrupt, inefficient and repressive Panchayat order. During the last 14 years, while managing to arouse popular aspirations for economic well being and social justice, the Parliamentary political system utterly failed to keep its promises.[19] In addition the military potential of Nepal should be kept in the backdrop before arriving at any abrupt conclusion. Moreover, the uniformity in the ethnic composition and the overall uniformity in their economic profile and hence lack of many classes in society makes it easier for Maoism to thrive in Nepal. But for many Maoists, even accepting to take part in elections of the Constituent Assembly in a bourgeoisie set up is a revisionist attitude, although it was the Nepali Maoists who forced the so-called bourgeoisie democracy to accept their terms and conditions. Monarchy has been abolished in Nepal and the Maoists have won the elections.

Politically, diplomatic relations between the People's Republic of China and Nepal was established in 1955, the year King Mahendra became the King of Nepal after the death of his father King Tribhuvan. It was the period when Nepal had a passionate quest for independence and status in international society and its big strategic understanding with China gave Kathmandu an opportunity to balance its relations with India. The new King Mahendra also appointed T.P. Acharya as the new Prime Minister of Nepal who was known for his pro-China and anti-India inclinations. Presumably India considered the immediate danger not from common border with China but from its extension in Nepal as the latter was a relatively weak country.[20] The new dispensation of Nepal introduced Panchayat system and put several restrictions on the activities of political parties. The system of panchayat continued in Nepal for next thirty years and after an intense movement for the restoration of democracy the existing system was replaced by the system of a constitutional monarchy based on multiparty formula. Political relations between China and Nepal touched a new height during the period.

Maoists activities remained limited to influencing public opinion in ways more than one. The left wing communist organisations kept themselves active and often raised voices in support of the popular grievances and also against the land reform policies of the government. Initially they had lacked mass support because of their violent means and ideological preoccupations.

In 1990 the Partyless Panchayat system was replaced by Parliamentary democracy and a fresh constitution was enacted which paved the way for competing party politics. Since the process of democratisation started in early nineties, Nepal witnessed a plethora of contentious activities, both violent and non-violent. Contentious activities include identity and gender movements, numerous public protests and strikes and the Maoist rebellion. But to a large extent these contentious activities were an urban phenomenon in Nepal. They occurred around Kathmandu and other urban centres. Many of the people engaged in these activities belonged to middle class or elite section of the society.

The Maoists stood first in the mobilisation of the rural poor and their issues. No political party or movement had mobilised the rural people more than the Maoists. This is significant because the mainstream movements and political parties, despite their claim of representing the rural people, were mostly led by urban and rural elite. If the mobilisation of hitherto largely neglected people is a contribution towards democratisation, the Maoists have played a significant role.[21] The Maoists controlled a large part of Nepal's geographical space and enjoyed public sympathy for their proposed socio-economic programme. However, the violent methods adopted by them undoubtedly undermined electoral democracy and put a question mark on the future of democracy.

Even in the first general elections held in May 1991 the Nepali Congress and the United Marxist Leninist Communist Party of Nepal (UML) shared most of the votes and Girija Prasad Koirala, leader of the Nepali Congress became the Prime Minister. But unfortunately factionalism soon engulfed the Nepali Congress and it became difficult for Koirala to implement policies and programmes of the government. He lastly resigned and called for mid-term election in 1994. The United Marxist Leninist Communist Party of Nepal won 89 seats in the general elections held in November 1994 and Man Mohan Adhikari of the UML formed a minority government with the help of small parties like the Nepal Majdoor Kisan Party and Communist Party of Nepal (Masal). Nepal, thus, became the first communist monarchy.

The minority government of Man Mohan Adhikari assumed power after an election campaign dominated by issues mostly India centred and based on anti-India planks; abrogation of the 1950 treaty, ending the special relationship with India, renegotiating agreements on cooperation in water resources, and ending the recruitment of Nepalese Gurkhas in the Indian Army-exactly the issues raised by the Maoist in 2008 when they formed the government under the Premiership of Pushpa Kamal Dahal 'Prachanda'. In his election campaign, before the polls, Adhikari was to seek the review of Nepal's 1950 treaty with India because it proved convenient to him in an atmosphere which was anti-India.[22] He found in the treaty a tilt in India's favour and declared it to be reviewed.[23] The new Prime Minister also refused to accept Indian security umbrella and expressed the wish to have free trade with both Pakistan and Bangladesh.[24] Going a step further the then Adhikari government of Nepal made an institutional arrangement at the Foreign Secretary level set up in March 1995; but after a few rounds of discussions, it became clear that India was not interested in amendment: the treaty had either to be abrogated or maintained in its present form, as the text of the treaty did not provide for modifications.[25] India made its stand clear either we keep it or you abrogate it. However Nepalese leaders did not go beyond making proforma noises about review of the treaty being under active discussion. At the moment the best New Delhi could do was to watch the new Nepal which had turned red recently[26] but at the same time India, on its part, took great care in not giving any impression of big brotherliness.

The Maoists of today were once a part of the mainstream politics under the banner of United Peoples Front of Nepal (UPFN) led by Baburam Bhattarai. In a split in the party, the Baburam faction failed to get the recognition of the Election Commission to participate in the mid-term elections in 1994. This group joined hands with the Communist Party of Nepal (Maoists). The declared aim of the Maoists is to establish a people's government through peoples war that is inspired by Marxism–Leninism– Maoism. In 1996 the Maoists launched the 'Peoples Movement or Jana Andolan by carrying out attacks in different parts of Nepal. Indeed they launched insurgency after the state repeatedly ignored their demands and received support from the population ignored by the state. Like other leftists, the Maoists of Nepal considered the states as a semi-feudal organisation and held it responsible for the prevailing socio economic ills within the country. The Maoists of Nepal have also projected India and the US as the imperialist powers trying to subvert the interests of the people of Nepal by aligning with the rightist forces within Nepal.

By the time the peoples movement was started by the Maoists the systems of the country as whole provided them a convenient phenomenon. With the democratic politics in Nepal being extremely factionalised successive governments in Nepal found it difficult to implement governmental policies and programmes. One result of this was that the rate of economic growth was modest, but it did not match the rate at which population grew. Particularly in the Ninth Plan (1998-2002) which was planned to make Nepal a competitive, competent and technologically oriented society failed to achieve the target due to the violence unleashed by the Maoist insurgency. The Peoples Movement cast a dark shadow on the development in all sectors. It resulted in massive unemployment and illiteracy in a society that had an ethnically and religiously fragmented population. It all favoured the Maoists because those who mobiiise often seek resources or comfortable policies from the state. This situation helped them in intensifying conflict among groups who control the state and its resources and those who want a voice in the state and a share of its resources. The Maoists used terror tactics to spread their influence in the rural areas and taken effective control of administration in several districts. By the end of 2000, the Maoists were active in over two thirds of the 75 districts of Nepal. They had set up Peoples government in five districts of western Nepal. In the areas under their control, the Maoists do local policing, settle local disputes, collect levies from the people and even set up banks.

In the early years of the Maoist movement, Nepalese politicians belonging to the leftist camp displayed a fraternal resistance to taking any harsh measures toward the Maoists. The Communist Party of Nepal Marxist-Leninist, the third largest political party in Nepal, openly endorsed the aims of the Maoists even while disapproving of its working style. The majority ruling party, the Nepali Congress, beset with internal problems, could not take concrete action to deal with the Maoist problem. The Maoist insurgency added confusion in the democratic politics of Nepal that was already reeling under factionalism which ultimately led to a constitutional crisis. The key problem for Nepal at the time was the absence of linkage between the people at large and their government. Consequently the formation of a healthy civil society in Nepal has been held in check. The conflicts in Nepal have been the outcome of incongruence between societal aspirations and state institution.[27]

The Maoists of Nepal took maximum benefit of the prevailing

political instability of the Kingdom and from 2001 onwards began to dominate the politics and political events of the country. It assumed grave proportions, became number one problem of Nepal and government's measures such as, force, persuasion and negotiation to tackle the Maoist problem proved both useless and counterproductive as well. Since March 2001, several rounds of peace negotiations have been held between the government and the Maoists. But due to irreconcilable differences and mutual suspicion, these efforts have not borne result. Terror and violence by the insurgents continued and the security forces have stepped up counter insurgency operations. However, the Maoists activities had restricted the democratic rights of the common people even when they were conducted in the name of protecting democratic rights. The most well-known public protests were the bandhs which called for closure of markets, towns, cities or the whole country. Those who dared to continue with regular activities were often violently stopped. The common people were thus denied their fundamental political rights and civil liberties.

For long the Maoists of Nepal had held normal political processes under seize as prescribed in the constitution of 1990. In May 2002, the Deuba government recommended the dissolution of the parliament but found it difficult to hold elections because of the Maoist insurgency. Taking advantage of the situation King Gyanendra invoked Article 127 of the constitution to dismiss the Prime Minister and his cabinet for incompetence in October 2002. He nominated Lokendra Bahadur Chand to head a nine-member interim government but in March 2003 the mainstream forces of the country launched a movement against the monarchic takeover. Since then, a tripartite power struggle has dominated Nepali politics, between the king, the mainstream political parties and the Maoists. Even during this period the Maoists remained adamant in their demand for the creation of a Constituent Assembly to draft a drastically revised constitution. As the Maoist insurgency raged, the King declared a state of emergency on 1 February 2005 arresting mainstream political leaders and assumed absolute power.

When King Gyanendra decided to dismiss the Government of Sher Bahadur Deuba and declare emergency in the Himalayan Kingdom in 2005, it was clear that his days were numbered. Although the country was passing from the worst form of political instability and dilemma, dismissing the government was not the best option.The Maoists have been able to grow, in part because of the factious nature of the mainstream parties but a major share of the blame surely rests on the king who had not given any administration in Kathmandu, room for negotiation.[28] The king had also betrayed the expectations that the country had from him following his incarnation in 2001. To falcify the king's calculations the Maoists and the democratic forces joined hands together and after a nineteen days mass demonstration in April 2006 the king had to left his executive powers and agree to work with an interim government. In a grand alliance of seven parties and the Maoists, the latter had consented to join the interim government. This grand alliance was entrusted to conduct elections to a Constituent Assembly. The interim government would have also to administer to country till the formation of a new government elected on the basis of the Constitution which will emerge from the Assembly's deliberations.[29] The 8 - point agreement between Seven Party Alliance (SPA) and the Maoists explicitly provided for the United Nations to help in the management of arms and armed personnel of both the sides and to monitor it in order to conduct elections for the Constituent Assembly in a free and fair manner.[30] It was the best chance ever provided for the peaceful democratic change in the Himalayan Kingdom.

The election to the members of Constituent Assembly was held on April 10, 2008 that saw more than 60 per cent participation of the 17.5 million-strong electorate in 21,000 polling centres. In results the Nepali citizenry surprised itself and the world on occasion with a show of people's will that was unprecedented and path-breaking. It had brought a rebel force barely out of the jungle into the driver's seat of national politics. The Maoists has achieved a massive win over its rivals, the Nepali Congress and the mainstream left Communist Party of Nepal (UML). By voting in the Maoists as the single largest party, the electorate has sent a clear message that it favoured the new. But voters tempered this message by denying the former rebels an absolute majority of their own. Under the rules of Nepal's interim constitution a two-thirds majority was needed for any major decision, including the election of Prime Minister and President. By giving the Maoists a little more than one-third of the seats, the electorate said that it wanted the Maoists to keep alive the principle of consensus that had served Nepal's parties so well in the struggle against the monarchy.

Several factors seem to explain the crushing success of the Maoists in Nepal. To begin with, the Maoist win is the result of a well-oiled campaign machinery worthy of a politico-military organisation. There was country-wide deployment of threat and intimidation during the run-up to the elections, which demoralised competing party activists and civil servants alike. A major reason for the win seems to be voter's desire to keep the Maoists from returning to the people's war and suffering attendant miseries. The imperfect peace process, made so by the absence of the rule of law and state administration over the last two years, left the population beleaguered and worried of a return to that horrific period. It is said that urban people were convinced of the Maoists popular promise in a country whose workforce continues to migrate in massive numbers to India and overseas because of high levels of poverty. The Maoists projected themselves as true agents of change.[31] Lastly they also filled their candidates from the members of the deprived communities, including the Dalits, the Janajati ethnic category and women. They laid claim with justification, to having introduced all the salient issues that had been placed before the electorate including the demands for inclusion, federalism, secularism and an overturning of economic relations to serve the underclass.

Emergence of the Maoists as the single largest party had paved the way for formation of a Maoist-led coalition government in Nepal. Having confirmed that he would lead the Maoists in the government Pushpa Kamal Dahal 'Prachanda' began to speak on its relations with neighbouring countries and at the same expressed his party's vision of a new Nepal. Apart from underlining his desire to follow the policy of 'equidistance' in relationship with giant neighbours–India and China[32] he also wanted to change the image of the Maoists among the middle classes in Nepal and among the international community. There was some suspicion about the Maoists' intentions, given their background as insurgents against the monarchy and it was thought that they would be autocratic when they assumed power. Initially there were doubts whether they would participate in the democratic process of elections as it was assumed their strength lay only in the power of arms. After emerging as the largest party there was still some concern that it would turn autocratic, Prachanda emphasised that they would again proved the critics wrong by demonstrating their commitment to multi-party democracy and democratic rights and freedoms.[33] However, with some delay in forging the alliance the Maoists had reached an agreement with the Communist Party of Nepal (UML) and Madhesi Janadhikar Forum (MJF), the two major parties, to support Prachanda's candidacy first and later the government. In afterwards his candidacy was also backed by other small parties. He took the oath of office of the Prime Minister with eight ministers in the third week of August 2008.[34] Now the time has come to rectify the past misdeeds and address the question of disjunction with utmost care and importance.

7.3 ORIGIN AND STATUS OF MADHESI IN NEPAL

The Madhesi

Madhesi is an amorphous term referring to caste categories of the eastern Terai in particular. The Terai belt is Nepal's most densely populated region and accounts for half the country's 29 million people. Not all of its residents are Madhesis, however, Janajati groups like the Tharus – the original inhabitants before the swamps were cleared and Avadhi, Bhojpuri and Maithili - speaking migrants moved up from India have a strong presence in the western planes districts. In addition to them there are Limbus and throughout the region, the Nepali-speaking Pahadis are present in significant numbers. The Madhesis in particular, form 31.2 per cent of Nepal's population and they are as stratified in terms of language and caste as the Pahadis, a shared sense of grievance inheres in all of them, 'We have never been accepted as Nepalis. Despite being Nepali citizens, we have always been called Indians.[35]

In past the people of the Terai region have sometimes opposed the policies of the government, but their resentment against it never developed to an extent which could be termed as a separatist movement. On many occasions after 1950 people of the Terai region raised their voices against the economic policies of the government. One of the major issue of their resentment has been the land reform policies of the government. In fact, the people of the Terai, most of whom have migrated from the Indian plains continued to maintain their socio-cultural links with their Indian counterparts. They also do not possess similar linguistic, ethnic and economic background. Because of different socio-economic background the interests of the people of the Terai do not coincide with each other. It had in turn, discouraged them from organising themselves into a cohesive group.[36] However, an organisation named Terai Liberation Front was formed in 1964 to fight the causes of the Terai. But as the movement was politically motivated it never gained mass support and faded out.

The turn of events moved fastly in Nepal at the close of the century and thereafter as well. Multi-party democracy with constitutional monarchy was adopted in 1990 and the Maoist's movement initiated in 1996 had changed the social feeling and political fate of the nation. Gyanendra, the last king of Shah dynasty who took over the throne following the palace massacre in which king Birendra was gunned down in June 2001, miscalculated three things : First, he thought the Maoists and mainstream parties would never join hands and form a collective front against him. Secondly he hoped that given a choice between the Maoists and the monarchy, the international community, particularly India and the United States, would eventually choose monarchy. And lastly, he underestimated the consciousness of the Nepali people, which had grown by leaps and bounds in the post-1990 open society and during the decade-long Maoist insurgency.[37]

After a long gap the Madhesi awakened in April, 2006 when the mass upsurge of the people's movement sought peace and pluralism, and mandated the writing of a new constitution to redraw state-society relations. The agitation of Madhes was a spontaneous uprising by the people of Terai plains origin who have long felt excluded amidst the high lander identification of the nation state. The exclusion that Madhesi activists speak about is not just nomenclatural. There is bitterness over the extent to which Madhesis have been kept out of the state administration, and over the fact that Hindi - the link language between Maithili, Bhojpuri and Avadhis finds no official recognition in Nepal. They in common with the rest of the erstwhile kingdom's citizens, wanted the Constituent Assembly to provide them the rights they have been denied all these years. Their demands included proportional representation in state organs including the army changes in electoral laws to enhance Madhesi participation and so on. Sensing the government's mood they have also enlarged their aspirations to the level of utopia and included self determination and the declaration of the 500 - by - 20 mile Terai plains as a single province "Ek Madhes, Ek Pradesh."[38]

Initially, the Maoists of Nepal kept a sympathetic view towards the problems of Terai region and in the areas where janajatis were dominant and demanded for a Constituent Assembly to be elected on the basis of proportional representation. It gave a wide mass support to the Maoists who were in keen contest with the Nepali Congress. But after the Jan Andolan-II of March-April 2006 when Parliament was restored and the Maoist joined the government, the Nepali Congress and the Communist Party of Nepal (UML) forced the former rebel to drop their demand for proportional representation. A compromise was struck among them for only half the seats to the Constituent Assembly to be allotted on proportional representation basis. By this understanding the Maoists were not in greater loss because they promised ethnic rights, but its impact on Madhesis became sparking and they immediately started their movement which paved the way for further developments in Nepalese politics.

There are three forces in Nepalese national life who are attached to the issue of Madhesis - the Maoists, the Nepali Congress along with Communist Party of Nepal (UML) and the palace politics. They all tried to compete and gain the favour of Madhesis for no other purposes but political. As the movement of Madhesis was erupted due to Maoists consensus with the other forces, they remained soft throughout the movement. On their part they have put forward a map which comprises more than a dozen provinces, including a part of the Terai called 'Madhes' which divided the region into three sub-provinces of Avadh, Bhojpura and Mithila. The Tharus and Limbus got their own provinces in the western and eastern Terai. The Nepali Congress and its allies, found the agitation of Madhes as useful since its immediate target was the Maoist but in due course they felt that it was unable to countenance the identity-led nature of the agitation in the Terai. Therefore, Girija Prasad Koirala, the Prime Minister became slow in addressing the Madhesi demands. The Nepali public across the country also doubted the sincerity of Nepali Congress to the republican cause. Earlier Koirala floated the idea of 'baby king' and his daughter Sujata who was contesting the election from Sunsari district in the Terai was also in favour of constitutional monarchy.

With the violent movement of the Madhesis, over night new political groups emerged which took up the demands for, inter alia, a fully proportional electoral system. Eventually, two armed groups also emerged – the Janatantrik Tarai Mukti Morcha (JTMM) and Jai Krishna Goit. While the Maoists wanted to tackle the problem of Madhesis domestically these extremist outfits have operated with impunity from Indian towns of Sitamarhi, Raxaul, Darbhanga and Gorakhpur. But having facilitated the discussions in New Delhi in the autumn of 2005 that brought the Maoists to an understanding with the parliamentary parties, New Delhi had been asked, specifically, to rein in militants who have been engaged in bombing and targeted killings in Nepal's Terai plains and taking refuge across the open border.[39] As time went on, it became clear that quite a few among the Madhesi leadership were seeking consortium with the royalists of Kathmandu, as well as the Hindutva forces across the border.

By these developments the Narayanhiti royal palace or Gyanendra seemed energised and viewed the events as a last silver line to save the fortunes of monarchy in Nepal. He sent emissaries to meet with Hindutva and BJP stalwarts in India in a bid to revive the near- end system of the country. But at this stage the Foreign Ministry in South Block played its card in favour of a pluralistic, representative evolution in Nepal. By extending the tenure of Indian Ambassador to Nepal until after the election the government had sent a message committing its own agenda and standing to the holding on elections on schedule in Nepal.

However, the demand of 'Ek Madhes, Ek Pradesh' is problematic because it will foreclose the real devolution and inclusion that Nepal's diverse ethno-linguistic groups aspire to. The three Madhesi parties – Madhesi Janadhikar Forum (MJF), Tarai Madhes Loktantrik Party (TMLP) and the Sadbhavna Party will also do their job differently making the situation bad to worse. An added cause for wariness is the interest some United Nations officials as well as U.S. government agencies and non–governmental organisations have begun to show in the Madhesis. Sensing the prospect of the larger payoff that internationalisation might bring, the Madhesi leadership and a section of the people are prepared that if Nepal fails to grant autonomy, they would look to India. 'We are offering Kathmandu control over only defence,[40] foreign affairs and communications and he also added further that if Kathmandu does not want this we can always offer Delhi the same.

In the circumstances all hopes pinned on the formation and efficiency of a 601- member House that has the dual responsibility of drafting a new constitution and serving as parliament during the interim. The Constituent Assembly is a necessary condition for the country to achieve political stability, peace and a return to pluralism. The general expectation is that the Constituent Assembly will define a democratic constitution that will simultaneously address the many conflicting and complementary demand of marginalised minorities and, at long last, provide politics as a platform for economic progress. Whatever the origins of the recent Madhesi movement, the Terai region is in ferment and will not settle for second class status. If the Constituent Assembly fail to design federal structures which guarantee autonomy and dignity to all regions of Nepal and economic justice for the poor and the landless, new faultlines and conflicts will emerge. With the right approach, Madhesi aspirations can easily be accommodated within the federal Nepal that all parties there are officially committed to. Earlier India played a good role in helping to broker the last agreement between the Nepal government and the Madhesi parties and now it should ensure that its territory is not used by extremist forces bent on sabotaging the possibility of a democratic solution in a peaceful way.

7.4 CHALLENGES AHEAD

Nepal was brought together territorially by the Gorkha conquest. It had not been unified psychologically and economically even after more than two centuries. This is partly because the Nepali state was captured and exploited by a small elite caste group ever since its formation. The ruling group defined the rights and duties of citizens towards the state to promote its own interests. This disjunction between the state and society has been the underlying cause for the eruption of many contentious activities in present day Nepal, which have directly or indirectly affected the recent trend towards democratisation.[41] The Maoists who are assigned to seat on driver's position by the power of the ballot have every right to feel betrayed and cheated, they must make one last attempt to foster a consensus. For the better or worse, the former rebels are the only party with the ability to manage the contradictions and faultlines which lie at the base of Nepali society. A just beginning initiated with cooperation from all corners need to be upheld.

Earlier the Maoists attempt to lead a coalition government was frustrated by the arch rivals the Nepali Congress, the Communist Party of Nepal (UML), and the Madhesi Janadhikar Forum (MJF) who banded together to defeat the candidature of Ram Raja Prasad Singh, the Maoist nominee for President in July 2008. In this month Ram Baran Yadav, a Madhesi and Nepali Congress candidate for President and parmanand Jha of the MJF were elected first President and Vice-President of the new republic of Nepal. However, internal politics in the Kingdom took a turn and in less than a month Pushpa Kamal Dahal Prachanda was elected the Prime Minister of the Federal Democratic Republic of Nepal by a four-fifth majority of the Constituent Assembly. It represents the ultimate victory of sobriety, accountability, and morality over the politics of cynicism and distrust.[42] Although governing Nepal at a time of global economic uncertainty will be challenging, the most important task is to lead the writing of a new constitution. The key challenges will be here to articulate robust mechanisms for the exercise of citizens' political, social, cultural, and economic rights working out a federal structure that can address the needs and aspirations of different ethnic groups, including the Madhesis; and ensuring that the army remains subordinate to civil authority.[43] The new government and Constitution are likely to place Nepal's relations with the outside world and with India on a sounder footing.

Despite instability of the successive governments the Nepali Congress and the Communist party of Nepal (UML) had in fact since 1990 developed values of responsible politics and Parliamentary practice and the expectation was that particularly with the new entrants the Maoists and the new the Terai/Madhes, the people now wait to see how the leadership takes the lead vis-à-vis the grave responsibilities of writing a new democratic constitution and running the state administration. It poses a challenge before the new dispensation to continue required majority in the Constituent Assembly to incorporate their radical reforms into the new constitution. Without sufficient number in the constituent the opposition would not be willing to be a party to the programme of the Maoists and would try to subvert any radical changes aimed at curtailing their own class interests. Hence no radical restructuring of the system is possible without the militant mobilisation of the vast masses into bitter class struggle. It is impossible to make changes through measures initiated from above; that is through state decrees and laws.[44]

Army integration is another issue that needs to be dealt with. The Maoists must also assure all on a sober and responsible approach to the national security forces – the Nepal Army, the Armed police and the Nepal Police. Related to it is the integration of the People's Liberation Army with the Nepal Army. Integration is a formal part of the peace process and the seven party alliance is formally committed to seeing it through. Until now, the Nepal army brass has publicly opposed integration. The Maoist leader Prachanda himself had said in the past that Nepal did not need such a large army but any drawing down of numbers will have to be accompanied by a plan to reabsorb those being demoralised in some kind of productive employment. What form integration will take and what the overall size of the Nepal Army should be are issues that need sorting out. The Maoist leadership needs to handle this question with a great deal of sensitivity and tact. Already, the decision to deploy the People's Liberation Army for the Prime Minister's security has irked the Communist party of Nepal (UML), MJF and Nepali Congress. Arjun Narsingh, the spokesperson of the main opposition party Nepali Congress, has also said that if the integration did not meet international standards, it could demoralise the Army.[45] He added further, how can they control both state and non-state armies? It has continued to be a deadlock point among the coalition-partners and needs to be handled carefully.

The Maoists faced an extremely difficult task ahead in balancing all the external forces and carrying on with their people's agenda. Basically the Maoists were apprehensive of the US and Indian motives and designs with whom it has to deal tactfully. As disclosed by Prachanda in May 2008 in course of an interview to The Hindu 'We will be living in a fool's paradise if we believe that the US and India will be comfortable with the Maoists in Nepal or that they will adjust to the new reality. Although they will continue diplomatic relations, they will create an adverse situation if the new government does not obey their dictates. The US tried its best to keep the monarchy alive as the king was a pawn to rule by proxy. As for India it received a slap in its face when G.P. Koirala and his NC faced a defeat'[46] However, he did not miss the opportunity to add the fact that both India and the US can hit at Nepal's belly – its economy by paralysing industrial production, blocking trade and supply lines thereby creating food shortages and shortage of consumer goods. Towards the US perhaps it is because of its continuing designation of the Maoists as a terrorist organization. Former President Jimmy Carter has publicly called for this designation to be withdrawn but no organization that has been so named has ever been taken off the terrorist list. From strategic points of view the Indian government should approach the US to get Nepal removed from the list of terrorist organisation. This designation is a major hurdle in developing Nepal's relations with many developed western countries.

Not only on several internal and foreign policy counts but the present dispensation will also face difficulty in solving its own party's problems. The major challenge for the Maoist-led government would be to reinstate hundreds of families displaced by their war. Of the estimated 2100 displaced families, only 700 have got their homes back. The Maoists also have to return the public and private land and properties seized during their war. Here, it is necessary to separate this issue into two. Certain properties such as private dwellings are easier to return but land seized from landlords is not. In the case of land that is being tilled by persons other than legal owners, a solution of a longer term nature can be found through the constitutional process itself rather than through bargaining outside the Constituent Assembly. Article 19 of the Interim Constitution speaks of compensation to be paid by the state for any property requisitioned as part of scientific land reform'. The question of land is central to the livelihood of millions of ordinary Nepalis and land reform will be a major pre-occupation of the Constituent Assembly. Earlier, on the day of Prime Ministerial election, senior leader Babu Ram Bhattarai reiterated the party's commitment to return those confiscated land and properties.

References

1. J.W. Bjorkman, 'Changing State/Society Relations : Broad - Brush Approaches and Analytic Models', Ramesh K. Arora, ed., Administrative Change, Vol. XXVIII, No. 2 & Vol. XXIX, No. 1,

January-December 2001 (Jaipur, 2001), pp. 12-13.

2. Rishikesh Shaha, Nepali Politics : Retrospect and Prospect (Delhi, 1978), p. 26.
3. Rajkumar Singh, Less Tasty Indo-Nepal Political Relations, 1947-1997 (Patna, 1998), p. 18.
4. Takashi Inoguchi, 'Political Security : Toward a Broader Conceptualisation', Bansidhar Pradhan, ed., International Studies, Vol. 40, No. 2, April-June 2003 (New Delhi, 2003), p. 114.
5. S.D. Muni, ed., Nepal : An Assertive Monarchy (New Delhi, 1977), p. 4.
6. Indra Deo Mishra, Systemic Strains and Political Development in Nepal (Varanasi, 1985), pp. 25-36.
7. Bhuvan Lal Joshi and Leo E. Rose, Democratic Innovations in Nepal (California, 1966), p. 316.
8. See, H.M. King Mahendra, Proclamations, Speeches and Messages, HMG (Nepal, 1969), pp. 1-3.
9. Rishikesh Shaha, op.cit., p. 16.
10. Bhola Chatterji, Nepal's Experiment with Democracy (New Delhi, 1977), p. 17.
11. V.N. Khanna, Foreign Policy of India (New Delhi, 2001), p. 150.
12. The Times of India, May 18, 1991.
13. Kuldip Nayar, 'Estranged Neighbour : The Arrogant India', The Indian Express, December 12, 1994.
14. S.D. Muni, 'On a Hot Tin Roof', The Hindustan Times, August 30, 2003.
15. Manoj Joshi, 'A Tale of Two Countries', Ibid., February 5, 2005.
16. Siddharth Varadarajan, 'The Countdown in Kathmandu has Begun', The Hindu, March 30, 2006.
17. Ibid., May 1, 2006.
18. Siddharth Varadarajan, 'The Rumblings in Nepal's Tarai', Ibid, April 9, 2008.
19. Dr. Ramakant and B.C. Upreti, 'Regionalism in Nepal : A Study of the Terai Region', in Ramakant, ed., Regionalism in South Asia (Jaipur, 1983), pp. 158-60.
20. Ameet Dhakal in The Hindu, June 22, 2008.
21. Kanak Mani Dixit, 'India and Nepal's Constituent Assembly', Ibid., March 7, 2008.
22. Ibid.
23. Siddharth Varadarajan, The Hindu, April 9, 2008.
24. Uddipan Mukherjee, 'Maoism and Its Future in India', Subhash C.

Kashyap, ed., South Asia Politics, Vol. 7, No. 3, July 2008 (New Delhi, 2008), pp. 26-27.

25. S.D. Muni, The Hindustan Times, August 30, 2008.
26. The Times of India (editorial), July 5, 1960.
27. Raj Kumar Kothari, 'Democratic Transition in Nepal Banes and Boons for India', Subhash C. Kashyap, ed., South Asia Politics, Vol. 7, No. 2, June 2008 (New Delhi, 2008), pp. 24-25.
28. Kuldip Nayar, 'Estranged Neighbour : The Arrogant India', The Indian Express, December 12, 1994.
29. The Times of India, November 21, 1994.
30. The Indian Express, November 22, 1994.
31. K.V. Rajan, 'Should the 1950 Treaty Be Scrapped?' The Hindu, May 3, 2008.
32. Ibid., November 22, 1994.
33. Raj Kumar Kothari, op.cit., p. 26.
34. The Hindustan Times (editorial), February 2, 2005.
35. Siddharth Varadarajan, 'In Nepal Times to Check the Dangerous Drift', The Hindu, September 20, 2006.
36. Ibid.
37. Kanak Mani Dixit, 'Enter Nepal's Maoist Establishment', The Hindu, April 14, 2008.
38. Ibid., June 14, 2008.
39. Ibid., June 30, 2008.
40. The Times of India (Nagpur), August 23, 2008.
41. Raj Kumar Kothari, op.cit., p. 26.
42. The Hindu (editorial), August 16, 2008.
43. Ibid.
44. K. Srinivas Reddy, 'Uphill Task for Nepal Maoists', Ibid., May 16, 2008.
45. Ibid., August 31, 2008.
46. K.Srinivas Reddy, op.cit.

8

THE TROUBLED WATERS OF FARAKKA: A FACTOR FOR UP AND DOWN IN INDO-BANGLADESH RELATIONS

The holy waters of Ganga have proved despair rather than a hope in relations between India and Bangladesh. It was after the initial differences in regard to the construction of Farakka barrage between India and Pakistan that the former had taken almost a unilateral decision to construct a barrage, in particular, to save the port of Calcutta from excess silting. Years after the independence of Bangladesh commissioning of the barrage took place and that was the starting point of a series of bilateral negotiations/agreements to determine the share of water that each side was to receive during the lean season of every year. In the start Indo-Bangladesh relations was marked as honeymoon phase of their relationship with no differing perceptions in sight. However it all took a 'U' turn when Sheikh Mujib was assassinated in August 1975 and a series of coup reigned in Bangladesh one after another. At a later stage the sharing of waters at Farakka had become more a matter of politics than of economy as the change over suited the military Generals of Bangladesh, who, apart from all, faced the problem of legitimacy. Difference of social, political, economic and religious bases in India and Bangladesh has added fuel to the fire and the waters of Farakka was paraded before the world community as the most blatant example of India's "intransigence" against a weak and small neighbour. In between the relationship of love and hate the two had signed three agreements on the sharing of Ganga Waters at Farakka respectively in 1975, 1977 and 1996.

Initial Developments

In pre and post independence phase the issue of constructing a barrage across the river Ganga at Farakka was alive and drew the attention of the people then in power. Continuous efforts were undertaken and committees of experts were appointed from time to time to formulate measures, to maintain uninterrupted navigation on Hooghly waterway. Opinions on the issue were sought by a large number of engineers of world repute like Stevenson Moore in 1919, Sir William Willcock in 1930, T.M. Oag in 1939 and A. Webster in 1946. At the time of partition Sir Cyril Radcliff, the chairman of the Bengal Boundary Commission, who was authorised to demarcate boundary between India and Pakistan, realised the importance of Farakka and saw to it that the entire Bhagirathi-Hooghly the off take from Ganga was given to India as it was a must for the existence of Calcutta city and the port. Keeping it in view, the Boundary Commission demarcated the district of Murshidabad, which was predominantly a Muslim-majority area in India, and in lieu awarded the region of Khulua, which was a Hindu dominated, to Pakistan.

In post-independence phase Dr. Walter Henson of Germany was first and final to suggest, in 1957, that proposal for the construction of a barrage across the Ganga was the best solution of this technical problem. It was the most purposeful measure with which the long term deterioration in Bhagirathi-Hooghly could be stopped and could possibly be converted into a gradual impovement.[1] Earlier a detailed report of Calcutta port prepared by Hydraulics Study Department of the port in 1957 was handed over to Dr. Henson in which it was said that in the monsoon season considerable volume of sand are brought down to the various bars and crossing the Hooghly and with the increase in the monsoon flows practical only with the sharp peaks, the river channel established by dredging during the dry season is disturbed. It also pointed out that the study improvement in depths over the bars and crossing occur when there are prolonged head water supply.[2] The suggestion of Dr. Walter was based on this exhaustive report.

Construction of a barrage at Farakka across the river Ganga was necessitated more from India's point of view that forced New Delhi to take a lead in its planning and execution. Ten million tonnes of silt entered the river every year from the sea with high tides. The monsoon floods in Hooghly flashes 6 million tonnes of silt back to the sea leaving behind an accumulating balance of 4 million tonnes every year which was slowly but regularly choking sections of the river. Massive dredging operations had been undertaken from time to time to keep the shipping channel clear. Calcutta port authorities were spending Rs. 75 lakhs per year preceding the year 1972 for dredging but in 1972 the expenditure went upto Rs. 10 crores : yet the silting continues unabated. The 126 miles voyage between Calcutta port and the estuary through the river Hooghly took as much as 26 hours because the ship had to wait at three points enroute for the high tide to cross the shallow points.

Calcutta is an important Indian port situated on the bank of the river Hooghly. The port is situated 126 miles away from the sea. It is through this Hooghly water way that ships of all states have to pass to reach Calcutta port and it is sustained by the supply of water from Ganga. After flood of an unprecedented magnitude in the year 1789, it abruptly changed its course and carved out the present day channel known as Padma that flows into Bangladesh territory. The upper reaches of its former channel became a distributory and consequently began to silt up, reducing the number of days in the year in which large vessel can use the port at a greater inland distance.[3]

Thus, the main objective of Farakka Barrage Project was the improvement of Calcutta port, and for the fresh water supply from Hooghly to adjoining industrial complex. The silt makes it impossible for the ships to reach Calcutta port throughout the year because there has been fast deterioration of sailing opportunities. In January 1957 the maximum drafts were 27 feet; in January 1959 the drafts fell to 24 feet.[4] The number of sailing opportunities has also been seriously affected. In 1938 ships of draught of 26 feet could use the port nearly 300 days a year, now such vessels could not use the port at all. The resulting decline in traffic handled by the port had been drastic. The port handled 11 million tonnes of traffic in 1964-65 but it declined to 7.5 million tonnes in 1974-75. The decline took place despite rapid industrialisation of the hinterland since India's independence in 1947. The deterioration of the Bhagirathi-Hooghly and consequent decline of the Calcutta port affected the health sanitation and economic life of the people not just on the banks of the river but a vast area of land historically dependent directly or indirectly on the river.[5]

Apart from decline in traffic and deterioration in sailing opportunities, the Government of India viewed the interests of the population of Calcutta city which was much more than the population of Bangladesh. Indeed, the rational of saving Calcutta city and the port impinges upon the economy of as many as 13 states of India as well as the neighburing countries Nepal and Bhutan.

The industrial and commercial activities located in the area cover some of the most vital sectors of the Indian economy including minerals and metals, transport machinery, steel, textile, tea, jute, food processing and leather industries. The utilisation of Ganga waters by India for such vital purpose, affecting the life of a large segment of the Indian society could by no stretch of imagination be characterised as wasteful.

Pakistan had, since the beginning of the plan, been opposing the construction of a barrage across the river Ganga at Farakka mainly on the ground that execution of the project would reduce East Pakistan's supply of water, deprive it of its share of water and further development. It also put forward seven points in favour of its argument for not constructing the barrage as it would cast an adverse effect on the overall development of its Eastern part.[6] India, on the otherhand, had repeatedly assured Pakistan that Farakka barrage scheme would not disturb the irrigation scheme of East Pakistan for the metrological conditions of East Pakistan were such that there was generally an excess of water and the problem was how to drain it away. Pakistan had also charged India that latter's approach to the issue had been contrary to international law and practice. S. Pirzada, the Foreign Minister of Pakistan, in reply to a question in Pakistan's National Assembly, declared on 18 July 1967 that the waters of the river Ganga should be equitably be shared by the two countries on the basis of genuine needs and in accordance with international law.

Despite differences between the two over the construction and purpose of the barrage, delegations of India and Pakistan met several time to resolve the issue. Four meetings of the experts of the two countries were held between July 1960 and January 1962 but failed to break the deadlock. In March 1961 when Jawaharlal Nehru, the then Prime Minister of India, and Ayub Khan, the President of Pakistan discussed the issue at the Commonwealth Conference of Prime Ministers, in London, the two dignitaries seemed poles apart. While Nehru assured Ayub Khan of a reasonable settlement, the latter had suggested to refer the matter to the technical experts.[7] Pakistan had also repeated its suggestion in July 1961, in mid 1962, in May 1963 and in June 1965, but the Government of India, in its reply, maintained that ministerial conference could only be held after the exchange of data regarding the project.

With a view to put pressure on New Delhi Islamabad tried to internationalise the issue by raising it at the International Water For Peace Conference, held in Washington, in May 1967. Again in 1968 it was raised at the Afro-Asian Legal Consultative Committee meeting held in Bankok. The year also witnessed bilateral talks between the two in the second week of May in which Indian side explained how the barrage would help East Pakistan in overcoming recurring flood menace.[8] However, it rejected the Pakistani delegation's suggestion that good offices of a third party like the World Bank should be used to resolve their differences over the utilisation of the water of the eastern rivers.[9]

Nothing concrete came out from the several round of talks that were held between India and Pakistan in 1969-70. Probably the domestic setting of Pakistan was not favourable during the 1968 to 1970 talks. It was during this period that President Ayub Khan had stepped down and Yahya Khan had taken the charge of the office. A movement in East Pakisan for autonomy had already been launched by the National Awami League Party. By raising unwarranted objections during the talks, the Government of Pakistan wanted to show that how much serious it was in resolving the crisis. It was, probably, an act to counter the autonomy movement and divert the attention of the opposition parties. The sincerity of Pakistan itself was not without doubt.

Differing Perceptions

The most crucial determinant of any policy, whether domestic or foreign, is the people constituting a nation, whose attitude reflecting the extent of their socio-economic and cultural development play a significant role in all policy matters.[10] Bangladesh is a geographical integrate of the subcontinent earlier known as Indo-Pakistan sub-continent. What formerly was a nation state as part of the big continent of Asia, became a sub-continent when the nation was partitioned forming two nations–India and Pakistan in August 1947. Bangladesh is a geographical unit of the sub-continent which before 1947 was one nation state. Apart from common inheritance in terms of culture, tradition and socio-economic and political legacies, the countries of the sub-continent have many more things in common than irritants among them. Even then irritants have had the upper hand and what was once a single nation state, has fallen apart divided into at least three independent nation states.[11] The physical proximity of Bangladesh with India and other neighbours is an important factor which at once, is viewed as the cause of irritation and a possibility of amicability between the two countries.

In comparison to West Pakistan, the socio economic structure of Bangladesh at the time of independence was in a advance stage because feudal relations had already made rooms for semi-feudal, semi-capitalist relations. The Hindus and the Muslims constituted two distinct sections of population in Bangladesh. There are social and religious differences between them. Yet, close association and system of fictive kinship have brought them in close contact with each other. It kept the nationalist ideology in the political culture of Bangladesh intact more or less before its independence in December 1971. As it was strong enough in its base, the separate ethno-cultural entity of Bengalis had contributed to the forming of political culture, particularly during the colonial days. After 1947 the idea of a distinct national group received political validity and was intensified by two leading events : the language movement of 1952 and the Six Point Programme of 1966.[12] The next remarkable phase in the Politics of Bangladesh was the period 1947-71 which witnessed solidification of this nationalism, Thus India commenced its relations in 1971 with a mature country from the view point of nationality.

In 1947, the Eastern Pakistan was economically stronger than its Western part but as latter's discriminatory policy continued in each and every sphere of economy, it lagged far behind the pace of development in united Pakistan. During two and a half decades of being part of Pakistan, Bangladesh was exploited by West Pakistanis almost in the same fashion, as had been by the British. The continued economic disparity finally brought forth the concept of two-economy to the forefront. The two-economy thesis was propounded by some East Pakistani economists and rested primarily on two points : first, because of its geographical peculiarity. Pakistan did in fact have two separate and distinct economy; and second, the economic policy of the Government of Pakistan always worked against the interest of East Pakistan and gave rise to economic disparity between the two wings of Pakistan.

Thus, the creation of Pakistan seriously damaged trade and economic activity in the eastern region and East Bengal was the worst sufferer. Bangladesh, in terms of national resources, is not such as to develop self-reliant economy. It has jute and natural gas. In terms of minerals it is very poor. For coal and iron it is thoroughly dependent on others. There is not much scope for hydro-electric power, as mostly the region is flat, despite huge availability of water.[13] The disrupted economy and the resultant chaos in East Bengal was one of the factors behind the demand for autonomy and subsequently the clamour for independence.

As a result of the differing perceptions in socio-economic sphere the purely bilateral problem of sharing the Ganga waters at Farakka was sought to be internationalised and attempts were made, though not very successfully, to malign India in every possible way. Backed by the call of jehad, against the "ungrateful Hindus" who were accused of not having accepted the sovereignty of Bangladesh over the distribution of Ganga waters, the Government of Bangladesh sought to make the Farakka issue a communal one. In the post-Mujib phase of Indo-Bangladesh relations, the new government did nothing to curb anti-Indian tirade in the communal press in Bangladesh. The supporters of the new regime sought to link the Farakka issue with general accusations against India and called for eliminating the last of the national traitors and their agents and for this they resolved to "stand by the armed forces".[14] Surprisingly, technical aspects and the problem of recurring floods due to uncontrolled river waters were side tracked and, instead, the so-called threat of India's aggression was projected at various international fora.

Apart from the religious affinity of the people of Bangladesh, the fact that they lived as citizens of Pakistan for over 24 years during which religion used to play a vital role in both the domestic and foreign affairs of the country had become one of the most important factors in the image formation of the people.[15] This image was negative one, and nurtured on the basis of the so-called fundamental difference between 'Muslim Pakistan and Hindu India'. The legacy of this long association with Pakistan remained in future an important aspect which has a definite bearing on Indo-Bangladesh relations.

Despite the fact that religion is very close to one's being, it has neither been a factor to unite diverse communities nor it has been a sole factor to create politically sovereign identities out of one social community. Though the first division of the Indian sub-continent was made on the basis of religion, substantial religious minorities remained in both the newly created nations-India and Pakistan. In India the leaders of national liberation movement had recognised the concept of unity in diversity and tried to carry forward the movement on secular lines. They were opposed to communal demand for the creation of Pakistan and denied the two-nation theory which was being proposed by the British colonialists.

Perhaps on being influenced from India, the national liberation movement in Bangladesh threw off the mask of religion and sought to unite the people with the aim of defending Bengali nationalism, language and culture. In this movement, the humanitarian role played by India, in contrast to the ghastly crimes perpetrated by the West Pakistani military rulers, brought the people of Bangladesh nearer to their Indian brethren into a bond of cordiality and friendship. During the entire period of liberation movement religion did not play even the minimal progressive role, as it had already proved its futility in keeping Pakistan united. Reintroduction of religion after the liberation of Bangladesh, as a political tool, was, therefore, not in tune with the objectives of national liberation movement.

Expressing total solidarity with the principles and objectives of the national liberation movement the first Government of Sheikh Mujibur Rahman, in its historic constitution of 1972 included nationalism democracy secularism and socialism. However, the later developments on the issue made it clear that the secular principle of Bangladesh was planted on a religious society where still people were not in favour of discarding it. Religion was too sacred a trust with the people, which could not be allowed to be polluted by political considerations. Unfortunately people failed to understand that Bangladesh had emerged as a secular state, not because the religion of the vast majority of the people was in danger, but to ensure fuller manifestation of its secular values like language and culture in the context of socio-economic development, free from foreign exploitation. Bangladesh's survival as an Islamic state kept it away from India and put nearer to powers, friendly neither to India nor to Bangladesh.

The Bangladesh war of independence was fought under the leadership of Awami League who shared almost the same framework of social philosophy as the Indian ruling party of the time. The mixture of a rather populist version of socialism with reformist vision of state capitalism, and an ideological adherence to the principle of secular and democratic state brought India under the Congress and Bangladesh under the Awami League within the same general framework of state ideology.[16] The perceived mutuality of interests between India and Bangladesh took concrete shape during 1971-1975 or till Sheikh Mujibur Rahman was all in all at the helm of affairs. The Post-Mujib period of Bangladesh nourished a strong anti–India feeling which became violent and did not spare even the bilateral issues, such as, the sharing of Ganga waters at Farakka. Keeping in view the geopolitical terms and also because of India's role in Bangladesh's national liberation movement it was a difficult task for any government in the country to go whole hog against India, nevertheless the fact remains that both, at the government level and with its abetment at the level of media serious attempts were made to undermine friendly relations with India.

However, this difficult task was made easy by the post-1975 regimes of Bangladesh. The new rulers had anti-Indianism as one of its plank, and they immediately embarked upon an anti-Indian tirade.

They used irritants not unusual between neighbouring countries as bases for their campaign and used every national and international forum to defame India. Dhaka's failure to make a point at the Colombo Summit of non-aligned nations was paraded as a success and India's just criticism of Bangladesh's attempts to internationalise Farakka issue was branded as an exhibition of frustration, disillusionment and defeat at the Colombo meet.[17] War hysteria was sought to be created in Bangladesh in which the then ruler Ziaur-Rahman was next to none and said, 'We are concerned about the aggression being carried out from across the border and also about the deliberate withdrawal of huge quantum of water from the Ganga to the deteriment of Bangladesh. We will face up these aggressions at all costs and shall stand up heads erect in full glory of a free nation. Each one of us shall fight arm in hand, if need be'.[18]

The anti-India tirade in the post-Mujib phase had a definite national as well as international support. Ruler's new plank was fully backed by the communal political parties, which had been rehabilitated after the coup. The ultra-leftists and pro-Beijing elements were also not lagging behind in supporting Zia's Government. The military rulers of Bangladesh while embarked upon India for latter's hegemonistic ambitions, they, as a balancing act, sought to improve country's relations with China. It is significant to note here that Beijing, along with Washington, was the instigator of the conspiracy that overthrew Sheikh Mujibur Rahman. In the changed circumstances both China and the US became the champion of Bangladesh's inalienable rights vis-a-vis India. Two goodwill delegations from Bangladesh visited China in May and June 1976 and Peking had officially condemned the Indian attitude towards Bangladesh on the Ganges river waters and border disputes. China gave full support to Bangladesh on the Farakka issue at the UN.

It was clear from the perception and attitude of the new rulers of Bangladesh that they formed the anti Indian policies in total disregard of the ground realities, prevailed in relations between the two countries. Failure of Bangladesh effort to carry the Farakka issue at Colombo and the UN, established the fact that the problems between the two countries could not be resolved on the crest of communal propaganda, and that to talk of war and military preparedness to face Indian transigence was, to say the least unrealistic. Having realised the disappointments, in the beginning of the year 1977 Bangladesh agreed to talk on the issue with India that made substantial agreements to be signed possible on the sharing of Ganga waters between India and Bangladesh.

Concluded Agreements on Farakka

After the independence of Bangladesh a major breakthrough came in the relations of the two countries when they signed a Treaty of Friendship, Cooperation and Peace during Indira Gandhi's visit to Dhaka in March 1972. Article VI of the Treaty maintained that the high contracting parties further agreed to make a joint study and take joint action in the fields of flood control, river basin development and the development of hydro-electric power and irrigation. The discussions of the two Prime Ministers on sharing of the waters of Ganga at Dhaka resulted in the formation of a Joint Rivers Commission (JRC) relating to which, statutes were signed in Dhaka on 24 November 1972. The JRC was entrusted with the task of discussing at length the approach to long term planning for development of the water resources of the Ganga and other river systems.

As a follow up of the good understanding between India and Bangladesh, the two had signed an Interim Agreement on the sharing of Ganga waters at Farakka on 18 April 1975. The Agreement came at the end of three-day negotiations between Jagjivan Ram, the Agriculture Minister of India, and his Bangladeshi counterpart Abdur Rub Sernibat. Under the agreement signed in Dhaka India was allowed to draw up to a specific volume of water for its feeder canal for the benefit of Calcutta port. The daily withdrawal of water ranged between 11,000 and 16,000 cusecs in the last ten days of April and May respectively. The remaining flow of water was allowed to go to Bangladesh.

Despite several lackings, the agreement was welcomed by most of the leading newspapers as it set an outstanding example of mutual understanding and accommodation.[19] The port of Calcutta required 40,000 cusecs of water throughout the year including the lean months, which was necessary to flush the silt up Hooghly. Secondly, there was no time limit in the agreement. It would have been better if some time limit would have been fixed. Thirdly, during the lean season heavy withdrawals would reduce the share of Padma in Bangladesh. But it is significant to mention here that it was done on an adhoc basis. Jagjivan Ram, a signatory of the agreement and India's Minister for Agriculture, in a statement in the Loksabha on 21 May 1975, maintained, 'Since the discussion regarding the allocation of the minimum flow of Ganga during the lean months are continuing between the two governments the present agreement is a provisional assignment to enable the running of the feeder canal.'[20] Lack of any agreement for the lean season flow of Ganga at Farakka made Bangladesh anxious more than that of India and therefore, it raised the issue at different international fora.

The Second Agreement on the sharing of Ganga waters at Farakka was signed on 5 November 1977 when a non-Congress government under the premiership of Morarji Desai had taken over in India. With the change of guard at New Delhi, a climate of mutual understanding and cooperation created that paved the way for such an exhaustive and liberal agreement between the two countries. The signed agreement contained fifteen articles divided into three parts. The first part covered Articles I-VII and dealt with the terms and conditions of the sharing of Ganges waters during the lean season. Article II of the agreement provided for the sharing of waters from 1st January to 31st of May every year which was to depend on the actual availability of waters at the barrage. It also gave a guarantee to Bangladesh of 80% of its share for ten days 21-30 April, every year. Articles IV-VII were related to the setting up of joint committees of the representatives nominated by the two governments to observe and record the daily flow below the Farakka barrage and in the Feeder Canal as well as at Hardinge Bridge. The Committee was to be responsible for supervising the implementation of the short-term aspects of the agreement relating to the division of the available waters during the lean season.[21] According to part II of the agreement the Joint Rivers Commission was reactivated with a view to finding a long term solution of the problem. The third part (Articles XII-XV) dealt with the provisions of review and duration of the Agreement.

Prime Minister Morarji Desai and Atal Bihari Vajpayee, the Minister for External Affairs, made an official statcment in the Loksabha and Rajyasabha respectively on 14 November 1977 in which they maintained that the agreement had to be based on the principles of shared sacrifices and mutual accommodation without affecting the right and entitlement of either country during the lean season when there was not enough water to meet the requirement of both the countries. Among other things, the statement also noted the Government of India's hope that the approach and spirit which made the agreement possible, if applied to larger spectrum of country's relations with Bangladesh, should lead to an ever-widening cooperation between the two countries. But as the good wishes of the new Janata Government was not sufficient to fulfil the needs of Calcutta port, the agreement drew critical references in both the Houses particularly from the members of West Bengal. They termed the agreement as 'nothing but an apologia for a political agreement entered into with the intention of appeasing a military regime'. They called the agreement a sellout for political purposes in which the interests of the port of Calcutta had been compromised.[22]

The Third and the latest agreement on the sharing of Ganga waters at Farakka was also signed during the reign of a non-Congress government on 12 December 1996. It was signed by Sheikh Hasina, the Prime Minister of Bangladesh, and her Indian counterpart H.D. Devegowda, who headed the government of a United Front. The treaty will be valid for 30 years with provision of review after every five years or earlier. The signed treaty provided that if the availability of water at Farakka is 70,000 cusecs or less, it will be shared between the two on 50-50 basis. If the quantum is between 70,000 and 75,000 cusecs, Bangladesh will get 35,000 cusecs while India will retain the rest. If the quantum rises above 75,000 cusecs, India will retain 40,000 cusecs, while the rest will go to Bangladesh. The lean period for both the countries starts in the first week of January and lasts 150 days. But the leanest period is between the middle of March to the first week of May. In addition, the 10-day hydraulic cycles giving the advantage to India and Bangladesh alternately, ensures that neither side will face a crisis during the period.[23]

The agreement of December 1996 on the sharing of Ganga waters at Farakka is for the longest period ever signed by the two countries. Jyoti Basu, played a very active and positive role in the negotiations and provisions have been made to take care that neither Bangladesh nor India or more precisely West Bengal is at a disavantage. It was welcomed in New Delhi and Dhaka where both sides expressed satisfaction over signing of the treaty.[24] Because the new government of Bangladesh is not committed to an anti-Indian programme, they seized the opportunity to begin a new chapter in India–Bangladesh relations. They put the relations on a stronger basis and hoped it to be so in future.

References

1. R.K. Dixit, 'Indo-Pakistan Talks on Farakka and Related Matters', Indian Journal of International Law, Vol. IX (1969), pp. 215-16.
2. Foreign Affairs Record, Vol. XXIII, No. 8 August 1977 (New Delhi, 1977), p. 151.
3. T.D. Vaishnav, 'Indo-Bangladesh Accord on Farakka Barrage : Background and Implications', Socialist India, Vol. XII, No. 2, June 14, 1975.
4. J.S. Bains, 'The Farakka Barrage : International Law Aspects', Modern Review, Vol. CXII, No. 5 November 1962, p. 367.
5. Indian Journal of International Law, Vol. XVI, No. 4, 1976, P. 526.

6. Financial Express, October 3, 1977.
7. Margret Alva, 'Janata Foreign Policy : A Critique' in Janata Foreign Policy, K.P. Mishra, ed. (New Delhi, 1979), p. 14.
8. Lok Sabha Debates, Vol. VII, No. 1, November 14, 1977, col. 298.
9. Ibid., col. 299.
10. Georgi Arbatov, The War of Ideas in Contemporary International Relations (Moscow, 1973), pp. 54-55.
11. Virendra Narain, Foreign Policy of Bangladesh (Jaipur, 1987), pp. 19-25.
12. S.R. Chakravarti, 'Bangladesh : Problems of National Liberation Movement', in S.R. Chakravarti Swaroop, Rani Dubey, P.C. Mathur and Virendra Narain, Turmoil and Political Change in South Asia (Jaipur, 1978), pp. 26-27.
13. Virendra Narain, op.cit., pp. 28-29.
14. Ibid., pp. 99-100.
15. A.F.M. Shamsul Bari, 'Image and Realities of Bangladesh-India Relations', Law and International Affairs, Vol. 1, No.I, January 1, 1975 (Dhaka), P. 45.
16. Jayadeva Uyangoda, 'Indo-Bangladesh Relations in the 1970s : Bangladesh Perspectives', in Shelton U. Kodikara, ed., South Asian Strategic Issues, Sri Lankan Perspectives (New Delhi, 1999), p. 69.
17. Saturday Post, August 21, 1976.
18. Bangladesh Observer, August 22, 1976.
19. Lok Sabha Debates, Vol. 2, No. 37, April 21, 1975, col. 235.
20. Ibid.
21. The Hindu, November 6, 1977.
22. Lok Sabha Debates, Vol. IX, December 15, 1977, col. 218. For detail see also cols. 232, 236 and 268.
23. Indian Recorder, Vol. IV, No. 3, January 15-21, 1997, p. 2543.
24. Ibid.

SELECT BIBLIOGRAPHY

Documents

Administrative Reforms Commission, *Report of the Study Team on Centre-State Relationships, Vols. I & II* (Delhi, Manager of Publication, 1970).

Agreement between His Majesty's Government of Nepal and the Government of India on the Gandak Irrigation and Power Project Kathmandu, 4 December 1959.

All India Congress Committee, *The Background of India's Foreign Policy* (New Delhi, 1952).

Asian Relations Organisation, *Report of the Proceedings and Documents of the First Asian Relations Conference,* New Delhi, March-April 1947 (New Delhi, 1948).

Bhasin, A.S. ed., *Documents on Nepal's Relations with India and China 1949-1966* (Academic Book, Bombay, 1970)., *Nepal's Relations with India and China, Documents 1947-1992*, Vol. I (Siba Exim, Delhi, 1994).

Bulganin, N.A., and Khrushchev, N.S., Visit of Friendship to India, Burma and Afghanistan : *Speeches and Official Documents, November-December 1955* (Foreign Languages Publishing House, Moscow, 1956).

Constituent Assembly Debates 1947-1949.

Communist Party of India, (Marxist), *People's Democracy,* December 1966-March 1968.

Cooperation for Progress in Nepal, Ministry of External Affairs Government of India (New Delhi, 1966).

Colombo Summit : *Documents and Selected Speeches of the Fifth Conference of Heads of State or Government of Non-aligned Countries, Colombo, 16-19 August 1976* (People's Publishing House, New Delhi, 1976).

Countries from Belgrade, 1961 to Georgetown 1972, Main Documents Ministry of Foreign Affairs (Georgetown, 1972).

Foreign Policy of India : Text of Documents 1947-58 (Lok Sabha Secretariat, New Delhi, 1958).

Foreign Affairs Record, Ministry of External Affairs External Publicity Division (Government of India, New Delhi).

Government of India, Ministry of External Affairs, *Kashmir: White Paper, Meetings and Correspondence between Prime Ministers of India and Pakistan, July 1953- October 1954* (Delhi, 1954).

Government of India, Administrative Reforms Commission, *Report of the Study Team on State Administration* (Manager of Publications, Delhi, 1970).

Government of India, *Indo-Nepal Economic Cooperation,* Kathmandu.

Government of Pakistan, *Constituent Assembly of Pakistan,* Debates, Vol.1, No. 4, 19 March 1956.

Government of Pakistan, *The Constitution of Islamic Republic of Pakistan* (1973).

Government of Pakistan, *White paper on the Performance of the Bhutto Regime* (Islamabad, 1979).

Government of Pakistan, *Economic Advisory Wing, Economic Survey : 1993-94* (Islamabad; Finance Division, June 1994).

Indira Gandhi, *Statements on Foreign Policy, January-April 1983* (External Publicity Division, Ministry of External Affairs, New Delhi, 1983).

India, Military Alliances, 1947-57: Text of Documents (Lok Sabha Secretariat, New Delhi, 1957).

India, Kashmir and the United Nations (External Publicity Division, New Delhi, 1948).

India, Muslims in India, Ministry of Information and Broadcasting (New Delhi, 1966).

India and Foreign Review, Ministry of Information and Broadcasting (Publication Division, Government of India, New Delhi).

International Commission of Jurists, *The Events in East Pakistan* (Geneva, 1971).

International Institute for Strategic Studies, *Military Balance, 1992-93 to 1999-2000* (London, 1999).

Khanal Yadunath, *Background of Nepal's Foreign Policy* (Department of Publicity and Broadcasting, Kathmandu).

Nehru, Jawaharlal, *India's Foreign Policy: Selected Speeches, September 1949-April 1961* (Publication Division, Ministry of Information and Broadcasting, New Delhi, 1961).

Press Conference, 1952-54, Information Service of India (New Delhi).

Nepal-India Relations (Department of Publicity and Broadcasting, Kathmandu, 1963).

Nepal-China Boundary Protocol (Department of Publicity and Broadcasting, Kathmandu, 1963).

New Developments in Friendly Relations between China and Nepal, Chinese Peoples Institute of Foreign Affairs (Foreign Language Press, Peking, 1960).

Notes, Memoranda and Letters Exchanged and Agreements Signed between the Government of India and China : White Paper: 1954-1959 (New Delhi, 1959).

President Nixon's *Report to Congress* (February 1972).

Progress of Nepal-India Cooperation Programme, Indian Cooperation Mission (Kathmandu, 1968).

Report of the Ministry of External Affairs, 1956-1959 (Government of India Publication, New Delhi).

Report, Ministry of External Affairs, Government of India Prime Minister's Statements and Foreign Ministers Statements (New Delhi, 1977-1979).

Resolution, Ministry of External Affairs (New Delhi, 1970).

Smith, Roger M., ed., *Southeast Asia: Documents of Political Development and Change* (Cornell University Press, Newyork, 1974).

Suhrawardy, H.S., *Statement on Foreign Relations and Defence* "(Government of Pakistan, Karachi, 1957).

Text of Joint Communiques, Lok Sabha Secretariat, *Foreign Policy of India. Text of Documents 1947-1964* (New Delhi, 1966).

Text of Graham Report, *Document S/3821, Supplement for April- May and June* 1957.

The World Bank, *World Development Report : 1990-2000* (Oxford, 2000).

United Nations Development Programme, *Human Development Report, 1990-1998* (Oxford, 2000).

U.S. Foreign Policy for the 1970s: Shaping a Durable Peace : A Report of the Congress by Richard M. Nixon, President of the United States, February 9, 1972 (Washington, 1972).

U.S. Central Intelligence Agency, *Report on Heroin in Pakistan : Sowing the Wind* (September 1992).

World Armaments and Disarmaments SIPRI, Year Book (Oxford 1974-2000).

World Press Review (Publication Division, Ministry of Information and Broadcasting, Government of India, New Delhi).

Books

Achin Vanaik, *The Painful Transition : Bourgeois Democracy in India* (London, 1990).

Acimovic L., ed., *Non-alignment in the World of Today* (Belgrade Institute of International Politics and Economics, 1969).

Aiyer, S.P. and R. Srinivasam, eds., *Studies in Indian Democracy* (Allied, Bombay, 1965).

Alexandrowicz, C.H., *Constitutional Developments in India* (Oxford University Press, Bombay, 1957).

Alker and Russell, *World Politics in the General Assembly* (Connecticut University Press, New Heaven, 1965).

Allen, Douglas, ed., *Religion and Political Conflict in South Asia* (Oxford University Press, New Delhi, 1993).

Almond, Gabriel A. and B.G. Powell, *Comparative Politics : A Developmental Approach* (Little Brown, Boston, 1966).

Almond, Gabriel A. and James S. Coleman, eds., *The Politics of the Developing Areas* (Princeton University Press, Princeton, 1960).

Alexander, P.C., *My Years with Indira Gandhi* (Vision Books, New Delhi, 1991).

Apter David, *The Politics of Modernisation* (University of Chicago Press, Chicago, 1965).

Appadorai, A., ed., *Selected Documents on India's Foreign Policy and Relations 1947-1972* (Oxford University Press, Newyork, 1982).

Austin, Granville, *The Indian Constitution : Cornerstone of a Nation* (Oxford University Press, Newyork, 1966).

Ayub Khan, Mohammed, *Friends Not Masters : A Political Biography* (Oxford University Press, London, 1967).

Azar, Edward E., and Chung In Moon eds., *National Security in the Third World: The Management of Internal and External Threats* (Edward Elgar Publishing, Aldershot, 1988).

Bandyopadhyaya, J., *The Making of India's Foreign Policy: Determinant Institutions, Processes and Personalities* (Allied Publishers, Bombay, 1979).

Bailey, F.G., *Caste and the Economic Frontier,* (Manchester University Press, Manchester, 1957).

Baldwin, David A., *Foreign Aid and American Foreign Policy* (Praeger, Newyork, 1966).

Bhaduri, Shankar and Afsir Karim, *The Sri Lankan Crisis* (Lancer International, New Delhi, 1990).

Bhambhari, C.P., *Foreign Policy of India* (Sterling, New Delhi, 1987).

Bhutto, Zulfikar Ali, *If I am Assassinated* (Vikas Publishing House, New Delhi, 1979).

Bowels, Chester, *Ambassador's Report.*

Brecher, Michael, *Nehru : A Political Biography* (Oxford University Press, London, 1959).

Nehru's Mantle : The Politics of Succession in India (Praeger, Newyork, 1966).

The Struggle for Kashmir (Oxford University Press, Newyork, 1953).

Brown, Michael E. and Ganguly, Sumit, eds., *Government Policies and Ethnic Relations in Asia and the Pacific* (Cambridge, 1997).

Brown W. Norman, *The United States and India and Pakistan* (Harward University Press, Cambridge, 1953).

Carras Marry C., *The Dynamics of Indian Political Faction* (Cambridge University Press, Cambridge, 1972).

Chanda, Asok, *Federalism in India: A Study of Union-State Relations* (George Allen and Unwin, London, 1965).

Chakravarty, P.C., *India's China Policy* (Indian University Press, Bloomington, 1962).

Chaudhuri, Nirad C., *The Continent of Circe : An Essay on the Peoples of India* (Oxford University Press, London, 1966).

Chavan, Yashwant Rao B., *India's Foreign Policy* (Somaiya Publishers, Bombay, 1979).

Chopra, Pran, *Uncertain India : A Political Profile of two Decades of Freedom* (Asia Publishing House, Bombay, 1968).

Cohen, Stephen P., *The Pakistan Army* (Himalayan Books, New Delhi, 1984).

Cohen, Stephen P., and Richard L.Park, *India : Emergent Power* (Crane, Russak & Company, Newyork, 1978).

Cormack, Margaret, *The Hindu women* (Asia Publishing House, Bombay, 1961).

Cressey, George B., *Asia's Lands and Peoples,* (McGraw-Hill Newyork, 1951).

Damodaran, A.K. and U.S.Bajpai, eds., *Indian Foreign Policy : The Indira Gandhi Years* (Sangam Books, London, 1990).

Dash, S.C. *The Constitution of India* (Chaitanya Publishing House, Allahabad, 1968).

Davis, Kingsely, *The Population of India and Pakistan* (Princeton University Press, Princeton, 1951).

Dean, Vera Micheles, *New Patterns of Democracy in India* (Harvard University Press, Cambridge, 1969).

Dixit, Aabha, *Ethno-Nationalism in Pakistan* (Institute for Defence Studies and Analysis, Delhi, 1996).

Dixit, J.N., *Anatomy of a Flawed Inheritance : Indo-Pakistan Relations: 1970-94* (Konark Publishers, New Delhi, 1995).

Dube, S.C., *Indian Village* (Routledge and Kegan Paul, London, 1955).

India's Changing Villages – Human Factors in Community Development (Routledge and Kegan Paul, London, 1958).

Easton, David, *The Political System : An Inquiry into the State of Political Science* (Scientific Book Agency, Calcutta, 1971).

Edwardes, Michael, *Nehru : A Political Biography* (Penguin, 1973).

Edmead, Frank, *Analysis and Prediction in International Mediation* (Unitar, Newyork, 1971).

Embree, Ainslie T., ed., *The Hindu Tradition* (Modern Library, Newyork, 1966).

Esposito, John L., ed., *Islam in Asia : Religion Politics and Society* (Oxford University Press, Oxford, 1987).

Falik, Richard A., *Global Approach to National Policy* (Harvard University Press, Cambridge, 1975).

Frankel, Joseph, *The Making of Foreign Policy : An Analysis of Decision Making* (Oxford University Press, London, 1963).

Gaan, Narottam, *Indira Gandhi and Foreign Policy Making : The Bangla Desh Crisis* (Patriot Publishers, New Delhi, 1992).

Gandhi, Indira, *Aspects of Our Foreign Policy : From Speeches and*

Statements (An AICC Publication, New Delhi, 1973).

Gandhi, Rajiv, *Statements on Foreign Policy : November 1984-April 1985* (Ministry of External Affairs, New Delhi, 1985).

Gopal, S., *Jawaharlal Nehru : A Biography* (Oxford University Press, Delhi, 1976).

Gupta, M.G., *Rajiv Gandhi's Foreign Policy : A Study in Continuity and Change* (M.G. Publishers, Agra, 1987).

Gupta, R.C., *US Policy Towards India and Pakistan* (B.R. Publications, Delhi, 1977).

Gupta, Sisir, *India and Regional Integration in Asia* (Asia Publishing House, Bombay, 1964).

Kashmir – A Study in India – Pakistan Relations (Asia Publishing House, Bombay, 1966).

India's Relations with Pakistan, 1954-1957 (Indian Council of World Affairs, New Delhi, 1961).

Harrison, Selig S., *India : The Most Dangerous Decades* (Princeton University Press, Princeton, 1960).

Hartmann, Horst, *Political Parties in India* (Meenakshi, Meerut, 1971).

Hassnain, S.E., *Indian Muslims : Challenge and Opportunity* (Lalvani Publication House, Bombay, 1968).

Holsti, K.J., *International Politics : A Framework for Analysis* (Printice – Hall, Englewood, 1967).

Hussain, Asif, *Elite Politics in an Ideological State* (Dawson, Folkestone, 1979).

Hutton, J.H., *Caste in India* (Oxford University Press, Newyork, 1963).

International Monetary Fund, *World Economic Outlook : April 1985* (External Relations Department, Washington, 1985).

Islam, Nurul, *Development Planning in Bangladesh – A Study in Political Economy* (C.Hurst and Co., London, 1977).

Israni, Kimat and Haku Israni, *India : A superpower* (Lancer International, New Delhi, 1989).

Jackson, Robert, *South Asian Crisis : India, Pakistan, Bangladesh* (Chatto and Windus, London, 1975).

Jain, R.K. *China-South Asian Relations 1947-1980* (Radiant Publishers, New Delhi, 1981).

Jalal, Ayesha, *Democracy and Authoritarianism in South Asia: A Comparative and Political Perspective* (Cambridge University Press, Cambridge, 1995).

The State of Martial Law : The Origins of Pakistan's political Economy of Defence (Cambridge University Press, Cambridge, 1990).

Jalal Ayesha and Sugata Bose, *Modern South Asia – History, Culture, Political Economy* (Oxford University Press, New Delhi, 2005).

Jansen, G.H., *Non-alignment and the Afro-Asian States* (Praeger, Newyork, 1966).

Jha, S.K., *Uneasy Partners India and Nepal in the Post-Colonial Era* (Manas, New Delhi, 1975).

Kapur, Ashok, *India's Nuclear Options : Atomic Diplomacy and Decision Making* (Praeger, Newyork, 1976).

Kapur, Harish, *India's Foreign Policy 1947-92, Shadow and Substance* (Sage Publications, New Delhi, 1994).

Kaul, T.N., *India, China and Indo-China* (Allied Publishers, New Delhi, 1980).

Diplomacy in Peace and War : Recollections and Reflections (Vikas Publishing House, New Delhi, 1980).

Kavic, Lorne, J., *India's Quest for Security : Defence Policies, 1947-1965* (University of California Press, Berkeley, 1967).

Kukreja, Veena, *Civil – Military Relations in South Asia : Pakistan, Bangladesh and India* (Sage Publications, New Delhi, 1991).

Military Intervention in Politics : A Case Study of Pakistan (NBO, New Delhi, 1985).

Kumar, D.P., *Nepal : Year of Decision* (Vikas Publishing House, New Delhi, 1980).

Kumar, Satish, *The New Pakistan* (Vikas Publishing House, New Delhi, 1978).

Lakdawala, D.T., *International Aspects of Indian Economic Development* (Oxford University Press, London, 1950).

Laxmi, Y., *Trends in India's Defence Expenditure* (ABC, New Delhi, 1988).

Lewis, John P., *Quiet Crisis in India : Economic Development and American Policy* (Doubleday and Co., Newyork, 1964).

London, Kurt, *The Making of Foreign Policy : East and West* (J.B., Lippincot Co., Philadelphia, 1965).

Lyon, Peter, *Neutralism* (Leicester University Press, Leicester, 1963).

Madan, Gopal, *India as a World Power : Aspects of Foreign Policy* (Sagar Publications, New Delhi, 1974).

Madhu, Limaya, *India and the World* (New Delhi, 1979).

Majumdar, Asis Kumar, *South East Asia in Indian Foreign Policy* (B. Mitra Naya Prakash, Calcutta, 1982).

Mallik, Dev Narayan, *Post-war International Politics – A quadripartite Survey* (Veena Mandir Publishers, Muzaffarpur, 1973).

The Development of Nonalignment in India's Foreign Policy (Chaitanya Publishing House, Allahabad, 1967).

Maniruzzaman, Talukdar, *Radical Politics and the Emergence of Bangladesh* (Bangladesh Book International, Dhaka, 1975).

Bangladesh Revolution and Its Aftermath (Bangladesh Book International, Dhaka, 1980).

Martin, Lawrence W., ed., *Neutralism and Non-alignment : The New States in World Affairs* (Praeger, Newyork, 1962).

Mason, Edward S., *Foreign Aid and Foreign Policy* (S.R. Suneja Publications, New Delhi, 1964).

Mason, Philip., ed., *India and Ceylon : Unity and Diversity* (Oxford University Press, Newyork, 1967).

Mirchandari, G.G., ed., *Reporting India 1977* (Abhinav Publications, New Delhi, 1978).

Mishra, Pramod K., *South Asia in International Politics* (Udh Publishers, Delhi, 1984).

Moore R.J., *Tradition and Politics in South Asia* (Vikas Publishing House, New Delhi, 1979).

Morris Jones, W.H., *The Government and Politics of India* (Butchinson & Company, London, 1971).

Muhith, A.M.A., *Bangladesh : Emergence of a Nation* (Bangladesh Book International, Dhaka, 1980).

Munir, Muhammad, *From Jinnah to Zia : A Study of Ideological Convulsion* (Vanguard Books, Lahore, 1980).

Naik, J.A., ed., *India in Asia and Africa-Documents : 1976-1978* (Avinash Reference Publication, Maharashtra).

The *Great Janata Revolution* (S.Chand and Company, New Delhi, 1977).

Pak Bomb and Rajiv's India (National Publishing House, New Delhi, 1986).

Nanda, B.R., *Indian Foreign Policy : The Nehru Years* (Vikas Publishing House, Delhi, 1976).

Nath, Tribhuvan, *The Nepalese Dilemma* 1960-74 (New Delhi, 1975).

Natarajan, S. *A Century of Social Reform in India* (Asia Publishing House, Bombay, 1959).

Nayak, Pandav, ed., *Pakistan : Society and Politics* (South Asia Publishers, New Delhi, 1984).

ed., *Pakistan : Dilemmas of a Developing State* (Aalekh Publishers, Jaipur, 1985).

Nehru, Jawaharlal, *The Discovery of India* (John Day, Newyork, 1946).

Glimpses of World History (L.Drummond, Newyork, 1949).

India's Foreign Policy (Publication Division, Ministry of Information and Broadcasting, Government of India, 1961).

Ohlson, T., and M. Brozska, *Arms Transfer to the Third World, 1971-85* (Oxford University Press, Oxford, 1986).

Overstreet, Gene D., and Marshall Windmiller *Communism in India*, (University of California Press, Berkeley, 1959).

Palmer, Norman D., *South Asia and United States Policy* (Houghton Mifflin, Boston, 1966).

The Indian Political System (Houghton Mifflin, Boston, 1961).

Palit, D.K., *War in the High Himalayas : India in Crisis – 1962* (Lancer International, New Delhi, 1991).

Pannikar, K.M., *The Principles and Practice of Diplomacy* (Asia Publishing House, Bombay, 1956).

The Problems of Indian Defence (Asia Publishing House, 1960).

Park, Richard L., and Irene Thinker, eds., *Leadership and Political Institutions in India* (Princeton University Press Princeton, 1959).

Patel, Surendra J., *Indian Economy : Towards the Twenty First Century* (Universities Press, Hyderabad, 1955).

Phadnis, Urmila, *Ethnicity and Natinal Building in South Asia* (Sage Publications, New Delhi, 1990).

Power, Paul E., ed., *India's Non-alignment Policy* (D.C. Health & Co., Boston, 1967).

Pye, Lucian W., *Asian Power and Politics : The Cultural Dimensions of Authority* (Harvard Universtiy, Cambridge, 1985).

Qureshi, M.L., *Survey of Economic Resources and Prospects for South Asia* (Marga Institute, Colombo, 1981).

Rahman, M.M., *The Politics of Non-Alignment* (Associated publishing House, New Delhi, 1969).

Rajan, M.S., *Nonalignment : India and Future* (University of Mysore Press, Mysore, 1970).

India in World Affairs, 1954-56 (Asia Publishing House, 1964).

Ramakant, *Nepal,China and India* (Abhinav Publications, New Delhi, 1976).

Rana, A.P., *Imperatives of Nonalignment : A Conceptual Study of India's Foreign Policy in the Nehru Era* (Macmillan, New Delhi, 1976).

Rasgotra M.Chopra, V.D. and Mishra K.P. eds., *India's Foreign Policy in the 1990s* (Patriot Publishers, New Delhi, 1990).

Rasgotra, M.K.,ed., *Rajiv Gandhi's World View* (Vikas Publishing House, New Delhi, 1991).

Rosenau, James, N., ed., *International Politics and Foreign Policy : A Reader in Research and Theory* (Free Press, Newyork, 1961).

Domestic Sources of Foreign Policy (Free Press, Newyork, 1967).

The Scientific Study of Foreign Policy (Free Press, Newyork, 1971).

Rosen, George, *Democracy and Economic Change in India* (University of California, Berkeley, 1966).

Rosen, Stephen Peter, *Societies and Military Power : India and its Armies* (Oxford University Press, Delhi, 1996).

Sardesh pande, Lt. Gen. S.C.*Assignment Jaffna* (Lancer, New Delhi, 1992).

Sathyamurthy, T.V., ed., *Region, Religion, Caste, Gender and Culture in Contemporary India* (Oxford University Press, Delhi, 1996).

Sengupta, Bhabani *India: Problems of Governance* (Centre for Policy Research, Konark, New Delhi, 1996).

Shaha, Rishikesh, *Nepali Politics : Retrospect and Prospect* (Delhi, 1975).

Politics in Nepal 1980-1991 (Manohar Publishers, New Delhi, 1992).

Shelly, Mizanur Rahman, *Emergence of a New Nation in a Multipolar World : Bangladesh* (University Press, Dhaka, 1979).

Singer, Milton, ed., *Traditional India : Structure and Change* (University of Texas Press, Austin, 1959).

Singer, Jasjit, ed., *Kargil 1999 : Pakistan's Fourth War for Kashmir* (Knowledge World, New Delhi, 1999).

Singh, Kuldip, *India and Bangladesh* (Anmol Publications, Delhi, 1987).

Singh, Maj.Gen. Sukhwant, *India's Wars Since Independence : General Trends* (Vikas Publishing House, New Delhi, 1982).

Singh, Rajkumar, *Less Tasty Indo-Nepal Political Relations, 1947-1997* (Novelty, Patna, 1998).

India-South Asia Minus Congress Regimes (Novelty, Patna, 2000).

Indo-Pak Nuclear Tension 1974-1998 (Samiksha Prakashan, New Delhi, 2001).

India's Foreign Policy- The First Study in Continuity and Change (Samiksha Prakashan, New Delhi, 2001).

Past, Present and Future of Kashmir (Gyan Publishing House, New Delhi, 2008).

India and Pakistan – Social, Political and Military Perspectives (Regal Publications, New Delhi, 2009).

Global Dimensions of Indo-Nepal Political Relations Post-Independence (Gyan Publishing House, New Delhi, 2009).

Relations of NDA and UPA with Neighbours (Gyan Publishing House, New Delhi, 2010).

Smith, Donald E. *India as a Secular State* (Princeton University Press, Princeton, 1963).

Smith, Wilfred Cantwell, *Modern Islam in India: A Social Analysis* (Ripon Printing Press, Lahore, 1947).

Sobhan, Rahman, *The Crisis of External Dependence : The Political Economy of Foreign Aid to Bangladesh* (Dhaka University Press, Dhaka, 1982).

Spear, Percival, *India, Pakistan and the West* (Oxford University Press, London, 1958).

Subrahmanyam, K., *Security in Changing World* (B.R. Publishing Company, Delhi, 1990).

Sutton, John L., *Arms to Developing Countries, 1945-1965* (Institute of Strategic Studies, London, 1966).

Syed, Anwar Hussain, *Pakistan: Islam, Politics and National Solidarity*

(Praeger, Newyork, 1982).

Tasser, Salman, *Bhutto : A Political Biography* (Vikas Publishing House, New Delhi, 1980).

Thakur, Janardhan, *All the Prime Minister's Men* (Vikas Publishing House, New Delhi, 1977).

Tharoor, Shashi, *Reasons of State : Political Development and India's Foreign Policy Under Indira Gandhi* (Vikas Publishing House, New Delhi, 1982).

Thompson, Edward John and Geoffrey Theodore Garratt, *Rise and Fulfilment of British Rule in India* (Macmillan, London, 1934).

Thomas, Raju, G.C. *Indian Security Policy* (Princeton University Press, Princeton, 1986).

Vajpayee, Atal Bihari, *New Dimensions of India's Foreign Policy* (Vision Book, New Delhi, 1979).

Varma, S.P., and Narain, V.ed., *Pakistan Political System in Crisis : Emergence of Bangladesh* (University of Rajasthan, Jaipur, 1972).

Varma, S.P. and Misra, K.P., ed., *Foreign Policies in South Asia* (Orient Longmans, New Delhi, 1969).

Vital, David, *The Survival of Small States : Studies in Small Power / Great Power Conflict* (Oxford University Press, London, 1971).

Victor, Cecil, *India : The Security Dilemma* (Patriot Publishers, New Delhi, 1990).

Vohra, Dewan, C., *India's Aid Diplomacy in the Third World* (Vikas Publishing House, New Delhi, 1980).

Weiner, Myron, *Party Politics in India : Development of Multiparty System* (Princeton University Press, Princeton, 1957).

Political Change in South Asia (Farma K.L., Calcutta, 1968).

Xinhua New Agency, *China's Foreign Relations: A Chronology of Events* (Foreign Languages Press, Beijing, 1989).

Zaidi, A.M., and Zaidi, S.G. eds., *The Encyclopaedia of Indian National Congress* (S.Chand and Company, New Delhi, 1981).

Zinkin, Taya, *Challenges in India* (Walker, Newyork, 1967).

Ziring, Lawrence, ed., *The Sub-Continent in World Politics* (Newyork, 1975).

Articles in Books, Periodicals and Newspapers

Ahmad, Emajuddin, 'Current Trends in Islam in Bangladesh', *Economic and Political Weekly,* Vol. XVIII, No. 25, 18 June 1983.

Ahmad, Kamaluddin, 'Six- Point Movement and the Emergence of Bangladesh', *South Asian Studies,* Vol. 13 (July- December 1978).

Ahmar, Moonis, 'The Role of CBMs in the Post Cold War Era', *ACDIS, Occasional Paper,* Department of International Relations.

Ahmed Naveed, 'The Non-Aligned Movement and Pakistan', *Pakistan Horizon,* Karachi, Vol.32, No. 4 (Fourth quarter, 1979).

Ahmed, Feroz, 'Ethnicity, Class and State in Pakistan', *Economic and Political Weekly,* 23 November 1996.

'The Rise of Muhajir in Pakistan', *Pakistan Progressive,* Vol. X, Nos. 2-3 (Summer-Fall 1989).

Aiyar, S.P., 'Structure of Powers in the Indian Federal System', *Journal of Constitutional and Parliamentary Studies,* Vol.3, No.4 (October-December, 1969).

Alam, Muhammad Badiul, 'The Concept of Non-alignment : A Critical Analysis', *World Affairs,* Vol. 140, No.2 (Fall, Washington, 1977).

Ali, S.M., 'Nepal at the Crossroads', *Far Eastern Economic Review,* 22 April 1965.

Anand, R.P., 'Role of New Afro-Asian Countries in the Present Legal Order', *American Journal of International Law,* Vol. 56.

Anderson Piers, 'India's Frontlines in the Himalayas', *Reporter,* 3-16 January, 1964.

Appadorai, A., 'Where India Faces China', *Foreign Affairs,* 4 July 1959.

'On Understanding Indian Foreign Policy', *International Relations,* Vol. 2, No.2, October 1960 (London, 1960).

'Centre-State Relations', *Eastern Economist,* Vol. 52. No. 23, 6 June 1969.

Ayoob, Mohammed, 'Two Faces of Islam', *Asian Survey,* Vol. 19, No. 6 (June 1979).

'India and Nepal : Politics of Aid and Trade', *The Institute of the Defence Studies and Analysis* (October 1970).

Bahadur, Kalim, 'India and Pakistan', Bimal Prasad, ed., *International Studies,* Vol.17 (Vikas Publishing House, New Delhi, 1978).

'Ethnic Problems in Pakistan', *World Focus,* Vol. XV, Nos. 4-5 (April – May 1994).

Bajpai, Girija Shankar, 'Nepal and the Indo-Nepalese Relations', *Indian Year Book of International Relations,* Vol.3, University of Madras (Madras, 1954).

Bajpai, Kanti and Ganguly Sumit, 'Transition to Democracy in Pakistan', *In Depth,* 23 (Spring 1993).

Bains, J.S., 'India's International Disputes', *Indian Journal of Politics,* Vol.2, No. 1 (Aligarh, January-June 1968).

Beri, H.N., 'Pakistan and CENTO'. *Strategic Analysis,* Vol. 1, No. 3 (New Delhi, January 1977).

Bhambhari, C.P., 'The Chinese Aggression and India's Foreign policy', *Political Science Review,* Vol.2, No.2 (October 1963).

Bista, K.N., 'Nepal and India Stand for Cooperation with All Nations', *The Rising Nepal,* 20 April 1972.

Blondel, Jean, 'Party Systems and Patterns of Governments in Western Democracies', *Canadian Journal of Political Science* (June, 1968).

Brecher, Michael, 'Elite Images and Foreign Policy – Choices', *Pacific Affairs,* Vol. 40, Nos. 1-2 (Spring – Summer, 1967).

'Neutralism : An Analysis', *International Journal,* Vol. 17, No. 3 (Summer Toronto, 1962).

Bull, Hedley, 'The Conduct of American Foreign Policy : A View from Abroad Consisting under Pressure', *Foreign Affairs,* Vol. 57 (1978).

Burton, J.W., 'Rights and Obligations of Nonalignment', *Austrilian Outlook,* Vol. 16, No. 3 (Melbourne, 1962).

Chakravarty, Nikhil, 'Foreign Ties : Why So Formal', *The Times of India,* 10 June 1990.

Chanda, Asok, 'Centre and the States Need for New Adjustments,' *The Times of India,* April 14, 1969.

Chari, P.R., 'India's Nuclear Policy,' ed., K.P. Misra, *Janata's Foreign Policy* (Vikas Publishing House, New Delhi, 1979).

Chauhan, R.S., 'Consolidation and Confrontation : A Study of Nepal Politics 1970', *South Asian Studies,* Vol. VI, No. 1 (January 1970).

Cheema, Pervez Iqbal, 'Impact of the Afghan War on Pakistan', *Pakistan Horizon,* Vol. XXXI (1988).

'China in Nepal' *Thought* Vol. XIV, No. 41 (October 1962).

Chopra Surendra, 'Prospect of Indo-Pak Trade', *Indian Journal of Political Science,* Vol. 38, No. 40 (Bombay, October – December 1977).

Chowdhury G.W., 'Bangladesh : Coup and Counter Coup : International Implications, *ORBIS,* Vol. XIX, No. 4 (Winter, 1976).

Dar, A.N., 'Mr. Bhattarai Plays Right', *The National Herald,* 16 June 1990.

'Need for a Cautious Approach in Kashmir' *The Hindustan Times,* 27 August 1997.

Dastur, Aloo J., 'India at Bandung and Belgrade', *Foreign Affairs Report,* Vol. 13, No. 7 (Indian Council of World Affairs, New Delhi, July 1964).

De Russet, Alam, 'On Understanding Indian Foreign Policy', *International Relations,* Vol. 1, No. 11 (London, April 1959).

Desai, Morarji, 'Farakka Agreement : An Acid Test of India's Foreign Policy', *India and Foreign Review,* Vol. 15, No. 4 (New Delhi, December 1977).

Dixit, Aabha, 'Developments in Pakistan', *Strategic Analysis,* Vol. XIX, No. 4 July 1996.

Dixit, J.N., 'A Difficult Neighbour', *The Hindustan Times,* 27 October 1999.

Dieter, Bram, 'Changes in South Asia Intra-regional and External Relationships', *The World Today,* Vol. 34 (London, October 1978).

Dutt, Vijay and Ninan Servanti, The Route of Discontent', *India Today,* Living Media, New Delhi, 16-31 July 1978.

Dyakov, A., 'Partitioned India', *New Times,* Moscow, No. 3, 14 January 1948.

Engineer, Asghar Ali, 'Pakistan's Policy and its Viability', *The Hindu,* 14 October 2000.

Fazal, M. Abul, 'Feudalism', *The Nation,* 10 and 11 June 1997.

Gandhi, Kishore, 'Kashmir – A Holistic Approach'. *The Hindustan Times,* 18 October 1994.

Gangal, S.C. 'Trends in India's Foreign Policy', ed., K.P.Misra, *Janata's Foreign Policy* (Vikas Publishing House, New Delhi, 1979).

'A Successful Visit', *The Indian Express,* 11 February 1978.

Guha, Seema, 'The Lankan Tug of War', *The Times of India,* 28 July 1997.

Gupta, Sisir K., 'Islam as a Factor in Pakistan's, Foreign Relations, *India Quarterly,* Vol. 18, No. 3 (July – September 1962).

'Moslems in Indian Politics 1947-1960', *India Quarterly,* Vol. 18, No. 4 (December 1962).

Hah, Chong-do, 'The Dynamics of the Cultural Revolution', *World Politics,* Vol. 24, No. 2 (1972).

Haksar, P.N., 'Non-alignment : Retrospect and Prospect', *Mainstream,* Vol. 17, No. 39, 26 May 1979.

Harrison, S.Selig, 'Troubled India and Her Neighbours', *Foreign Affairs,* Vol. 43 (Newyork, 1964-65).

Hers, Peter, 'Nepal between India and China', *Swiss Review of World Affairs,* Vol. 17, No. 6 (September 1967).

Hossain, Mosharaf, 'Nature of State Power in Bangladesh', *Journal of*

Social Studies, No. 5 (Dhaka University, Dhaka, 1979).

Huq, Abdul Fazal, 'The Problem of National Identity in Bangladesh', *The Journal of Social Studies,* No. 24 (Dhaka, April 1984).

Husain, Syed Anwar, IOZP and SAARC : A Comparative Analysis, *Regional Studies,* Vol. 9, No. 3 (Summer 1991).

Jain, Girilal, 'Jana Sangh : Back to Unadulterated Pro-Americanism', *Link,* 7 (43), 6 June 1965.

'Foreign Policy Consensus – Some New Factors at Work' *The Times of India,* 6 April 1977.

Jain, N.P., 'Cooperation Among Non-aligned Countries', *India and Foreign Review,* Vol. 15, No. 6, 1 January 1978.

Kamal, A. Nazir, 'Karakoram Highway – A Nation Building Effort', *Strategic Studies,* Vol. II, No. 3 (Islamabad, Spring 1979).

Kapur, Ashok, 'Emerging Problem in India's Foreign Relations in the Seventies', *Foreign Affairs Report,* Vol. 20, No. 7 (New Delhi, July 1971).

Morarji's Signal to President Carter, *The Indian Express,* 23 December 1977.

Khanal, Y.N., 'Nepal 1972 : A Search for a New Base-Camp', *Asian Survey,* Vol. XIII, No. 2 (February 1973).

Kumar, D.R., 'Nepal's Road to China', *Far Eastern Economic Review,* Vol. 53, No. 8, 20 February 1964.

Kumar, Satish, 'Nepal and China', *Indian Journal of Political Science,* Vol. 24 (January – March 1963).

Kumar, Sumit, Pakistan's Jehadi Apparatus : Goals and Methods, *Strategic Analysis,* Vol. XXIX, No. 12 (March 2001).

Kurve, Mavin, 'Nepal's Peace Zone Move : Attempt to Change 1950 Treaty', *The Times of India,* 14 January 1981.

Laport, Jr. Robert, 'Pakistan in 1995 : The Continuing Crisis', *Asian Survey,* Vol. XXXVI, No. 2 (February 1996).

Lasswell, Harold, 'The Scientific Study of International Relations',

Yearbook of World Affairs, Vol. 12 (London, 1958).

Low-Beer Francis, 'The Concept of Neutralism', *American Political Science Review,* Vol. LVIII (Washington, 1964).

Madhu, Limaya, 'India's China Policy', *The Illustrated Weekly of India,* Vol. XIIX (The Times of India Press, Bombay, November 12-18, 1978).

Malhotra, Babita and Kumar S., 'Thaw in Indo-Bangla Relations', *The National Herald,* 10 January 1991.

Malhotra, Inder, Beyond the Bangla Poll-New Delhi Dhaka Relations, *The Times of India,* 8 June 1978.

'China's Stance on Kashmir', *The Times of India,* 22 February 1990.

Manandher, R.P., 'Some New Light on Early Nepal-China Relations', *Bulletin Indian Institute of Advanced Study* Vol. III, No. 4 (July 1970).

Mehta, Swadesh, 'The Organisation of an International Force : The Indian View', *International Studies,* Vol. 7, No. 2 (New Delhi, October 1963).

Menon, N.C., 'An Unequal Bargain', *The Hindustan Times,* 3 November 1997.

Menon, V.K.N., 'Caste Politics and Leadership in India', *Political Science Review* (October – December 1964).

Mohanty, Manoranjan, 'China Commentary : Course of Sino-Indian Normalisation', *The Amrit Bazar Patrika,* 19 May 1978.

Morris-Jones, W.H., India's Political Idioms', C.H. Phillips, ed., *Politics and Society in India* (George Allen and Unwin, London, 1963).

'Stability and Change in Indian Politics', Saul Rose, ed., *Politics in South Asia* (Macmillan, London, 1963).

Mukherjee, Dilip, 'Ms, Bhutto's Predicament : Sharing Power to Survive', *The Times of India,* 4 May 1990.

Muni, S.D., 'Chinese Arms Pour into Nepal', *The Times of India,* 1 September 1988.

'A Common Destiny, *The Times of India', Patna,* 23 April 1989.

'Internal Political Problems', *World Focus,* No. 115 (July 1986).

"South Asian Summit : Primacy and Politics, *Mainstream,* Vol. 24, No. 15, 15 December 1985.

'SAARC: As an Approach to Mutual Confidence Building', *SAARC Perspective,* Vol. 2, No. 4 (December 1988).

Narain, Virendra, 'Bangladesh and Changing International Context : An Analysis of Perceptions', S.P. Verma and Virendra Narain, eds., *Pakistan Political System in Crisis : Emergence of Bangladesh,* (South Asia Studies Centre Jaipur, 1972).

Narayan, Sriman,'India-Nepal', *United Asia,* Vol. XIV, No. 4 (July 1967).

Nayar, Kuldip, 'Estranged Neighbour : The Arrogant India', *The Indian Express* 12 December 1994.

Newman, K.J., 'The Constitutional Evolution of Pakistan', *International Affairs,* Vol. XXXVIII, No. 3 (July 1962).

Noorani, A.G., India – Nepal Relations: The Heart of the Matter, *The Indian Express,* 11 April 1989.

Pant Pushpesh, 'Major Developments in India's Foreign Policy and Relations', *International Studies* (January-June 1979).

Podgaonkar, Dileep, 'Pak Crisis and India's Choices', *The Times of India,* 9 August 1990.

Pattanaik, Smruti S., 'Islam and the Ideology of Pakistan', *Strategic Analysis,* Vol. XXII, No. 9 (December 1998).

Patterson, Gorge N., 'A Himalayan Confederation', *Far Eastern Economic Review,* Vols. 47-48 (1968).

Poole, Peter A., 'Communist China's Aid Diplomacy', *Asian Survey,* Vol. 17, No. 11 (November 1966).

Poulose, T.T., 'The Politics of Nuclear Freezone in South Asia', *Pacific Community,* Vol.6 (Tokyo, April 1977).

Power, Paul F., 'India's Foreign Policy : The Age of Nehru', *Review of*

Politics, Vol.6, No.2 (April 1964).

Prasad, R.C., 'Social Polarisation and Political Instability', Iqbal Narain, ed., *State Politics in India* (Meenakshi Prakashan, Meerut 1976).

Puri, Rakshat 'Delhi's Kowtowing to Beijing', *The Hindustan Times,* 12 November 1997.

Pylee, M.V., 'States Under Constitutional Emergency', *Journal of Commonwealth Political Studies,* Vol.1, No. 2 (1967).

Rahman, M.Anisur, 'East Pakistan: The Roots of Estrangement', *South Asian Review,* Vol.3, No.3 (April 1970).

Rajan, M.S., 'Bangladesh and After', *Pacific Affairs, Summer,* Vol. 45, No. 2.

Ramakant, 'Nepal's Foreign Policy and China', *India Quarterly,* Vol. XXVI, No. 3 (July-September 1971).

Raman, A.S., 'India : Democracy in Danger', *Contemporary Review,* Vol. 233, No. 1355 (December 1978).

Rao, P.V. Narasimha, 'Nepal-India Relations' (*Nepal Council of World Affairs,* Journal, Souvenir Issue, December 1981).

Rashid, Ahmed, 'Bhutto's Burden : Pakistan in Deep Economic Crisis', *The Times of India,* 23 September 1996.

'Pakistan's Coup : Planting the Seeds of Democracy', *Current History* (December 1999).

Ray, Heman, 'Communist China's Strategy in the Himalayas', Nepal, A Case Study *Orbis,* Vol. 2, No. 3 (1967).

Sahay, S., 'A Close Look Indo – Nepal Relations', *The Statesman,* 10 December 1981.

Sareen, Rajendra, 'Dimension of Turmoil', *The Tribune,* 5 February 1990.

Sengupta, Bhabani, 'Towards Good Neighbourliness', Bimal Prasad, ed. India's Foreign Policy – *Studies in Continuity and Change* (Vikas Publishing House, New Delhi, 1979).

'A Deeply Divided Nation,' Pran Chopra ed., *Contemporary Pakistan*

New Aims and Images (Vikas Publishing House, 1983).

'After IPKF is Out', *The Hindustan Times,* 23 February 1989.

Singh, S.Nihal, 'India – China : Time to Move Forward', *The Statesman,* 22 May 1979.

Subrahmanyam, K., 'India's Relations with Her Neighbours', *Strategic Analysis,* Vol. II, No. 12 (March 1987).

Talbot, Phillips, 'Kashmir and Hyderabad', *World Politics,* Vol. I (April 1949).

Victor, Cecil, 'Busting Terrorist Bases no Solution', *The Patriot,* 18 May 1990.

Vishwanathan, 'Indo-Sri Lanka Relations', *India Quarterly,* Vol. XLVI, No.1 (January-March 1990).

Wallace, Paul, 'India : The Dispersion of Political Power', *Asian Survey,* Vol VII, No. 2 (February 1968).

Weiner, Myron, 'The Politics of South Asia,' Gabriel A. Almond and James S. Coleman, *The Politics of Developing Areas* (Princeton University Press, Princeton, 1960).

Wriggins, W. Howard, 'Pakistan's Search for a Foreign Policy After the Invasion of Afghanistan', *Pacific Affairs,* Vol. 57, No. 2 (The University of British Columbia, 1984).

Zhurkin, V., 'India a Great Power', *New Times,* No. 5, 26 January 1956.

Newspapers

The Amrit Bazar Patrika (Calcutta).

The Ceylon Daily News (Ceylon).

The Commoner (Kathmandu).

The Dawn (Karachi).

The Dainik Nepal (Kathmandu).

The Financial Times (London).

The Gorkhapatra (Kathmandu).

The Hindu (Madras).

The Hindustan Times (New Delhi).

The Indian Express (Delhi).

The Indian Nation (Patna).

The Nagpur Times (Nagpur).

The National Herald (New Delhi).

The Newyork Times (Newyork).

The Rising Nepal (Kathmandu).

The Sunday Standard (New Delhi).

The Statesman (Delhi).

The Times of India (New Delhi).

The Times (London).

The Tribune (Chandigarh).

The Xinhua (Beijing).

Periodicals

American Political Science Review (Newyork).

Eastern Economist (Bombay).

Economic and Political Weekly (Bombay).

Foreign Affairs (Newyork).

Foreign Policy Report (New Delhi).

Illustrated Weekly of India (Bombay).

India Today (New Delhi).

Indian Journal of Political Science (Hyderabad).

International Affairs (Moscow).

International Studies (New Delhi).

Link (New Delhi).

Pacific Affairs (Newyork).

Political Science Quarterly (Newyork).

Time (Newyork).

SAARC News (Calcutta).

World Politics (Princeton).

World Today (London).

INDEX

L

O

P

Q